CHRISTIANOPOLIS

An Ideal of the 17th Century

JOHANN VALENTIN ANDREAE
FELIX EMIL HELD, TRANSLATOR

COSIMOCLASSICS

NEW YORK

[I]n this respect the inhabitants are especially blessed because no one can be superior to the other in the amount of riches owned, since the advantage is rather one of power and genius, and the highest respect, that of morals and piety. They have very few working hours, yet no less is accomplished than in other places as it is considered disgraceful by all that one should take more rest and leisure time than is allowed.

—from "Occupations"

Jo: Valentinus
Andrea. D.

JOHANN VALENTIN ANDREAE

PREFACE

Iт is my belief that Johann Valentin Andreae represents a
very important step in the development of the principles of
education and scientific investigation, and that his works,
now very little known, deserve worthy recognition in the
history of literature. It is the purpose of this investigation to show the value of his writings as those of a great
teacher and reformer; and especially to establish his utopia,
Reipublicae Christianopolitanae Descriptio, in its proper
place among the ideal states of the sixteenth and seventeenth centuries. As the Latin original of this utopia has
become quite rare I have made an English translation of
it, hoping that thereby the attention of students of literature, philosophy, pedagogy, and sociology may be attracted
to this remarkable document. Recognizing the great value
of Andreae's work Robert Boyle, as early as 1647, in a letter
to Samuel Hartlib, expressed the wish that an English
version of it might be made.

For my introduction to the subject, and for his assistance
and direction in its development, I wish to express my
gratitude and appreciation to Professor Julius Goebel, my
adviser and teacher. I also acknowledge my sincere thanks
to other members of the department of German of the
University of Illinois for their interest and helpful suggestions.   F. E. H.

CONTENTS

PREFACE iii

PART I

ANDREÆ'S "CHRISTIANOPOLIS," ITS ORIGIN AND INFLUENCE

CHAPTER   PAGE

I. INTRODUCTION 3

> Plato's *Republic*. Discovery of America and its effect on European thought and literature. Robinson Crusoe and forerunners of the same. Andreae and the shipwreck motif. More's *Utopia*. Andreae's life and works; his relation to education and to educators of the past. Summary of the purpose of the present investigation.

II. MORE'S "UTOPIA," CAMPANELLA'S "CIVITAS SOLIS" AND THE "CHRISTIANOPOLIS" . . 16

> Views and opinions of Hüllemann, Mohl, Sigwart, and later commentators regarding the originality of the *Christianopolis*. The *Christianopolis* compared and contrasted with the *Utopia* and the *Civitas Solis*. Is it a "copy" of either? The several purposes of More, Campanella, and Andreae. Herder's opinion. Andreae impressed with the government of Geneva. Analysis of the *Christianopolis*. Andreae's object, educational and religious reform. The founding of a "college." The *Christianopolis* original in form and content.

III. THE "CHRISTIANOPOLIS" AND FRANCIS BACON'S "NEW ATLANTIS" 41

> Opposition to Aristotle's deductive reasoning. Francis Bacon's life and works. The *New Atlantis*—date of composition. Bacon's ambition; his relation to scholars on the Continent. Casaubon, Weckherlin, Matthew. Analysis of the

CHAPTER PAGE

New Atlantis and a comparison with the *Christianopolis.* Salomon's House and the College of Six Days' Works. Seeking after "light." Earlier works of Andreae which contain his views—the *Fama,* the *Confessio, Die Christenburg.* Bacon's conception of a college is not the first in utopias. External as well as inner evidence make a knowledge of Andreae's works on the part of Bacon extremely likely.

IV. THE "CHRISTIANOPOLIS" AND "NOVA SOLYMA" 75

Immediate effect of Andreae's work more noticeable in England than in Germany. *Nova Solyma* a utopian romance; date and author. Life of Gott. His association with scholars in the circle of Andreae's friends. The theme and purpose of *Nova Solyma.* Its close similarity to the *Christianopolis.* "Light."

V. ANDREÆ, THE ROYAL SOCIETY OF LONDON, AND EDUCATIONAL REFORM 100

Disciples and followers of Andreae. Comenius's efforts to carry on regular correspondence with Andreae; his relations to Andreae. Similarity of their programs for educational reform. Hartlib; his unique position in England. Dury, religious and educational reformer; his acquaintance with Andreae. Figulus. Hübner. Comenius and Dury invited to England. Robert Boyle. The Invisible College. The Philosophical College. Haacke, a charter member of the Royal Society. Sprat. The Royal Society of London, 1662. Its aims. Relation to similar academies on the Continent. Some important features of the Royal Society could not have come through the *New Atlantis,* which is usually given as its model.

BIBLIOGRAPHY 126

PART II

CHAPTER		PAGE
	CHRISTIANOPOLIS	129
	DEDICATORY	131
	TO THE READER	133
I.	THE REASON FOR THE JOURNEY, AND THE SHIPWRECK . . .	142
II.	DRIVEN TO THE ISLAND, CAPHAR SALAMA	143
III.	THE ORIGIN OF CHRISTIANOPOLIS . .	144
IV.	EXAMINATION OF THE STRANGER, FIRST, AS TO HIS IDEAS OF LIFE AND HIS MORALS	145
V.	EXAMINATION, SECONDLY, AS TO HIS PERSON	146
VI.	EXAMINATION, THIRDLY, AS TO HIS PERSONAL CULTURE . . .	147
VII.	DESCRIPTION OF THE CITY . . .	149
VIII.	AGRICULTURE AND ANIMAL HUSBANDRY	150
IX.	MILLS AND BAKERIES . . .	151
X.	THE MEAT SHOP AND THE SUPPLY HOUSE	153
XI.	METALS AND MINERALS . . .	154
XII.	DWELLINGS	155
XIII.	MECHANICS	156
XIV.	PUBLIC PRAYERS	158
XV.	FOOD	159
XVI.	OCCUPATIONS	160
XVII.	VACATION PERIODS . . .	162
XVIII.	REWARDS	163
XIX.	PENALTIES	164
XX.	NOBILITY	165
XXI.	OFFICIALS	166
XXII.	PUBLIC WORKS	168

CHAPTER		PAGE
XXIII.	THE HOMES	169
XXIV.	FURNITURE AND FURNISHINGS	170
XXV.	NIGHT LIGHTS	172
XXVI.	THE COLLEGE	173
XXVII.	THE TRIUMVIRATE	174
XXVIII.	RELIGION	175
XXIX.	ADMINISTRATION OF THE STATE	177
XXX.	THE MINISTER OR PRESBYTER	179
XXXI.	CONSCIENCE	180
XXXII.	THE MINISTER'S ASSISTANT OR THE DIACONUS	181
XXXIII.	THE JUDGE	183
XXXIV.	UNDERSTANDING	184
XXXV.	MEASURE	185
XXXVI.	THE DIRECTOR OF LEARNING	186
XXXVII.	TRUTH	188
XXXVIII.	THE TONGUE	189
XXXIX.	THE LIBRARY	190
XL.	THE ARMORY	192
XLI.	THE ARCHIVES	193
XLII.	PRINTING	194
XLIII.	THE TREASURY	195
XLIV.	THE LABORATORY	196
XLV.	THE DRUG SUPPLY HOUSE	198
XLVI.	ANATOMY	199
XLVII.	THE NATURAL SCIENCE LABORATORY	200
XLVIII.	PAINTING AND PICTURES	202
XLIX.	MATHEMATICAL INSTRUMENTS	203
L.	THE MATHEMATICS LABORATORY	204
LI.	THE DEPARTMENTS OF LEARNING	205
LII.	THE TEACHERS	207
LIII.	THE PUPILS	208
LIV.	THE NATURE OF INSTRUCTION	209

CHAPTER		PAGE
LV.	GRAMMAR, THE FIRST DEPARTMENT .	210
LVI.	ORATORY	212
LVII.	THE VARIOUS LANGUAGES . . .	213
LVIII.	LOGIC, THE SECOND DEPARTMENT .	215
LIX.	METAPHYSICS	216
LX.	THEOSOPHY	217
LXI.	ARITHMETIC, THE THIRD DEPARTMENT	219
LXII.	GEOMETRY	220
LXIII.	MYSTIC NUMBERS	221
LXIV.	MUSIC, THE FOURTH DEPARTMENT .	223
LXV.	MUSICAL INSTRUMENTS	224
LXVI.	THE CHORUS	225
LXVII.	ASTRONOMY, THE FIFTH DEPARTMENT	227
LXVIII.	ASTROLOGY	228
LXIX	THE HEAVEN OF THE CHRISTIANS .	229
LXX.	NATURAL SCIENCE, THE SIXTH DE-PARTMENT	231
LXXI.	HISTORY	232
LXXII.	CHURCH HISTORY	233
LXXIII.	ETHICS, THE SEVENTH DEPARTMENT .	235
LXXIV.	THE GOVERNMENT	236
LXXV.	CHRISTIAN POVERTY	238
LXXVI.	THEOLOGY, THE EIGHTH DEPARTMENT	240
LXXVII.	PRACTICE OF THEOLOGY	242
LXXVIII.	PROPHECIES	243
LXXIX.	MEDICINE	245
LXXX.	JURISPRUDENCE	246
LXXXI.	THE DWELLINGS OF THE YOUTH . .	247
LXXXII.	THE TEMPLE	249
LXXXIII.	VOCATION	250
LXXXIV.	SERVICES	252
LXXXV.	SACRED PSALMODY	253
LXXXVI.	THE SACRAMENTS	255

CHAPTER		PAGE
LXXXVII.	ABSOLUTION AND EXCOMMUNICATION	256
LXXXVIII.	MATRIMONY	258
LXXXIX.	WOMEN	260
XC.	CHILDBIRTH	261
XCI.	WIDOWHOOD	263
XCII.	THE COUNCIL HALL	265
XCIII.	THE COUNCILMEN	266
XCIV.	THE GARDENS	268
XCV.	WATER	269
XCVI.	THE AGED	270
XCVII.	FOREIGNERS AND PAUPERS . . .	272
XCVIII.	THE SICK	273
XCIX.	DEATH	275
C.	BURIAL	276
	CONCLUSION OF THE DESCRIPTION AND DEPARTURE OF THE STRANGER. .	277

ILLUSTRATIONS

Johann Valentin Andreae . . . . *Frontispiece*

FACING
PAGE

Ground Plan of Christianopolis—Christianopolis . 129

Title Page of the Original Edition of the "Christianopolis" 143

PART I

CHAPTER I

INTRODUCTION

THE conception of an ideal state comes down to us from the time of the ancients. Plato's *Republic* is the expression of the ideal of a philosopher, the representative of the highest culture of his age, who in the time of his maturity, after long association with one of the greatest teachers of his country, after years of travel among different peoples, and a life of close attention to the study of social and political conditions, reduced the results of his observations and experiences into concrete form. He pictured to his countrymen a state, free from the corruptions of extreme license and the dangers of tyranny, and embodying in its laws and institutions the two fundamentals of his governmental ethics—man's individual life and personal morality, and his relation and obligations as a member of state and society. Plato was a prophet—a prophet of evil, because he saw clearly and truly the inevitable outcome to which the trend of events in the Athenian state was leading; a prophet of good, in that he foretold a better time, analyzed the problem, and offered his solution. But the *Republic* is a utopia in the literal sense. Plato's state exists nowhere—it is a purely ideal conception which the author cannot locate in any definite place.

The Renaissance marks the time when men's thoughts again were called to the subject of reform. The practical turn given by Humanism away from sophistical, disputing, dreamy abstractions, toward the affairs of life; the enlightenment of the world, spiritually and mentally, due to the revival of learning; and especially the discovery of the western world, all tended to give man and society a new impetus—a swelling, crowding, longing desire for a fuller, freer, larger life.

The century after the discovery of America, and the explorations and voyages of the Spanish and Portuguese which followed, opened the mind of all Europe to a realization of the narrowness of its former point of view. New continents inhabited by unheard of and unthought of races of people; conditions of life never before known to the civilized world, or if known, forgotten through centuries of artificiality; men living in freedom, without extreme or noticeable restrictions of law, and yet in reasonable harmony and order—these were new conceptions which, though they by their suddenness struck hard and with stunning effect, yet cleared a new and immeasurably broader horizon, and brought out the contrast between the degenerating artificiality of civilization and the natural, original condition of man. And while it is true that tales and legends as wild as those brought back by the Argonauts to the Grecian world circulated for a century and more, and found fertile soil in the imaginations of Europeans, yet in the course of time and in the light of more definite information, the public mind returned to a normal balance, and sifted out of the mass of reports, the facts that could be relied upon. The fountain of eternal youth became a healthy climate, fresh air, and cool springs; the fabulous rivers of gold took the form and shape of cultivated fields and limitless stretches of timber; and the phantastical, mythical race of beings resolved itself into a simple people, an example of human life close to nature.

Then followed slowly the discovery of the folk-song

and folk-poetry as the original language of pure human nature, and with it, all succeeding attempts to determine the true character of man. This movement, however, did not reach its climax until much later—in the eighteenth century and in the writings of the classical period of German literature. Experiences of the Moravian and Jesuit missionaries among the American Indians and association with the wild tribes led to further investigations into their nature and customs. A feeling developed that civilization could be redeemed only by stripping it of all useless and vain conventionalities; and in order that this might be done, primitive man would have to furnish the model. Hence there followed a study of primitive man wherever he could be found, and a rehearsal of literature which dealt with primitive races. Herder translated the poems of Ossian, the Irish bard, the poetic efforts of the Finns and Lapps, and collected folk-lore from all nations. Goethe, in his *Westöstlicher Divan,* turned to the primitive life of the Orient. Even Hölderlin, in his *Hyperion,* had his hero, when all else failed him, seek after the "inmost parts of Asia" and exclaim, "Man cannot deny that he was once happy even as the deer in the forest; and after countless years there still glimmers within us a longing for the days of the primitive world, when everyone trod the earth like a god, before (I do not know what) tamed man; and when instead of walls and dead timber, the soul of the world, the holy atmosphere everywhere present, embraced him."[1] Homer and the primitive Greeks were studied with renewed energy and from an entirely different point of view. The Hebrews were investigated as a primitive people and new researches made in the Old Testament. Rousseau and his "back to nature" were a part of the same move-

[1] Hölderlin: *Gesammelte Dichtungen* (Cotta), II, pp. 161, 162.

ment. The literature of the eighteenth century is full of such expressions as " a whole man," " the complete man," " natural man," and the like. The whole problem was an effort to find the secret of happiness in man as he was put into the world, pure and uncontaminated by the artificialities and conventionalities of over-civilization. And furthermore, now that the eyes of Europe were opened to the immensity of the newly discovered world, and a definite locality was provided where such plans could be realized, the utopian idea sprang up again, and the distant islands of the sea [1] were represented as the homes of people living

[1] An important and well represented type of literature had its origin in this movement—the *Robinsonaden,* first definitely represented by Defoe's *Robinson Crusoe,* including Robinson stories in all languages and literatures, and finally culminating in Schnabel's *Insel Felsenburg.* In a dissertation, Wackwitz (see bibliography) summarizes the forerunners of Defoe's *Robinson Crusoe* with a view toward determining his sources. Kippenberg (see bibliography) discusses the Robinson tales in Germany up to the appearance of *Insel Felsenburg.* Finally Brüggemann (see bibliography) in his *Utopie und Robinsonade* analyzes the two types of productions, lists the elements essential to each type, and shows the presence of both in such works as *Histoires des Sevarambes* of Vairasse, *Robinson Crusoe,* and *Insel Felsenburg.* In these discussions all three writers take notice of the purely political utopias, and Brüggemann and Kippenberg make mention of *Christianopolis.*

The *Histoires des Sevarambes, Insel Felsenburg,* to a certain extent even the *Life of Joris Pines,* and other Robinson tales are composite productions. There is the shipwreck, the casting upon an uninhabited island of one or more persons, the gradual development and improvement of the place (thus far the pure Robinsonade), and the ultimate forming of an ideal state, the utopia.

These two types as independent productions are mutually exclusive; the Robinsonade is necessarily ended when the ideal state begins, for, as the latter represents a condition of contentment from which outside elements are to be excluded, so the former pictures essentially an exile, no matter what sentimental reasons the individual or individuals may have for regretting departure when the rescuing ship finally comes.

Brüggemann analyzes the *Insel Felsenburg* and selects as three under reformed systems of government, society, and education. It is not surprising that the new world with its freshness and wealth of beauty should have instilled life and vigor into the old. It is not strange that Europe should have been seized with a longing desire for homes in a new

important factors of the whole, 1) the motif of compulsory separation from the world, 2) the feeling of safety in an asylum from the interferences of civilized society rather than that of exile from a desirable community, and 3) the problem of sex relations. While Andreae's *Christianopolis* is mentioned in Brüggemann and Kippenberg, it is only to take passing notice and to add that Andreae has contributed little or nothing to the development of this class of literature. A few words will, therefore, not be out of place to show that the *Christianopolis* plays a more important part than has been heretofore shown.

It is generally supposed that the shipwreck motif is common to all utopias. Thus Hüllemann (II, p. 5), in attempting to prove Andreae's dependence upon More, mistakenly says: "Both ideal states are situated upon an island at which *both* authors arrive after having been *shipwrecked.*" In *Schlaraffia Politica* (p. 122) it is stated concerning Bacon's *New Atlantis:* "Like *all the other poets,* Bacon tells us how a ship . . . is struck by a storm and *wrecked*";—and again (p. 94), this time speaking of the *Christianopolis,* "The description begins *as usual* with a *shipwreck.*"

There is a Spanish account in 1609 of a shipwrecked mariner, one Serrano, whose experiences were reproduced by Happel in 1682 in his *Insulanischer Mandorell.* The original (translated into English in 1688 by Rycaut, and into German by Boll still later) has no features of a utopia. The *Tempest* of Shakespeare (1610 at earliest) describes the landing of a shipwrecked party and the subsequent life of the survivors upon an island. This is probably (Introduction to editions of the *Tempest* by Hudson and by Boas) based upon the account of the wreck of a vessel in the Bermudas, which was printed in 1610. But in the history of utopias there is no such experience. More, in his narrative, simply "travels on and eventually reaches Utopia." Campanella's hero "is compelled to go ashore" (p. 5), and so arrives at Civitas Solis. Both are very vague. Of these early utopias, *Christianopolis* alone clearly mentions the details of the arrival of the traveler at the island and of all utopias is the first to make use of the wreck. Bacon has no *wreck* at all, land. It was only natural that the literature of the time was crowded with utopian ideas, and that a new impulse was given toward improving the corrupted civilization in which men were living.

Thomas More is the first in this new period to give the world a picture of such an ideal state, and his *Utopia* is the beginning of a literature that played no small part in the

but after Andreae it is an essential part of utopias and Robinson stories.

Of the three essential factors of *Insel Felsenburg* as pointed out by Brüggemann, sex plays no part in the *Christianopolis* in the sense in which it forms a "problem" in the Robinson stories. Neither is absolute "separation" from the outer world a possible factor, as the traveler is thrown upon an island whose inhabitants are already out of the "Robinsonade" stage. However, as is partially admitted in Brüggemann (*Christianopolis,* chaps. iv, v, vi), there is a strict examination which would eliminate all but a very small per cent of casual visitors; and the cordial invitation to return is extended at the close, only because this visitor has proved himself unusually fit to be an adopted citizen in Christianopolis. But Brüggemann (p. 151) is wrong (as also Voigt, p. 75) in attributing the impossibility of a "separation" motif to the allegorical character of the *Christianopolis.* Just as certainly is it a gross injustice to the *Christianopolis* to say that "throughout the whole, more stress is laid upon laws than upon the individuals' interrelation and behavior, which latter condition is a result rather of the laws under which they live than of a natural, inner development" (Brüggemann, p. 150). The spirit in Christianopolis is not that of the "narrow-mindedness of church prudery" (Brüggemann, p. 150).

Brüggemann, strangely enough, does not find in the *Christianopolis* suggestions of the very factors which he selects from the *Sevarambes* as having influenced *Insel Felsenburg* after it ceases to be a Robinsonade. Yet *Sevarambes* is undoubtedly dependent upon the *Christianopolis* for many of these. First, there is the shipwreck already mentioned. In the second division, "Human beings have a natural bent toward evil. Good laws and examples must overcome this, else the evil within will choke the good. The government of the *Sevarambes* and the principles of education have, therefore, great influence upon the social life of the community" social and scientific programmes of the sixteenth and seventeenth centuries. The sudden impetus given to science, the wonderful advance in this field in Italy, Germany, and England, produced a desire for a new and more practical system of education. In Germany the unsettled conditions of church and state, the feeling on the part of Protestants that the Reformation had not been a complete success, the counter-reformation among the Catholics, the fore-mutterings of the long struggle of the Thirty Years' War—these all combined to give impulse to reform. Speaking of this period and the forces which led to the production of the utopias, W. Windelband says: "A new epoch of culture seemed to have been opened and an exotic agitation seized the imagination. Unheard of things were to be attained; nothing was to be impossible any more. The telescope unlocked the secrets of the heavens and the forces of the earth began to obey the investigator. Science strove to be the leader of human thought in its victorious course

(Brüggemann, p. 156, *Sevarambes*, p. 190, *Christianopolis* throughout). By the seventh year the children (girls as well as boys) are taken in charge by the state (*Sevarambes*, p. 192, *Christianopolis*, chap. liii). Ideas of community right (*Sevarambes*, p. 150, *Christianopolis*, chap. liii and elsewhere), rank not one of blood but of virtuous behavior (*Sevarambes*, p. 149, *Christianopolis*, chap. xx), honesty and good example, the only heritage (*Sevarambes*, p. 173, *Christianopolis*, chap. xx), and scores of others in the utopia of Vairasse, find their exact duplicates in *Christianopolis*. And the conclusion, "The visitor leaves the land with the firm determination to return and spend his last days there" (*Sevarambes*, p. 359), already occurs almost verbatim in *Christianopolis*. In other words, the third factor, that of the "asylum" which Brüggemann finds (before *Insel Felsenburg*) primarily in *Sevarambes*, is as strongly emphasized in *Christianopolis*, half a century earlier. It seems clear, then, that the *Christianopolis* of Andreae gave considerable (and hitherto unacknowledged) incentive to, and furnished some of the essentials of the Robinsonade and particularly of Schnabel's *Insel Felsenburg*.

through nature. Through her discoveries human life was to be completely transformed." [1]

One of the first to divine the dawn of a new epoch in the history of human civilization and to give expression to the secret hopes and aspirations of his time by the creation of a utopia was Johann Valentin Andreae,[2] preacher

---

[1] W. Windelband: *Lehrbuch der Geschichte der Philosophie*, IV, pp. 323 ff.

[2] The effect of Andreae's works on education will be emphasized in succeeding chapters. His relation to the past can be briefly told. The history of education from the Reformation to the beginning of the Thirty Years' War is to a great degree one of education in Germany. The educational reforms of Luther gave an impetus that could not easily be checked and that bore fruit most readily in his own country. After his, the names of Melanchthon, Sturm, Ratke; of Loyola, later of Campanella and Bacon, take prominent places. Andreae was a great admirer and a loyal follower of Luther. He speaks of him often and praises the work Luther did in church and school. But he seriously felt the need of a "second reformation" in both; not a return merely to the teachings of Luther but, as civilization had a century of additional experiences, a step ahead, a better system for the next generation. Moreover, Andreae had the scheme for such an advance. While at the university, he planned a reform of educational methods—his first published production and his last are pedagogical works. Nothing lay so near his heart or occupied so much of his time and energy as education. Bacon, in England, bent his energies on scientific research; Comenius strove to improve the school systems. Andreae had elaborate and perfected plans for *all* phases of instruction, from the primary grades to the highest, for the individual and for the state, including development spiritual, intellectual, moral, and physical.

Andreae, as has been said, was a staunch supporter of Luther's educational and religious doctrines, and a careful student of the whole field in the period following Luther. But he was not dependent upon these for all his material or his methods.

Andreae's pedagogical principles, as outlined in the *Christianopolis* and *Theophilus,* show an advance over Luther (who influenced him most)—an advance as shown in a more complete and rounded-out system of education as well as in the subject-matter of the courses. Luther stood too much under the shadow of Humanism,

and teacher at Vaihingen, Calw, and Stuttgart, founder of the " home " at Calw, traveler, writer, and finally general philanthropist. And his utopia, *Reipublicae Christiano-politanae Descriptio,* shows originality in plan of government and education, as well as advancement and progress beyond its predecessors and indeed beyond some of its immediate successors in the field; while a decade earlier in his *Fama Fraternitatis* [1] he outlines a plan for scientific investigation and gives the model for a " college " or society of fellows which shall institute a " general reformation " of the whole civilized world. Andreae's many-sided education and experiences, his deep interest in and clear insight into the affairs of men and humanity, his strong desire to uplift human society and to alleviate pain and suffering, gave his works recognition and careful considera-

and was too deeply engrossed in the church of his time, to be able to see the value of the study of any foreign language except Hebrew and the classics. Hence, although his religious reforms embraced all nations, his educational system was much less cosmopolitan. The educational system of Andreae, just as faithful and tried a Christian, is broader and considers the world. In questions of incentives, breadth of curricula, illustrative material, and like matters, he is far beyond his predecessors, while " he is the *first* who requires a regulated gymnasium " (Brügel, p. 174). It is with reference to matters of this kind that Vogt (p. 166) says, " Especially the elaborately developed pedagogical principles of Andreae are entirely his incontestable property." It must be added that many reforms existing merely " on paper " were revived by him.

[1] The *Fama Fraternitatis,* one of the so-called " Rosenkreutzer-schriften " of Andreae, is briefly outlined later (p. 72). The volume was received with the greatest enthusiasm, and soon appeared (Maack: *Geheime Wissenschaften,* Intro., xxxvii) in several languages: Latin, 1614; Dutch, 1615; French, 1616; Italian, 1617; English, 1652. As will be shown in the course of the following pages, Bacon and other English scientific investigators may easily have had access to the Latin or the French edition. For references to the *Fama,* see pp. 39, 54, 59, 72, 119, 120, 121.

tion in his own day, and make them effective even to the present time and worthy of closer attention. His life and activity may be briefly outlined as follows : [1]

Johann Valentin Andreae was born on the seventeenth of August 1586, the son of Johann Andreae, Dekan at Herrenberg and later Abt von Königsbronn. After his father's death (Valentin was fifteen years old) the boy, accompanied by his mother, whose quiet, religious temperament left an indelible stamp upon his life, moved to Tübingen, where he spent six years at the university. These years were of the greatest importance to him. He perfected himself in Latin, Greek, and Hebrew ; French, Spanish, Italian, and English. He also read widely in contemporary history and literature, and he became well acquainted with Erasmus, Lipsius, Scaliger, Heinsius, and De Thou—the library of Christopher Besold being at his disposal at this time. Not the least of his interests was the study of mathematics under Mästlin, the teacher of Kepler. In 1614 Andreae published a series of lectures, *Collectanea Mathematica,*[2] and in several of his later educational writings, mathematics play an important part. He kept up a correspondence with Kepler till the latter's death.

Not completing his work at Tübingen, Andreae spent seven years in travel. During these years, supporting himself to a considerable extent by private tutoring, he visited Strassburg, Heidelberg, Frankfurt, and several towns in Switzerland. His stay in this country seems to have impressed him strongly. Andreae makes especial reference in his autobiography to the social conditions in Geneva ; but

---

[1] *Allgemeine Deutsche Biographie; Realenzyklopädie f. Protestantische Theologie u. Kirche; Andreae und sein Zeitalter,* W. Hossbach; Andreae's *Vita.*

[2] Discussed at length by Carl Hüllemann: *Valentin Andreae als Pädagog,* I. Teil.

he could not tolerate the Calvinistic teachings. "If differences in religion (*religionis dissonantia*) had not restrained me, the harmonious unity of their customs and morals (*consonantia morum*) would have bound me to the place forever." [1]   And so he continued his wanderings, this time through France, Austria, and Italy. At last (1614) he obtained a position as Diakonus in Vaihingen, which he retained until 1620. Though full of trials and calamities, these years were among the most productive of his life. Some of his best works fall within or just before this period, as, for example, his *Theophilus,* which was composed during this time, though not published until 1649. He was outlining the theories which he put into practice during the last half of his life.

Next he was called to Calw on the Nagold, as Dekan and Spezialsuperintendent. Here he tried to establish a social system such as had existed in his imagination since his visit to Switzerland. He made his own congregation the starting point of his activities, and the children his material. Thence his efforts spread to the working classes in the city, whether in his church or not. He founded a mutual protective association among the workmen in the cloth-factories and dyeworks, and supported it from the voluntary subscriptions of his parishioners and friends. The organization exists today in flourishing condition and is well endowed. At the time of the sack of Calw by Johann von Werth's troops in 1634, and again four years later, Andreae lost heavily—not only in money and property, but especially from the destruction of his private collection of valuable manuscripts, paintings, and other works of art. The year following the last raid, Andreae accepted the urgent invitation of Duke Eberhardt III and became Hofprediger and Consistorial-Rat at Stuttgart. All Würtemberg was in a state of absolute

[1] *Vita,* p. 24.

devastation. His task was to reëstablish the Tübinger Stift and the Gymnasium at Stuttgart, as well as to fill the many vacant pulpits with worthy men, and to provide for the support of the latter. His personal income was exceedingly scant; and it was only through the encouragement and material assistance of Duke August von Braunschweig-Lüneberg that Andreae could support his family and the numerous refugees who always found a welcome in his home. After 1650 he withdrew to the Abtei von Beben-hausen, and four years later to that of Adelburg, where he died June the twenty-seventh of the same year.

The works of Andreae to be especially considered are mentioned in the bibliography; of these the *Descriptio* and the *Fama Fraternitatis* are of greatest importance for the present purpose. The commentators whose opinions will be discussed in the following chapter are W. Hossbach,[1] Robert von Mohl,[2] G. E. Guhrauer,[3] Christoph Sigwart,[4] Carl Hüllemann,[5] J. P. Glöckler,[6] *Schlaraffia Politica*,[7] W. Gussmann,[8] Andreas Voigt,[9] Joseph Prys,[10] J. Brügel,[11] and C. Vogt.[12] Of these the earlier ones take up the subject from a philosophical-religious point of view; while those

[1] *Andreae und sein Zeitalter.*

[2] *Die Staatsromane,* in *Geschichte u. Literatur d. Staatswissen-schaften,* I, p. 165.

[3] *Der Erste Deutsche Staatsroman.*

[4] *Kleine Schriften,* Freiburg i/B und Tübingen.

[5] *Valentin Andreae als Pädagog,* I, II.

[6] *Johann Valentin Andreae: ein Lebensbild,* Stuttgart, 1886.

[7] Anonymous: *Geschichte der Dichtungen vom besten Staate,* Leipzig, 1892.

[8] *Reipublicae Christianop.* Desc., in der ZkWL, Jahrg. 1886, pp. 326 ff., Leipzig, 1886.

[9] *Die Sozialen Utopien,* Leipzig, 1906.

[10] *Der Staatsroman des 16. u. 17. Jahrhunderts u. sein Erziehungs-ideal,* Würzburg, 1913.

[11] Schmidt: *Geschichte der Erziehung.*

[12] *Euphorion,* 1910, pp. 38-48.

which come in the latter part of the nineteenth century or later, that is, since the rise and rapid development of the principles of socialism and communism, have for their evident aim the lessons of common ownership and socialistic reform. To a considerable extent the prejudiced and erroneously formed conclusion of Mohl [1] as to the relation of the *Christianopolis* to earlier utopias, and the comments in *Schlaraffia* and of Sigwart have been taken over literally or in slightly modified form by most of the later writers on the subject. The number of arguments that have to be dealt with is, therefore, limited.

It is the purpose of this investigation to prove 1) That the *Christianopolis* is not a copy or direct imitation of earlier utopias, but an independent and original production. 2) That a close comparison of the *Christianopolis* with Francis Bacon's *New Atlantis* shows some striking similarities in form and content; and that external circumstances, also, make a knowledge of the *Christianopolis* on the part of Bacon extremely probable. 3) That *Nova Solyma*, a utopia appearing anonymously in 1648, attributed (1902) by the Rev. Walter Begley to John Milton, but since known to be the work of Samuel Gott, shows direct influence of the *Christianopolis*. And 4) that the principles of a general reformation in education and the plan of a " college " as outlined in the *Christianopolis* and other works of Andreae, were an important factor through J. A. Comenius, Samuel Hartlib, John Dury, and their associates, in the founding of the Royal Society of London.

[1] Mohl came upon the German translation of the *Christianopolis* first, and not knowing the original, considered it a production of the eighteenth century—" the work of some pietist." Having once expressed an unfavorable opinion on the work, he did not see fit to withdraw the same even after Guhrauer discovered the real author.

CHAPTER II

MORE'S *UTOPIA,* CAMPANELLA'S *CIVITAS SOLIS,* AND THE *CHRISTIANOPOLIS*

OF the commentators mentioned in the introduction Carl Hüllemann [1] does not think that Gussmann and Brügel lay sufficient emphasis upon the influence of More's *Utopia* upon the *Christianopolis.* He cites a number of passages showing similarities between the two, chiefly in external matters such as the description of the town, houses, gardens, and so forth, and in a few details of daily customs and habits. He also shows that in some cases both authors used the same vocabulary in dealing with similar subjects. From this he draws the conclusion, " We see then that the *Descriptio* is only in part an imitation of More's *Utopia,* but for the rest a remodeling." [2] The author of *Schlaraffia Politica* would make More the " father of all modern utopias " and continues, " For practically all sketches of ideal states, which have been written up to the present time, seem to be direct copies (*Abklatsch*) of the work of More." [3]

Robert von Mohl,[4] on the other hand, sees in the *Descriptio* only a recasting of Campanella's *Civitas Solis.* He admits that the contrast between real life in state and society, and a life based upon an exclusively religious-moral philosophy, would be an excellent motive for a work such as

[1] *Valentin Andreae als Pädagog,* II. Teil.
[2] P. 7.
[3] P. 43.
[4] *Geschichte und Literatur der Staatswissenschaft,* Bd. I, S. 187 ff.

16

(he insists) Andreae *tried* to compose. But he denies the latter's poetic and imaginative ability to do so. "Unfortunately the good Diakonus of Würtemberg did not know how to handle the thought cleverly and with inspiration (*Geist*). He believed he had done enough when he had substituted pious reflection for the dissoluteness of the Calabrian, and the prosaic reality of an orthodox Protestant country for offensive institutions and the artificially-composed religions of the same. His imagination was not lively enough to embody his teaching in living forms. Excepting the fact that he introduces prayer meetings and the like into his *Christianopolis,* and that he quietly restores the order of marriage and family into Christian society, he depends almost slavishly upon the *Civitas Solis.*" Mohl then cites a few points of similarity between the *Christianopolis* and the *Civitas Solis*—plan of the city and forms of government—and closes triumphantly with the argument, "At any rate, Andreae's version (*Überarbeitung*) of the *Civitas Solis* is a book very little known; while the original is still being republished and translated." [1]

Christoph Sigwart, careful and reliable as his criticism usually is, judges the *Christianopolis* harshly and, it must be added, very incorrectly when he says: "Inasmuch as temporal welfare and the abundance of material goods which serve its ends, not only have no value in themselves but are even dangerous to piety, every inner impulse to penetrate into the material activity of work is wanting; for where knowledge of the world is foolishness, and to know and love Christ the essence of all wisdom, a noble desire to

---

[1] A revival of interest in the *Christianopolis* in the eighteenth century is evident from the German translation appearing in 1741, and again in 1754; and Herder saw in Andreae a prophet whose influence would be a blessing to any age.

rule all nature wisely and aggressively must be lacking." [1]
It is hoped that the falseness of this implication will be
made clear in the succeeding pages. Sigwart, like Mohl,
considers the *Civitas Solis* a pattern for the *Christianopolis.*
"Andreae was given incentive to write an imitation of the
Civitas Solis, setting up in his *Descriptio* an ideal state on
the principles of his Protestant-pious philosophy of life." [2]

Andreas Voigt [3] likewise finds in the *Christianopolis* only
an adaptation of Campanella's Catholic notions to the
Protestant Church, and furthermore considers the work of
only second-rate importance. " In all exterior matters," he
says, "especially in the form of the city, his (Andreae's)
utopia coincides with Campanella's. The inner differences
are to be designated throughout as weaknesses and modera-
tions, and besides, are based upon Andreae's stricter ad-
herence to the doctrines of his church."

Joseph Prys [4] also insists that in important questions, as
in the pansophic character of intellectual education, the
depreciation of the languages, emphasis upon teaching by
observation of pictures, and so forth, Andreae coincides
with Campanella. " The supposition (that is, of borrow-
ing) becomes a certainty," he adds, " when we remember
that Andreae knew the *Civitas Solis* in manuscript form,
and that it was first of all through this fact that he was
given the incentive to write his prosaic *Descriptio.*" Exception will have to be taken also to the following: " Common to both utopias is a certain utilitarian tendency in
their pedagogy. In the final analysis, education serves in
both for the advancement and strengthening of the con-

---

[1] *Kleine Schriften von Christoph Sigwart,* I, p. 175.
[2] *Kleine Schriften von Christoph Sigwart,* p. 174.
[3] *Die Sozialen Utopien,* pp. 73 ff.
[4] *Der Staatsroman des 16. u. 17. Jahrhunderts,* p. 114, and p. 32
of this chapter.

trolling idea of government." [1]   Reference will be made to this later.

Carl Vogt, in his discussion of Johann Balthasar Schupp, devotes a number of pages [2] to the relation of the *Christianopolis* to other utopias.   His point of view seems clearest and perhaps least prejudiced of all commentators on this subject excepting, possibly, Brügel in his short but excellent paragraph.   He finds similarities in *Civitas Solis* and the *Christianopolis* as also in Plato, More, and Campanella, which he attributes more to the time or likeness in subject-matter than to literary dependence.   He also grants that there are some features in the *New Atlantis* which resemble the *Christianopolis,* although he is not willing to concede [3] evidence of any influence of Andreae upon Bacon. He sees a closer connection, for instance, between the *New Atlantis* and More's *Utopia;* but the passages [4] he cites in defense of his point of view are not convincing.   Neither is his criticism of Kleinwächter's opinion [5] sufficiently defended.   Furthermore, in his argument opposing the theory of an influence of *Christianopolis* upon *New Atlantis,* he seems to misinterpret a passage in *Christianopolis.*[6] The passage in the examination does not read as he would have it, " Are you a member of the Rosicrucians? ", but the government of Christianopolis must be constantly on guard not to admit into the city "beggars, jugglers . . . and impostors who *falsely say* they are Rosicrusians " (. . . *impostoribus, qui se Roseae Crucis Fratres mentirentur* ").

[1] *Der Staatsroman des 16. u. 17. Jahrhunderts,* p. 115.

[2] *Euphorion,* XVII, pp. 38-48.

[3] The statement that Bacon was influenced by *Christianopolis* is merely made without proof (*Realenzyklopädie f. Prot. Theol. u. K.,* 3. Aufl., Bd. I, S. 507).

[4] *Euphorion,* XVII, pp. 42, 43.   [5] P. 38.   [6] Chap. iv.

Now, it is hardly reasonable that the *Descriptio* should be an "exact copy" of both More and Campanella, especially as the productions of these two differ in many respects from each other. On the contrary it is not very difficult to show that this statement is true in neither case. To offset the likenesses in detail, one might also suggest a number of radical differences in detail. More's island is crescent-shaped; Caphar Salama is triangular. The dimensions of the former are two hundred by five hundred miles; the circumference of the latter but thirty thousand paces. Utopia includes fifty-four cities; Caphar Salama only one. The cities of Utopia are one-man governments at whose head stands a prince; the government of Christianopolis is a triumvirate, this being considered safer and more fair. Common tables are the custom in the *Utopia*. In the *Descriptio* each family eats alone, to avoid confusion and waste of time. The *Utopia* has an elaborate system of slavery; in the *Christianopolis* all citizens are free. In the *Utopia* the dead are burned; in the *Descriptio* they are buried. Though we read that "they detest war as a brutal thing,"[1] the *Utopia* lays great emphasis upon preparations and methods of conducting it, devoting, in fact, one-tenth of the whole work thereto; yet it passes over education in a few words. In the *Descriptio,* war is hardly mentioned, while education of the youth and scientific research permeate almost every chapter. The religion of the one is a confused mixture; the other is a Christian state. And the ethical standards throughout, hardly admit of comparison.

Campanella gives no description of the island on which his Civitas Solis lies. His Genoese sea-captain " is compelled to go ashore " and, on emerging from a wood, " finds himself on a large plain." His city is circular and built on

[1] More's *Utopia*, p. 75.

the slope of a hill. Seven concentric walls give repeated means of defense against an enemy. One ruler has supreme authority, temporal and spiritual, over all. He settles all disputes. Boys learn the sciences from magistrates by observing pictures, "without toil and as if for pleasure." Marriage and love are based on the principle of advantage to the state, not to the individual. The *Utopia* and *Civitas Solis* are in dialogue form; the *Descriptio* is a letter, in which the writer tells his own personal experiences. Such teachings and practices as, respect toward one's elders, hospitality to strangers and travelers, simplicity in dress and manners of life, moderation in all things, and so forth,—these are very naturally common to all utopias.

That Andreae knew both More and Campanella is certain. He mentions the former in his introduction to the *Descriptio*. In 1619 he translated several of Campanella's sonnets;[1] and speaks of him as "the talented, untiring, heroic champion against the heathen Aristotle"[2] and against all hypocrites, sophists, and tyrants.[3] With the manuscript of the *Civitas*, Andreae became acquainted in

[1] Sigwart, p. 174.
[2] Gussmann, p. 437.
[3] Campanella in a poem, probably one of those translated by Andreae, speaks of himself as "born to fight Tyranny, Sophistry, and Hypocrisy." In his *Die Christenburg* (see Grüneisen in *Zeitschrift für die historische Theologie*, VI, pp. 239, 246, 257), Andreae introduces the three chief generals of the enemy as Tyrannus, Hypocrita, and Sophista. The composition of this epic poem antedates Andreae's translation of Campanella's sonnets several years. In the introduction of the *Christianopolis* (p. 11, p. 136 in the appended translation) he speaks of hypocrisy as having usurped the place of religion, tyranny that of government, and sophistry that of letters. And it is to escape the dominion of these three that the hero in the *Christianopolis* undertakes his journey (chap. i).

1619 through his friend Tobias Adami, who, being Campanella's editor, was at that time having the manuscript printed in Germany as a part of *Philosophia Realis*.[1]

But the chief differences between the works of More and Campanella as compared with Andreae, are not to be superficially sought in such external characteristics as those mentioned above. The plan and conception of the three seem to be essentially different.

More was closely in touch with political conditions in England and on the Continent. Political reform and his favorite principle of communism are the nucleus of his *Utopia*, and in direct connection with this principle is the problem of the source of supply for the necessities of life. Hence More makes agriculture the chief occupation, and states that while there are various trades and crafts, agriculture is known to all; and all have training therein, in school and in the fields.

The *Utopia* is written in two books, the first of which consists of a discussion carried on by three persons, as to what constitutes the best form of government, and what practices are undesirable. Two abuses are especially censured—exorbitant taxes intended to swell the coffers of wasteful monarchs, and monopoly of land and property granted to privileged classes. So there are rehearsed the various methods of collecting money from the general public—methods common in England in More's own time. And the Genoese captain is quoted as saying, " To speak my real sentiments plainly, I must freely own that as long as there is any property, and while money is the standard of all other things, I cannot think that a nation can be governed either justly or happily." [2] This leads directly to a

[1] Dr. Emanuel Wessely: *Der Sonnenstaat*, Introduction, vi.
[2] P. 30.

description of the government of Utopia, where "people are governed better than anywhere else." And at the close, as a summary of the whole, four pages are devoted to a rehearsal of the reasons for the happiness of the Utopians, the trend of which is the following: "Thus I have described to you, as particularly as I could, the constitution of that commonwealth, which is the only commonwealth deserving the name. In all other places it is noticeable that while people talk of common wealth, everyone seeks his own wealth. But in Utopia there is no unequal distribution; and though no man has anything, yet they are all rich." [1] It is not difficult to see the chief point in More's mind.

Just what is the model for the *Civitas* is not very clear. Of the various interpretations, Gussmann agrees with Sudre when the latter says: "The monastery is the model for his (Campanella's) social organization. The priestly power and the church hierarchy are the foundation for the government of his new society. The sun-cities are groups of cloisters in which men and women live under a strict system of government." [2]

It must be admitted that parallels are not wanting. The head authority (Metaphysicus), as has been said, the judge in matters of both church and state, represents the pope, he with his three subordinate rulers appointing the rest. While political freedom and religious toleration are repeatedly mentioned, both are restricted by law and custom. Occasionally one even finds a phrase or sentence which smacks decidedly of the cloister—as when describing the common dining-room, "On one side sit the women and

[1] P. 95.
[2] W. Gussmann: *Reipublicae Christianopolitanae Descriptio,* in der ZkWL, Jahrg. 1886, p. 439.

on the other the men; and, as in the refectories of the monks, there is no noise." [1]

As in the *Utopia,* common ownership of property is an important feature. But carrying the point to a greater extreme, Campanella would make women part of the "*Gemeingut*" of the state. And his point of view is very clear. In the *Civitas* the individual exists for the state, not the state for its citizens. Hence, that the state may be of a high standard physically and intellectually, that it may be able to defend itself against possible attack, that the race may continue to be powerful, he has those in authority mate men and women, even as cattle are bred, considering only physical and temperamental characteristics, and thus assuring a stalwart offspring; for sexual love, as we have it between husband and wife, is not known. Should a man and a woman be inspired with a natural feeling of love, " it is permitted them to converse, joke, crown each other with wreaths and garlands, and even to write verses in one another's honor." But in general " they know in their love nothing other than feelings of friendliness." [2]

While at the Dominican monastery of Stilo, Campanella—then about seventeen years of age—met an old rabbi to whom he felt strangely attracted. During the week they spent together, Campanella was instructed in the mysteries of the occult sciences—alchemy, astrology, and magic. Of these astrology exerts the strongest influence in the *Civitas* of Campanella. On the walls of the temple, representations of the stars are to be seen; and verses describing their size, courses, and secret influences are added. [3] Another set of verses explains the homes of trees and plants, their chief characteristics and *their relation to the stars.* Trees are planted by the gardeners, cattle are bred

[1] *Sonnenstaat,* p. 22.   [2] P. 30.   [3] P. 10.

by their care-takers,[1]—even men and women are allowed to mate, only *when certain heavenly bodies are in conjunction.* Inventions and scientific discoveries are made,[2] calamities are averted,[3]—in fact " we do all things under the influence of the heavens." [4] As More's *Utopia* closes with a lengthy summary, which is to a great extent an elaboration of the principles of communism, so the closing pages of the *Civitas* are a tribute to the accomplishments of astrology—beginning with an exclamation on the part of the sea-captain, " O, if you but knew what they have learned from astrology . . . ! "

The question is raised by Voigt [5] whether the *Descriptio* is to be considered at all seriously, or whether Andreae intended that it should be taken in a purely allegorical sense. In support of the latter hypothesis, Voigt quotes a fable of Andreae's in which Truth, wandering about nakedly, and complaining of ill-treatment at the hands of those whom she would like to assist, is given this advice by Aesop: " Clothe your form in fable and fairy-tale, and you will be able to do your duty by God and man." [6] Voigt continues : " If Andreae was here thinking of his *Descriptio,* then we cannot class the latter with those utopias which were intended to represent a practical execution of an ideal; but we must rather look upon it as a mere poetic expression of his wishes."

Andreae learned early that the safest and most certain way to fix an argument and to secure the acceptance of a doctrine, is to give it a touch of poetic fancy. In commenting on this characteristic, Herder says: " All that Andreae writes takes the form of the fable—the expression in clever garb (*Einkleidung*) ; he speaks truths to which

[1] P. 45.   [2] P. 67.   [3] P. 70.   [4] P. 68.
[5] *Die Sozialen Utopien,* p. 75.
[6] Andreae: *Apologorum Christianorum Manip.,* VI, No. 29.

we hardly venture to give utterance now, after a hundred years' advancement. He speaks them with as much love and honesty, as brevity and sagacity; so that even yet he stands new and fresh in this quarreling, heretical century, and blooms in delicate fragrance like a rose among thorns." [1] We need only refer to the *Fama Fraternitatis*, the *Confessio, Die Christenburg*, or the *Chymische Hochzeit*. Is this sufficient reason for concluding that Andreae was not serious, nor hoped to outline a plan according to which a real social community and city government could exist? Or shall we think that Bacon was not in earnest with his utopia, when he called it "The *Fable* of the New Atlantis"? In explaining his purpose in the use of satire in the *Menippus*, Andreae says: "I call upon God to witness that I have not persecuted anyone, nor made sport at the expense of another, wantonly; but the cause of Christianity lay near my heart, and I desired to advance that cause by all means. As I could not do this directly, I tried a roundabout method —not, as it seemed to some, for the love of satire as many pious people do; but that I might accomplish something by means of jest and biting wit, and inspire love for Christianity." [2] Shall we regard More less seriously because his *Utopia* is an ill-concealed satire on the conditions existing in his own country? This view would seem to be just as unwarranted as that of Mohl when he, going quite to the other extreme, accuses Andreae of a substitution of the "*prosaic* realities of an orthodox-protestant country" for Campanella's more imaginative efforts, and denies a sufficient tact and spirit (*Geist*) on Andreae's part to handle the subject.[3] As a matter of fact, the two decades he spent

---

[1] Glöckler: *Johann Valentin Andreae: ein Lebensbild*, p. 42. (Quotation adapted from Herder, XVI, pp. 591 ff., and *Teutscher Merkur*, March, 1782.) [2] *Vita*, p. 46.
[3] *Geschichte u. Literatur d. Staatswissenschaft*, p. 188.

at Calw as Dekan and Spezialsuperintendent, represented a continuous effort, in spite of the most discouraging conditions, to put into execution the ideals which he had long cherished and which he had stated in his utopia. His efforts were not successful. The Thirty Years' War sapped the life and strength of the community, but his perseverance and his renewed efforts, after each interference, to realize the very principles taught in the *Descriptio,* give evidence of the place the latter held in his own opinion. There is reason to believe that More, Campanella, and Bacon, as well as Andreae, looked upon their respective utopias as the embodiment of the teachings they desired to give to the world.

In his autobiography [1] Andreae gives the following very interesting and suggestive description of the impression made upon him by conditions at Geneva—which city he visited on his journey of 1610. " When I was in Geneva, I made a notable discovery, the remembrance of which and longing for which will die only with my life. Not alone is there in existence an absolutely free commonwealth, but as an especial object of pride (*ornamentum*) a censorship of morals (*disciplina*) in accordance with which investigations are made each week into the morals and even into the slightest transgressions of the citizens—first by the supervisors of the wards, then by the aldermen, and finally by the magistrate, according as the case demands. As a result, all cursing, gambling, luxury, quarreling, hatred, conceit, deceit, extravagance, and the like, to say nothing of greater sins, are prevented. What a glorious adornment— such purity of morals—for the Christian religion! With our bitterest tears we must lament that this is lacking and almost entirely neglected with us; and all right-minded men must exert themselves to see that such is called back to

[1] *Vita,* p. 24.

life." One cannot help feeling that this "ideal state" of affairs—as it seemed to him—was the germ which gave incentive to his efforts of succeeding years. And there can be little doubt that his ideas of a utopia date from this time, especially as his *Descriptio* paints just such a picture of moral purity as here described.

The introduction of the *Christianopolis* is by no means its least interesting or suggestive division. Andreae sees two classes of persons in the world, one class composed of those who constantly admire and defend conditions as they exist; the other, of those who bear patiently the burdens which are heaped upon them, but who continually sigh for an improvement of society. The one in its misguided zeal keeps stirring up trouble and confusion, but accomplishes nothing; the other by sense and modesty acts as a conservative balance. Some have thought that God purposely permits the one class to be covered by mental darkness, that those who see the light from above may, when matters arrive at too evil a stage, overturn the corrupt system. And this is actually what was done by Dr. Luther, when his pleadings for reform were not heeded. In the meantime another darkness has fallen upon Christians; the success of the former reformation is not complete. There is need of another "general reformation" which shall accomplish what was missed before. The Devil is trying to persuade even Christians that no further efforts are necessary. But greed, extravagance, envy, laziness, and a whole catalogue of sins have again crept into the lives of men. Some still retain the light of the new religion, a proper conception of learning and art, of the rules of daily life;[1] but these are surrounded by tyrants, sophists, and hypocrites. Recently

[1] Andreae mentions several of these reformers, and includes Johann Arndt, to whom he dedicates the book.

when a so-called " *Brüderschaft* " [1] was suggested, whose teachings were exactly the reform the world needs,—what a disturbance was created among those who feared the overthrow of their power, and an abolishment of their deceitful performances, juggleries, and sophistries. And when it was discovered that the " *Fraternitas* " was secret and could not include the world in general, and when people became confused as to its real meaning, then one praiseworthy man called out, " Why do we wait for the coming of such a fraternity? Let us rather make a trial ourselves of that which seems good to us." Whereupon Andreae suggests the possibility of persons forming together a community where the principles of right living and freedom may be practiced, unhampered by the enemy. " An example of this rest and safety " is to be found in the lives of the inhabitants of Christianopolis now to be described,— not merely as they ought to be, but as they actually live. No one is compelled to come to this place ; but all who desire to do so, if found to be of proper character, are welcome. This invitation is repeated at the close of the work when the pilgrim returns to his native land, and at parting from the inhabitants of the island, asks permission to return and bring along his friends.

A beautiful opening chapter, which probably is partly responsible for the opinions of some, that the *Christianopolis* is a mere allegory, introduces the hero, a stranger in the realm of the authorities of tyranny, false art, and hypocrisy, as about to set out anew upon the " *Mare Academicum* " in search of enlightenment and a peaceful abode. The weather, fair and favorable at first, soon begins to darken ; and the ship, " *Phantasia,*" is beaten about by the storms of envy

[1] Andreae refers to the so-called Rosicrucian brotherhood.

and slander, driven into the sea of darkness, and finally wrecked.

Caphar Salama [1] is the island upon which one of the survivors of the wreck is thrown. Before he can be taken up into the city, he is subjected to a close examination [2] by each of three officials. This is an entirely new feature in utopias, and serves among other things to give the impression of a more complete and finished production. Later utopias make use of and expand this point. The first examination is preliminary, and a satisfactory conclusion of the same is necessary before the visitor may be fed or refreshed. This is a guard against the admittance of tramps and professional beggars. The second examiner [3] is without peer in shrewdness and ability•to read character. It is his duty to obtain information regarding the stranger's family, history, manner of life, health, and so forth. He makes no pretensions toward learning, but leaves this field to the third. [4] This examination proves to be the most embarrassing of all. The visitor, though by self-confession a scholar, finds himself irretrievably beyond his depths in the discussions of language, art, science, investigation, natural history, as also in that of charity, church, and the-

---

[1] The name is that of a village in Palestine noted on account of the battle in which Judas Maccabaeus conquered Nicanor (Wahl: *Clavis Librorum Vet. Test. Apochrif. Philol.*, Lips, 1853, p. 497). Reference to the battle is found in *Macca.*, I, pp. 7, 31. O. Kemper (*Der Inselname Capharsalama in J. V. Andreae's Schrift, Christianopolis*, M. C. G., VIII, p. 186) has traced the history and interpreted the meaning of this term. He defines the Hebrew words respectively as "place," "spot," or "village," and "salvation" or "peace," and the combination as "Friedensdorf," or "village of peace." This, with the term "Hierosolyma" (Jerusalem, Friedensstadt), which Andreae uses in the introduction to *Christianopolis*, referring to his "*minuta colonia*," and again in his *Vita*, pp. 258, 278, is entirely in keeping with the purpose of his utopia as expressed therein.

[2] Chap. iv.   [3] Chap. v.   [4] Chap. vi.

ology. He is now given an escort of three men who accompany him upon a tour of inspection and instruct him in all matters. An examination into the facts thus obtained and an analysis of material used will help give an idea of Andreae's conception of an ideal state, and will be a second proof of the comparative lack of dependence, in essentials, upon More and Campanella.

The most important and the most oft-recurring theme in the *Christianopolis* is that of education and training of the youth, and it is this which contains most of Andreae's personality. The teaching profession[1] is highly honored, and rightly. For instructors are not chosen from the lower classes—men who have not the ability to be useful in other lines, and who are therefore willing to teach for little pay— but they are selected on account of being remarkable for character and information. The teachers are of reasonable age, clean in life, upright, industrious, and gentlemen in every way. They are equipped with skill, shrewdness, and sense, and the ability to apply these virtues. For the citizens of Christianopolis realize that to intrust their sons and daughters to worthless or careless instruction, is to ruin the individual and the state as well. " For certain it is that no ones serves youth well except he likewise be able to care for the state; and he who proves himself of value to youth, has already benefited the state." Boys and girls are sent to the boarding school at six years of age. Parents do not hesitate to send their children from home, for they have the best possible care and attention. Education is threefold: worship of God with a pure soul, practice of a moral life, intellectual development. Boys recite in the morning, girls in the afternoon. The other half of the day is spent in mechanical occupation and household science and art.

[1] Chap. lii.

Their physical training consists of running, wrestling, riding, fencing, throwing, and the like.

Intermediate education [1] is given in institutions of fine arts, classed as schools of grammar, rhetoric, and languages. Foreign—modern and ancient—languages are studied and learned much more rapidly than in other countries. The chief object is not so much the attainment of learning as a means of boastfulness, but the ability to hold intercourse with other peoples, " both the living and the dead." This is a chapter out of Andreae's life. With all his study of science, mathematics, and theology at Tübingen, he was deeply interested in foreign languages, ancient and modern; so that before he was out of university, he was master of seven or eight. He gives as one object of his trip through France in 1610, the chance it would give to perfect himself in French. Prys is hardly justified [2] in comparing the *Christianopolis* with *Civitas Solis* on the basis of lack of appreciation of the value of languages. On the contrary, in Andreae's state it is required that all pupils perfect themselves in languages, as has already been seen. However, it is considered a serious mistake to neglect the mother tongue. For in this a student will express himself most naturally, and natural development of the mind and soul are especially to be desired. In rhetoric and oratory the same argument carries weight. While eloquent speakers and forceful writers are trained, *mere polish* and beauty of address are scorned.

Advanced studies are pursued in seven other auditoria or lecture halls. Dialectics, metaphysics, and theosophy may be studied in the second. The practical application of a good method is the aim of dialectics. Observation of the True, the Good, and the Beautiful, of unity and harmony, is

---

[1] Chaps. lv, lvi, lvii.   [2] *Der Staatsroman*, p. 114.

the essence of metaphysics. Theosophy is the highest form of this group. " Where nature ends, theosophy begins; it is the last resort, the finding in God what cannot be obtained by physical experiment." And only a few, comparatively, attain this. What fools men are who try to prove through Aristotle what God alone can fathom! Here Andreae proves that he is neither a sophist nor an unreasoning believer in astrology or alchemy. His philosophy of life is suggested in a number of instances throughout this and other works: Gain all possible information by sensible and reliable experiment and investigation; but thereafter leave the impossible, and *accept* nature and God.

The third auditorium is that of mathematics. Arithmetic, algebra, geometry, surveying, and mystic numbers are important as affording good mental training and also for their practical use when applied to the experiences of everyday life. Under the term " secret and mystic numbers " are not meant the cabalistic and deceiving combinations of jugglers, but rather the proportions of higher mathematics, then but dimly understood. " Harmony," " symmetry," " measurements of calculation " are favorite terms with Andreae to suggest the divine plan of the universe. He distinctly states here and elsewhere that faith in God, and not in *superhuman* endeavor, must be the test of our efforts. " Into these matters which seem to give forth such brilliant light let us not pry, unless the light of Christ leads the way and calls us into the sealed secret." [1]

Music [2] is treated scientifically and artistically. This is the fourth division. A knowledge of mathematics is an essential requisite. Combination of tones—harmony—is practiced, and produces almost unbelievable results. Musical instruments are manufactured and kept on hand—all pos-

[1] Chap. lxiii.   [2] Chaps. lxiv, lxv, lxvi.

sible kinds and of the finest quality. Hardly a citizen can be found who does not play one or the other of them. The voice is not neglected. But vocal music is restricted almost entirely to sacred song. The chorus is splendid, and passes singing through the streets of the city each week.

Astronomy and astrology are the departments of the fifth auditorium, and these are treated in close relationship to each other.[1] It is of importance to observe the heavens and the heavenly bodies; for man is directly dependent upon them for light, heat, rain, and so forth. He would be a fool, according to Andreae, who would deny the practical use of such a science; but there is so much difference of opinion and quarreling among scientists as to the mystical effect of the planets upon human beings, that the inhabitants of Christianopolis think it safer to look toward the spiritual heavens than upon the visible, for prophetic information. One brief sentence will serve to explain. "Experience strengthens faith, but reason is ever in doubt and confusion." Andreae is here entirely consistent with his views as expressed in other writings and, though he lived in an age when the wisest were strongly affected,[2] is singularly free from contamination with the extreme teachings of astrology and alchemy.

Natural history,[3] secular and church history furnish the subject-matter for the teachings of the sixth lecture hall. "It is needless to tell why they are so interested in natural history, since the very necessity of the science demands it. For through it we arrive at a general, as well as a specific, exact knowledge of the world; and investigate the movements, characteristics, behavior, and passions of creatures; what are the elements, form, measure, place, and time of

[1] Chaps. lxvii, lxviii.   [2] See page 121, footnote 2.
[3] Chaps. lxx, lxxi, lxxii.

things; how the heavens are moved, the elements are mixed, how things grow, what metals are useful. . . ." Natural history accompanies the science of human history—the relation of the experiences of man.

Ethics, political science, and Christian humility are in the seventh auditorium. Theology, gift of prophecy, and sanctification are in the eighth. Three principles stand out in the political and public life of Christianopolis: preserving the peace, equality of citizens, and contempt for large possessions. The practice of these principles guards the state and its citizens against the three greatest evils: war, slavery, and corruption in public affairs. The school of prophecy is intended not to teach the ability to prophesy, as has deceived so many, but to observe the harmony and truth of the prophetic spirit, as well as to be able to interpret the workings of the holy spirit and recognize inspiration from above.

The library, the armory, and the college must yet be mentioned as important features of the town.[1] The two former are in the central keep, and are opposite each other. The one is a storehouse of learning. Ancient books, lost to Europeans, are to be found here. Most of the citizens, however, care for only a few reliable books (including, of course, the Bible), and prefer to get knowledge directly from the "book of nature." The armory might better be called a museum. While cannon and guns are on hand in great numbers and ready for use in case of need, they are looked upon with horror, and the necessity for their usefulness is considered an invention of the Devil.

"Now it were time that we should approach the very center of the city, which you might well call its soul and life, . . . Here religion, justice, and learning have their abode, and theirs is the control of the city. They have elo-

[1] Chaps. xxxviii, xxxix, xxvi.

quence associated with them as their interpreter. Never have I seen such an amount of human perfection collected in one place, a fact which you will all acknowledge as soon as you have heard the description." [1]

The art of painting is very highly prized. Like Campanella, Andreae has his city thoroughly fitted out with paintings. Even the private rooms of the school children are appropriately adorned. Furthermore, taking a decided step forward, Andreae causes painting to be taught to the youth as an auxiliary to his education. The pupils improve their time with the brush, as one form of recreation, while among us, time is wasted in cards, dice, and so forth. To this, architectural drawing is added, and all necessary instruments are supplied. It should be noted that in the *Civitas* of Campanella the *observation* of pictures *is* the education; and it is distinctly stated that pupils learn " as in play and without any effort on their part." [2] This is, in the extreme, a dangerous method. Education, by means of sugar-coated and predigested capsules of knowledge, is too much the tendency in our own day. Andreae could give us a wholesome warning. His young people, it is true, use pictures for illustration, but they *make their own* illustrative material, and learn by trial and experiment. [3]

The introduction of experimental investigation and inductive teaching in utopias, practically begins with Andreae; and this is the foundation of his chapters on science and invention. Among these are descriptions of the laboratory,[4] the drug shop,[5] anatomy,[6] the theater of physics,[7] the study of nature,[8] and medicine.[9]

[1] The college will be further discussed in succeeding chapters.
[2] *Sonnenstaat*, p. 13.
[3] Chap. xlviii.
[4] Chap. xliv.
[5] Chap. xlv.
[6] Chap. xlvi.
[7] Chap. xlvii.
[8] Chap. lxx.
[9] Chap. lxxix.

Religion is the leaven of Caphar Salama, for its colony is a practical Christian city. There is no hypocrisy nor compulsion. The inhabitants are here by choice, and live voluntarily according to the principles of the Christian religion. Freedom, the keynote of government, is also the essence of the religious life. Religion has taken up her abode here to escape persecution.[1] Though Andreae's worst experiences came later than 1619, persecution and the horrors of a religious war were not unknown to this time. And the name of his " place of refuge " already referred to,[2] is typical of his own lifelong desire for a home of religious peace and rest.

Two plates of bronze, one [3] giving at some length the confession of faith, and the other [4] setting forth the aims and rules of daily life, are publicly posted—not merely that visitors may become acquainted with their creed, but that the latter may be ever before the inhabitants. Herein they pledge themselves to a pure, temperate, and active life, subject only to the commands of Christ and His representatives. As will be naturally supposed, prayer takes an important place—at the tables, in school, and in all meetings; a fact which gives occasion for Mohl's ironical remark already referred to, namely, that Andreae merely adds " prayer meetings," and for the rest, copies Campanella directly.

With such principles of education and religion, the government and social and family life of Christianopolis will be readily understood. The officials are not feared but respected. Their offices are performed in kindness and co-operation. A direct influence of the government of Geneva (as quoted above from Andreae's *Vita*) is found in the

---

[1] Chap. iii; pp. 58, 59 of the following chapter.
[2] See footnote 1, p. 30 of this chapter.
[3] Chap. xxviii.   [4] Chap. xxix.

description of the office of chief judge.[1] This individual makes it his business, and it is also his pride, to guard against the temptations that come to the citizens, and to help them to resist the same. Lawsuits [2] do not occur, as property rights are not involved. The jurists are teachers of political science and Roman law. They are the official scribes of the community. The senators [3] are truly old, wise men. They study carefully the history of the past and look ahead to plan and meet emergencies.

The family is the unit of social life. Chastity is the highest virtue, and transgressions are abhorred and punished. Marriage is a sacred institution. There being no property endowment, the emphasis is laid upon character and personal worth. Moderation in the relations between husband and wife is practiced—there is such a thing as chastity even in married life. " The crown of woman is motherhood, in the discharge of which duty she takes precedence of all heroes of the world." [4] If one compares the delicacy of Andreae's chapters relating to woman, with the almost bestial principles of the purely physical marriage in the *Civitas,* an idea of the difference in ethical tone which pervades the two works will be obtained. It is not the liberal and modern " eugenic " view of *Civitas Solis,* readjusted to the " prosaic monotony of an orthodox-protestant town," but fundamental differences in the spiritual make-up of the two men. Though nowhere as noticeable as in these chapters, yet the difference of standards and fineness of feeling are evident throughout.

If, in looking over the content of the *Christianopolis,* those features are selected upon which Andreae lays most stress, and which for him form the essential parts of an ideal state, and condense them into groups, the following will appear:

[1] Chap. xxxiii.   [2] Chap. lxxx.   [3] Chap. xciii.   [4] Chap. xc.

education, science, and investigation; religion, music, and art; government and social connections. A comparison of the above headings with the emphasized factors in the *Utopia* and the *Civitas Solis,* and also the method of treatment of these items, will show, 1) that between the *Christianopolis* and the *Utopia* there is slight or partial agreement only in some matters of social laws, government, and religion, though even in these fields the differences are greater than the likenesses; 2) that the *Civitas* lays emphasis upon objective methods of teaching, failure of the Aristotelian method, scientific investigation of nature, mathematics, and the value of painting. To say, however, as several do who have been quoted, that this coincidence necessarily means a copy, is absurd. For these principles of education were a part of Andreae's system long before he saw any of Campanella's manuscript. This will be evident from an inspection of the *Fama* and the *Confessio,* which were in print respectively in 1614 and 1616, and the former of which was circulated in manuscript form as early as 1610. The introduction of the *Fama* contains this prophecy: "The blessed dawn will soon appear, which, after the passing of the gloomy night of moonshine or the scanty glimmerings of the sparks of heavenly wisdom which may still linger with men as presagers of the sunshine, will usher in the pure day, with which all heavenly treasures will become known. This will be the genuine carbuncle, of which we have learned that it will give forth light in darkness—a welcome medicine to take away all ills and anxieties of men." Other parts of these earlier works will be used on later occasions.[1] Besides showing Andreae's early interest in the "wisdom which should reveal all invisible things in the world-secret" (knowledge by experi-

[1] See pp. 72, 119, 120, 121.

mental investigation), this section is also important because it shows that even in 1610 the philosopher's stone as such was for him a myth and merely symbolical of enlightenment.

In defense of the originality of the *Descriptio* (not considering minor likenesses in form and detail) it may then be briefly stated:

1) Andreae's notion of a utopia dates from his visit to Geneva, and his seriousness in the matter of a realization of such an ideal state is proved by his own personal efforts in the communities in which he lived.

2) The principles inculcated are not duplicated in preceding utopias—his conception of an ideal state is a new one; and the system of education as outlined, a marked improvement over all preceding, and, as far as utopias are concerned, is strictly his own.

3) In matters of science and education where the *Christianopolis* and the *Civitas* have important points in common, there is no proof of copying, as the same principles are found in Andreae's earlier works, especially the *Fama,* which antedates the *Civitas.*

4) As a final argument it may be said with Gussmann, " It would indeed speak but badly for Andreae's historical greatness, if his work, which fits so exactly into the frame of his other writings, and which is so thoroughly filled with his own peculiar soul (*Geist*), were nothing more than a dry recasting, the trivial bowdlerization (*Verballhornung*) of the work of another." [1]

[1] W. Gussmann: *Christianopolis,* in der ZkWL, Jahrg. 1886, VII, p. 438.

CHAPTER III

THE *CHRISTIANOPOLIS* AND FRANCIS BACON'S *NEW ATLANTIS*

THE story of the revolt against the Aristotelian method of arriving at conclusions, is one too often discussed to require lengthy repetition. Suffice to say that many scientists of the sixteenth century (among them especially Telesio Bernardino in Italy) were restive under the restrictions of the old system, and were striving, independently and in cooperation, to pave the way for a new philosophy of nature. Among those who fought most strongly against Aristotle and his teaching as it had passed down from his day, and one to whom the greatest credit has been given for overturning an old and instituting a new system of philosophy, is Francis Bacon. It would seem that he early conceived a dislike for Aristotle's system. If we can trust a statement from Dr. Rawley, which the latter says Bacon made to him in commenting upon his early student life, Bacon expressed this dissatisfaction as early as his sixteenth year when a student at Cambridge—namely, that at that time " he first fell into a dislike of the philosophy of Aristotle, on account of its unfruitfulness; it being a philosophy only strong for disputations and contentions, but barren of the production of works for the benefit of the life of man." [1]

Bacon was born in 1560. His father, Sir Nicholas Bacon, had been Lord Keeper of the Royal Seal, to which office Bacon also later attained. Francis Bacon entered Cam-

[1] Rawley's *Life of Bacon*, in *Spedding*, I, p. 4.

41

bridge at twelve, and completed the regular course in the liberal arts. Being destined by his father for service to the state, he accompanied an embassy to France and spent some time at Calais. At his father's death he returned to England and studied law and political science, which became his regular profession in life. It must be added, however, that law as such was never his greatest pleasure. In explanation of this fact a statement of his own may serve. "I possessed a passion for research, a power of suspending judgment with patience, of correcting false impressions, of arranging my thoughts with scrupulous pains. But my birth, my rearing, and education had all pointed toward politics, not philosophy, and, as is not unfrequently the case with young men, I was sometimes shaken in mind by other men's opinions. I also thought that my duty toward my country had special claims upon me. Lastly I conceived the hope, that, if I held some honorable office in the state, I might thus secure helps and supports in my labors, with a view toward the accomplishment of my destined task. . . . With these motives I applied myself to politics." [1] Under Elizabeth and later under James I, Bacon made great advancement in his profession, and held the highest offices in the government, until his disgrace and removal from the chancellorship in 1621. But during this time and especially during the five years of his life in retirement, he seems to have spent all his spare moments and to have devoted his best efforts (if we may judge from his letters and works, and also from comments of Dr. Rawley, his very intimate friend and the editor of his works) to the breaking down of what remained of the old method of Aristotle, and to the building up of a "new system" or

[1] Introduction to G. C. Moore Smith's edition, Bacon's *New Atlantis*, p. 11.

" new instrument " (*organum*).   This was to free the intellectual world from the fetters of pure logic and sophistry
and to open up unknown mines of truth and information—
a system which Bacon maintained was entirely his own and
which would cause a complete revolution in thought.   Of his
many works, those which deal especially with the subject
before us are: *The Advancement of Learning,* published in
English in 1605, the *Novum Organum* in Latin in 1620 and
the *De Augmentis,* Latin, in 1623.   The *Novum Organum*
or *Instauratio Magna* included the *Advancement of Learning* in revised and translated form.   The *Great Instauration* also includes the *Sylva Sylvarum,* or *Natural History,*
and to this was appended the *New Atlantis* when the former
was published for the first time by Rawley after Bacon's
death.   The *Sylva* was the last thing that occupied Bacon's
time.

Whether Bacon was entirely unprejudiced and unselfish
in his scientific efforts is a disputed question.   Wolff paints
Bacon as an antagonist of Aristotle, endeavoring to displace the latter from his world-throne and to establish himself in the vacated place.[1]   In so doing, he maintains that
Bacon fails to realize or at least to confess that his method
is after all not entirely new, but one which eliminates from
Aristotle his purely deductive reasoning, and merely de-
velops and adapts the inductive.   Certain it is that induction so often ascribed to Bacon did not begin with him ;
that the attainment of knowledge through experimental
means and the compiling of masses of detailed facts were,
as already stated, suggested and practiced long before.   But
Bacon was keen and quick-witted enough to grasp the value
of this method and first formulated it into definite principles.   He insists, furthermore, that *his* induction does not

[1] Wolff: *Francis Bacon und seine Quellen,* pp. 235 ff.

consist merely in simple enumeration of details and collection of facts but in an additional process of exclusion and
rejection.[1] This feature is not discoverable in his earliest
works, as for instance *Valerius Terminus,* but as a result of
his own experience, and perhaps suggestions from others,
gradually appears. So that his final scheme, as described
by Spedding,[2] provides for three steps: the ministration of
the senses, of the memory, and of the reason, under which
heads he includes the gathering of facts and material, and
the proper checking of results.

Of all Francis Bacon's works none has created more interest or has been more commented upon than the *New
Atlantis*—partly because of the uncertainty as to the date of
its composition, partly because of its content, and again,
because it is, as distinguished from Bacon's usual attempts,
a work of fiction. The *New Atlantis* was first written in
English, not in Latin as stated by Henry Morley in his
Ideal Commonwealths, and others, and was among the
works [3] translated into Latin during the last five years of
Bacon's life to assure their preservation.[4] There was no
date on the manuscript (it was published in 1627, a year
after Bacon's death, at the end of the *Sylva*) and the work
is a fragment. We are told by Rawley, "That his lordship thought also in the present fable to have composed a
frame of laws of the best state or mold of a commonwealth.
But foreseeing it would be a long work, his desire of collecting the *Natural History* diverted him, which he preferred many degrees before it." [5] In his summary of the

[1] Bacon's *Life and Works,* I, p. 34.
[2] *Life and Works,* I, p. 40.
[3] *Hist. of Henry VII, The Counsels, Civil and Moral, Dialogue of
the Holy War.*
[4] Rawley: *Life of Bacon,* p. 10.
[5] *Works,* III, p. 127, Pref. to the *New Atlantis.*

works of Bacon's last five years (those of his retirement) Rawley puts the *New Atlantis* between the *History of Henry VII* and *De Augmentis*. This would make the date of its composition about 1623. No one disputed this date until in comparatively recent years, when, due to the discovery of some papers in the *Harleian Charters,* which were attributed to Bacon, the date was suddenly pushed back seven to nine years. In the paper referred to [1] the *New Atlantis* is mentioned twice. The contents of the paper would point to a date between 1614 and 1617, according to which the *New Atlantis* must at least have been begun at that time. Dr. S. R. Gardiner took this view, and in his *Life of Bacon* in the *Dictionary of National Biography* states ". . . *New Atlantis,* formerly supposed to have been written as late as 1623, but now known to have been composed before 1617." This change was accepted by all authorities, and was copied in encyclopedias and " lives," until a full analysis of the case appeared in the *Athenæum* [2] in an article by Dr. G. C. Moore Smith. Dr. Smith pointed out that the paper, representing an address given by Bacon before the houses of parliament, was probably the work of Thomas Bushell,[3] written after the death of the former, and put into his mouth for personal reasons. The argument of the article was accepted by Dr. Gardiner in the next issue of the *Athenæum* [4] and the

---

[1] *Harleian Charters,* III, D, 14.

[2] Feb. 3, 1900.

[3] Thomas Bushell (1594-1674) entered the service of Bacon at the age of fifteen years. His habits were those of a spendthrift. When introduced at the court, his extravagant clothes were noticed by King James. He was always in debt, and Bacon came to his rescue often. When the latter was impeached, Bushell retired from public life, but returned after Bacon's death and promoted several mining schemes. In this capacity he seems to have used Bacon's name for his own private ends.

[4] Feb. 10.

matter now stands as formerly. The fact that Dr. Rawley, the private secretary of Bacon, definitely assigns the work to the last five years of Bacon's life, furnishes the strongest possible argument. His statement, just quoted, on the title page of the *New Atlantis,* suggesting that " it was unfinished because Bacon, being pressed for time, preferred to continue the *Natural History,"* would seem to be an additional proof, especially when one remembers that the part in which Bacon was most interested, that of science and invention, was already completed. It can readily be seen why Bacon, having finished that part of his ideal state, and feeling, as he stated several times, that his death would cut off some of his productions, preferred to leave the rest and take up his former task—that which lay nearer to his heart. At any rate Dr. Smith's statement may be accepted: "Accordingly, any attack on Dr. Rawley's date, on the ground of the *Harleian* paper, may be considered to be now abandoned." [1]

It cannot be doubted that Bacon set a high value on the *New Atlantis,* and commentators have not hesitated to attribute to it and to the ideals for which it stands a very prominent place in literature and in the development of modern natural philosophy. First of all Rawley, " Certainly the model is more vast and high than can possibly be imitated in all things. Notwithstanding most things therein are within men's power to effect." [2]

For those who have written on the subject, the *New Atlantis* is the most perfect form of ideal state up to the time of its publication, and for some, the scheme of a college and outline for research therein contained, the one and only model for the Royal Society of London and other

[1] Smith's edition of the *New Atlantis,* Introduction, p. 9.
[2] Title page of the *New Atlantis, Works,* III, p. 127.

similar institutions. Furthermore, that this model of a college and the plans for " investigating nature " appear first in the *New Atlantis* and are entirely original with Bacon has not as yet been much contested. It will be made clear further on, that the former contention is not entirely true; and to show that the latter statement may be seriously doubted, will be the purpose of the discussion immediately succeeding. There are certain undeniable likenesses in the *New Atlantis* and the *Christianopolis* of Andreae, and circumstances point to a relation between them. But before we take up a comparison of the two, the question as to whether it is at all possible that Bacon may have known Andreae's works will be looked into.[1]

Bacon had regular correspondence with men of letters in different parts of Europe, and he kept in as close touch as possible with all available contemporary literary and scientific productions. This cannot be doubted. For although his personal references to such correspondents, those whose interests were scientific rather than political, are comparatively few, certain incidental remarks give evidence of the facts. Only once, so far as is known, does he mention Campanella. But in this brief reference [2] he plainly suggests his acquaintance with him and with his ideas. A letter to Father Redemptus Baranza at Anneci, preserved in the collection of J. P. Niceron,[3] deals with Baranza's opinion on parts of the *Novum Organum*, which was published the second year previous and which Baranza had evidently carefully perused. Bacon's letter asks the latter to take up and develop certain phases of natural

[1] Simon Goulart translated some of Andreae's works into French. Andreae's *Fifty-two Discourses,* translated into French in 1622, are in the Stadtbibliothek at Zürich.

[2] Bacon's *Works,* II, p. 13.

[3] *Life and Letters,* VII, p. 374.

philosophy, and expresses, as he often does, the desire for " fit assistants " in the work he was undertaking. He adds the very suggestive clause, " I have seen those of your works that are published, works, certainly, of great subtlety and diligence in your way. The novelists (regularly at that time for innovators, inventors, and investigators) whom you name, Patricius, Telesius,[1] *besides others whom you do not mention,* I have read. . . . Let our acquaintance be now established." Scaliger [2] is mentioned in the *Sylva.*[3] " Therefore Scaliger does well to make the pleasure of generation a sixth sense," referring to Scaliger's *Exercitationes Adversus Cardanum.* And direct influence from the same source is traceable in the description of the chameleon [4] and elsewhere. Scaliger was in England in 1566 and kept up relations with the Continent while at the University of Leyden.

Among Bacon's memoranda of July 26, 1608,[5] is found this item: " Q. of learned men beyond the seas to be made, and

---

[1] Telesio Bernardino, the Italian philosopher, was born a Calabrian in 1508. He died in 1588. His philosophy is founded on experience, his researches including physics, chemistry, and astronomy. An academy founded by him in Naples, being intended to educate scientists and displace Aristotle's method, is still in existence. His chief work is *De Natura,* which appeared in fragment at Rome in 1568 and in Naples in 1586.

[2] Joseph Justus Scaliger (1540-1609) was perhaps the most famous philologian of the sixteenth century. He studied in Bordeaux and Paris, specializing in the classics and Hebrew literature. In 1566 he was in England, and spent the next twenty-five years in various places in South France. He was converted to the Protestant church, and succeeded Lipsius as professor at Leyden in 1593. He died in 1609. Among his very numerous and various writings are several on scientific subjects. Heinsius, and later Casaubon, were intimate friends and comrades of his.

[3] *Works,* II, p. 556, no. 694.

[4] II, p. 460, no. 360, from Scaliger's *Adversus Cardanum,* p. 196.

[5] *Works,* XI, p. 64.

hearkening who they be that may be so inclined." He was endeavoring to find help in the work of his *Great Instauration* from among the learned men of his own country and the Continent. Shortly after this he tried to interest Casaubon (who was then at Paris), as is plain from a letter Bacon wrote him. [1] Bacon knew of Galileo, and, according to Mr. Ellis' preface to the *Descriptio Globi Intellectualis,* " listened eagerly for news from the stars brought by the latter's telescope." [2]

A letter to Sir Henry Wotton [3] is of especial interest. In this letter Bacon says: " The letter which I received from your lordship upon your going to sea, was more than a compensation for any former omission, and I shall ever be glad to entertain a correspondence with you." [4] Spedding tells us that the letter went in company with three copies of the *Novum Organum.* Wotton was at the time on an embassy to Germany; and having a considerable acquaintance with the men of learning in Europe, could do much to advertise the book. He was so well acquainted with German, that for years in Ingolstadt and Vienna he was mistaken for a German. [5]

[1] *Works,* XI, p. 146.   [2] *Works,* III, p. 511.

[3] Sir Henry Wotton (1568-1639), diplomat and poet, was educated at Oxford, and went upon an extensive tour of Europe in 1588. He visited Altdorf, Linz—where he met Kepler—Vienna, Rome, and other cities in Italy. In 1593 he was with Casaubon at Geneva and later in France. In the service of Essex he accomplished diplomatic missions in France and Germany. After James' ascension to the throne, he was given posts as ambassador in various places in France and Spain. In 1619 he returned to England by way of Germany. He was present at James' funeral and went to parliament under Charles. In his acknowledgment of Bacon's letter and the three copies of the *Novum Organum* he promised to give one of the latter to Kepler.

[4] *Works,* XIV, p. 130.

[5] Lucy Aiken: *Memoirs of the Court of King James I.* London, 1822, I, pp. 117 ff.

A study of the lives of three men would seem especially to point toward a possible connection between Bacon
and the circle of friends and acquaintances of Andreae on
the Continent. These will be taken up separately.

Isaac Casaubon was born at Geneva in 1559. He was educated, and afterwards taught the classics at the university
in his native city. In 1593 he became acquainted with
Sir Henry Wotton, already referred to, who was at that
time on his travels through Europe; and the latter stayed
for some time at the home of Casaubon while in Geneva.
Casaubon soon had a world reputation among scholars.
The French, especially through the efforts of De Thou,[1]
tried hard to win Casaubon for France, by establishing him
at one of the French universities, and in 1596 he went to
Montpellier. Even earlier than this he had formed a close
friendship with Scaliger, then professor at Leyden. They
had been introduced by Richard Thomson, an Englishman.
Scaliger, who was eighteen years Casaubon's senior, did
not at first look upon his overtures with favor, but in the
end came to think very highly of his scholarly attainments,
calling him the " most learned man in Europe." They corresponded regularly until Casaubon's death in England.
From Montpellier Casaubon went to Paris, taking up a position under Henry IV, under the title of *Lectureur du Roi*.
With James he had already been in communication while
the latter was James VI of Scotland, and he was long
desirous of taking up his abode in London. The death of
Henry in 1610 released Casaubon from any obligations to
stay longer; and the same year he started for England in
the suite of Lord Wotton of Marley, the half-brother of

---

[1] De Thou, historian and statesman (1553-1617). His home was
in Paris, and during the reign of Henry IV, beginning in 1594, he
was president of the parliament. He had a wide circle of professional acquaintances, including Scaliger, Heinsius, and Bacon.

Sir Henry. With James he was very intimate. The latter spent hours in conversation with him and supported him with a considerable pension. The Bishop of Ely and the Dean of St. Paul's were his closest friends, and he also spent much time at Oxford and Cambridge. After his death in 1614 he was buried at Westminster. His very numerous publications deal to a considerable extent with the classics, and include translations from Greek into Latin. Among the "learned men beyond the seas,"[1] Casaubon is to be counted.[2] He had become acquainted with some of Bacon's writings and had written to Sir George Cary, expressing his appreciation of them. Bacon took advantage of this fact to open a correspondence with him, and this was at least partly responsible for the call which Casaubon received from James the following year. This letter[3] expresses the desire for friendship and coöperation in the great work of scientific research.

The second individual whose life may have formed a link between those of Bacon and Andreae is Georg Rodolf Weckherlin. He was born at Stuttgart in 1584, and entered the University of Tübingen in the spring of 1601, pursuing the study of jurisprudence. During the years immediately following his graduation from the university he entered the diplomatic service and discharged several missions in Germany and France. The three years following 1607 he spent in England, as secretary of a legation to James I, and in 1614 he is mentioned as acting as private secretary to the Duke of Würtemberg. His marriage to the daughter of Francis Raworth of Dover called him to England in 1616, and after 1624 he was under-secretary of state in England, having charge of the correction and examination of all

[1] Cf. p. 48 of this chapter.   [2] *Works*, XI, p. 145.
[3] *Works*, XI, p. 147.

official correspondence. During the civil wars he took his stand with parliament, though in the expedition against Scotland he followed Charles. In 1644 he was made secretary of foreign tongues, which office he held until displaced by Milton in 1649. In 1652 when Milton's sight began to fail, Weckherlin was his assistant. He died the following year. Weckherlin is known first of all as a poet, and has left a collection of several hundred poems. Among these there is one of some length dedicated to " Heinrich Wotton, dem Engelischen Ritter," while another is an adaptation of one of Wotton's odes.[1] This, it is to be remembered, is the Sir Henry Wotton who lived with Casaubon in 1593 at Geneva, with whom Bacon corresponded and to whom he sent his *Novum Organum* in 1620. It will also be noted that Weckherlin entered the University of Tübingen the same year as did Andreae, and that they spent the following four years there together, the one in jurisprudence, the other in theology. And furthermore Weckherlin was a close friend and for years the secretary of Benjamin von Buwinckhausen, Stadthalter of Alençon, an intimate friend of Andreae. At the death of Buwinckhausen, *Andreae* conducted the funeral services and in his sermon speaks of him as " a man of the greatest worth, of whom I shall never speak except with great honor." [2] Andreae mentions Buwinckhausen in his *Vita,* in various connections.[3]

The third to be considered is Sir Toby Matthew, courtier, diplomat, and writer. He was born in 1577 and was educated at Oxford. In 1598 he visited a friend in France but returned soon after. In 1601 he went to parliament and there

---

[1] Nos. 44 and 11 of Goedeke's collection of Weckherlin's poems, Leipzig, 1873.

[2] Weckherlin's *Oden und Gesänge* in Höpfner, and *Vita,* p. 113.

[3] *Vita,* pp. 103, 113, 119, 126, 150, 158, 159, 242.

became acquainted with Bacon. The next few years he spent in Europe, visiting especially Italy and Spain. While abroad he became converted to the Catholic faith. This, though he kept the fact secret for a while, made permanent residence in England impossible, as he refused to take the oath of allegiance. He was therefore on the Continent more than in England, though he made several attempts to be permitted to live at home, attempts in which Bacon earnestly took his part. While in Brussels he received a copy of the *Advancement of Learning* and, in 1610, the *De Sapientia Veterorum*. During the next few years he translated into Italian several of Bacon's works, among them the *Essays*. At a later period again at Brussels he translated into English *The Incomparable Dr. S. Augustine* and *The Penitent Bandito*. In 1624 he was appointed one of the eighty-four " Essentials " or original working members of an Academe Royal, the scheme of which had been completed by Edmund Bolton.[1] In 1625, as a mark of especial favor to Matthew, Bacon added his *Essay on Friendship* to the series, referring in his letter to the friendship existing between Matthew and himself. In Bacon's will was found a clause by which he left thirty pounds to be expended in purchasing a ring for Matthew. The latter died in the English College at Ghent in 1655. During Matthew's extensive travels in Europe he visited many towns in Italy, France, Switzerland, Spain, and Germany. During the whole period of their association, from the time he became acquainted with Bacon in 1601 until the latter's death, a regular correspondence was kept up between them. Many of these letters are preserved,

---

[1] Edmund Bolton (1575-1633), historian and poet. In 1617 he proposed a scheme for a college, and its fellows were actually chosen— the Academe Royal. But James died, and his successor showed no great interest in the institution. Hence the organization dissolved.

some quoted by Spedding. All show the closest friendship between Bacon and Matthew and a great appreciation on Bacon's part of the literary and critical ability of Matthew. As Bacon's books came out, copies were at once sent to Matthew, with a view toward getting the latter's opinion as well as having them circulated on the Continent. As is evident from the letters, Matthew was on the lookout continually for literary men whose acquaintance he would be glad to make, and whose scientific investigations could be of service to him in his own researches.

It will be evident from the foregoing pages that a knowledge on the part of Bacon of Andreae's *Christianopolis* and the *Fama*, and some of the other works, which appeared from 1614 to the time of Bacon's death, and some of which were circulated even earlier in manuscript form, is not by any means out of the question. Rather it would seem almost impossible that Bacon should *not* have heard of them through one or the other of their mutual acquaintances. The problem then becomes one of inner evidence in the works in question, to determine, if possible, whether they are kindred. This matter will be taken up now.

G. C. Moore Smith, in the introduction to his edition of the *New Atlantis*, devotes some pages to the tracing of the name " New Atlantis " to its sources. In the fable itself, Bacon refers to the " Atlantis," the island mentioned in the *Critias* of Plato. This island and the sea around it were named after Atlas and inhabited by his children and their descendants. Francisco Lopes de Gomara in his *History of the Indias* [1] made Plato's Atlantis the continents of America ; or rather the present America is all that is left of Atlantis after having been partially sunk into the sea as a result of an earthquake. Bacon refers to the same Atlantis as hav-

[1] 1552.

ing been almost depopulated by a great local flood; and locates his island of New Atlantis between the Great Atlantis and the Orient. Of greater interest for the present discussion, however, is the name of the city built upon the island. This is Bensalem, Son of Peace or Salvation. The names *Village of Peace, Caphar Salama,* and the *Hierosolyma* in the utopia of Andreae seem to have been directly transferred to *Bensalem* and to *Nova Solyma, A New Peace,* the latter being the Ideal City of Samuel Gott which will be discussed in the next chapter.

In form and general style the two works under consideration are the same. In each case it is the experience of an individual as the latter relates it to his hearers or readers, not a dialogue as was the case in the ideal states of both More and Campanella. Smith [1] comments favorably upon Bacon's beginning. "How natural an opening! No introduction, no account of persons spoken of, merely, 'We sailed from Peru.'" Bacon's introduction continues, "We had good winds at first. But then the winds came about and settled to the west. Next, strong and great winds came from the south. Finding ourselves in the midst of the greatest wilderness of waters in the world, we gave ourselves up for lost men and prepared for death." Now if we disregard for the time the allegorical form of the *Christianopolis,* however effective this may be, we have almost the identical words. "I set sail again upon the sea. I left the port with many others and exposed my life to a thousand dangers. For a short time the weather favored us; then adverse winds drove contrary currents against us and we despaired. The sailors did their best, but we soon saw destruction before our eyes and stood in readiness for death." [2]

[1] *New Atlantis,* Introduction, p. 23.
[2] Chap. i.

Then follows the landing. In the *Christianopolis*[1] it is a wreck and a violent casting ashore. In the *New Atlantis* a voluntary landing in boats. But in both cases the adventurers are kindly taken up and cared for. In the *Christianopolis*[2] the stranger passes three distinct examinations before he is given full privileges to use the city. In the *New Atlantis* the examination and the questioning on the ship are begun before landing is permitted, and are continued on shore. The first question, " Are ye Christians? ",[3] the most important, is followed by an oath, giving evidence that no blood has been shed, and that the party is not a band of pirates. In the *Christianopolis* the first examination is likewise a caution against vagabonds and tramps. A further suggestion of the same is expressed in the address given to the crew in the strangers' house by the leader.[4] After dwelling upon the miracle of their escape and rescue he adds: " Yet there is more. For they have by commandment, though in form of courtesy, cloistered us within these walls for three days. Who knoweth whether it be not to take some taste of our manners and conditions? And if they find them bad, to banish us straightway; if good, to give us further time." The parallel can be traced throughout the whole story. A mere detail of difference lies in the fact that Andreae divides his work into short chapters, but they are so well arranged and so closely connected that we get the idea of an uninterrupted relation of experiences and a description of impressions as the visitor passes through the city, even as is the case in the *New Atlantis*. In the *Christianopolis* the division is merely one of print.

The strangers' house and the fund for strangers in the *New Atlantis* is but an elaboration of Andreae's simpler

[1] Chaps. i, ii.
[2] Chap. iv.
[3] *New Atlantis*, p. 131.
[4] *New Atlantis*, p. 134.

method of showing kindness to strangers and caring for them after the proof of their worthiness has been established.   And the latter fact is also carefully investigated in the *New Atlantis*.   The rather lengthy and somewhat unnecessary description of the rooms in which the strangers are kept, and the preparations made for their reception and nursing, are very naturally suggested by the fact that here a whole ship's crew is to be accounted for, instead of but one individual.   The principle of humanity and charity, however, seems to be brought out just as clearly in the *Christianopolis* in a less boastful manner, though Smith[1] sees in Bacon's detailed account poetic means to greater " naturalness " in the description.   The latter part of the *New Atlantis*[2] is taken up with a description given by one of the Fathers of Salomon's[3] House as to the purposes and aims of this " college."   At the close of this, or rather in the midst of it, the narrative breaks off, and it remains for one to guess under what circumstances the visitors left the island and returned home to tell their story.   But the fact that they were by especial act merely permitted to stay longer than the usual time, and not allowed to remain permanently as a whole party, together with the farewell statement of the father of Salomon's House, " I give thee leave to publish what I have told thee, for the good of other nations "—these would naturally lead to a conclusion much like that of the *Christianopolis*.   This will suffice for a comparison of the narrative form of the two works.

[1] Introduction, p. 23, of his *New Atlantis*.

[2] Pp. 156 ff.

[3] Bacon regularly spells the word as it appears in the *Vulgate* and in Luther's translation of the Bible.   Though the name is similar to that of Solamona, the lawgiver of Bensalem, yet the inhabitants are convinced that he named the place in honor of the Hebrew king (*New Atlantis*, p. 145).

A strong point of similarity is found in the religious conditions in the two places. Bensalem, like Christianopolis, is a Christian state. A history of the island gives in substance the following mystical account of the introduction of the Christian religion into the place.[1] Twenty years after the ascension of Christ, the inhabitants of the east side of the island saw a great pillar of light in the night. Upon investigation with boats it was found that the pillar was unapproachable, until one of those present, a wise man of the society of Salomon's House, recognizing the miracle, prayed to God for light, and thereupon found *his* boat free to move ahead. The column disappeared as he approached; but at its base were found an ark containing the canonical books of the Old and the New Testaments and a message to the following effect: " I, Bartholomew, a servant of the Highest, and apostle of Jesus Christ, was warned by an angel that appeared to me in a vision of glory that I should commit this ark to the floods of the sea. Therefore I do testify and declare unto that people where God shall ordain this ark to come to land, that in the same day is come unto them salvation and peace and good will, from the Father and from the Lord Jesus." The implication of the message is that a safe place was to be found where God might establish His religion, and have it bear fruit in the hearts and lives of an honest and wise people. Now we find a strikingly similar idea expressed in the *Christianopolis.* First ". . . the church, which has been tossed about so many thousand years on the world-sea." [2] Again, " When the church wandered as a stranger from east to west . . ." [3] But especially in answer to the question " What blessedness set up its abode here?" the stranger is told, " When the

---

[1] *New Atlantis,* p. 137.   [2] Chap. xxxvi.

[3] Chap. lxix.

whole world raged against the good, and forced them to depart out of her boundaries, then Religion, an exile, taking along her most faithful friends, after crossing the sea and searching here and there, finally chose this land where she put her associates ashore; and later she built a city which we call ' the Christian city,' and desired that it should be the abode or refuge, if you like, of honesty and uprightness." [1] Compare with this also *Die Christenburg*, which was composed in 1615: " In the world-sea there is an island, much favored of God. . . . When evil took possession of the earth, religion fled hither." [2] Even the questions which bring out these explanations are strangely alike. It is the first question for information in both cases. " Who was the apostle and how was the place converted to the Christian faith?" The guide in the *New Atlantis* answers: " Ye knit my heart to you by asking this question in the first place; for it sheweth that ye seek first the kingdom of heaven." [3] And he then, like the guide in the *Christianopolis*, proceeds to explain the manner of the conversion of the island. A strange and unexpected development for Bacon is the mystical, mysterious description of the ark containing the letter and Bible. One is unconsciously reminded of the secret vault described in the *Fama*.[4]

Innumerable are the references to prayer and worship which correspond in the two works: thanks to God for rescue from the storm and safe landing among a Christian people; oaths in the name of God and Christ as pledge for past and future behavior. There is no mention of daily meals and church attendance in the *New Atlantis*. But the prayers at the Feast of the Family,[5] to be spoken of again,

---

[1] Chap. iii.   [2] Grüneisen, p. 254.
[3] *New Atlantis*, p. 137.   [4] *Fama*, p. 58 (Geheime Wissenschaften).
[5] *New Atlantis*, p. 147.

the only festivity of the sort described, and the benedictions at the close, are all suggestive of table and family prayers, as is the case in the *Christianopolis*. The father of Salomon's House, as he passes through the city, raises his hand and silently blesses the people. He begins his discourse about the college with the words, " God bless thee, my son," and closes with the same phrase. So also the officer of the strangers' house [1] comes " as a priest and a Christian " to bring what assistance and comfort he can to the afflicted. And the leader of the crew says in his address to his comrades, " Let us look to God, and every man reform his own ways. Besides we are come here amongst a Christian people, full of piety and humanity." [2] Again, " It seemed to us that we had before us a picture of our salvation in heaven; for we that were a while since in the jaws of death, were now brought into a place where we found nothing but consolation." [3] In like manner in the *Christianopolis* the stranger is addressed: " How fortunate you are, because after so vengeful a storm and shipwreck, you have happened to be landed at this place." [4] The religious, the Christian element in both the *New Atlantis* and in the *Christianopolis* is a very essential part of the whole.

Socially the two utopias are closely akin. The family is the unit of society, and upon it is built the whole social fabric. This conception is very far developed in the *New Atlantis*. The Feast of the Family is instituted and celebrated in honor of him whose family counts at least thirty living members. On an appointed day the head of the family, having previously chosen several friends to assist in the celebration, meets with the members of his family according to a stated ceremony. The occasion is made use of

[1] *New Atlantis*, p. 135.
[2] *New Atlantis*, p. 134.
[3] *New Atlantis*, p. 136.
[4] Chap. ii.

to settle all petty disputes between members, to impress lessons of morality, piety, patriotism, and obedience; and to bring all into close association with each other. The ceremony, rather elaborate and impressive, does not especially concern us here. The important features are these: the feast is religious in character, including invocation, hymns, prayer, and benediction. It bears also direct relation to the state; for the expenses are supplied from the state treasury, and the head of the family hereafter wears a medal presented by the king. Socially it emphasizes two important points: first, the principle of family unity. Toward the close of the ceremony, one of the sons is chosen who shall henceforth live with the father in the latter's house, assist him in the affairs of his household, and so hold the family together by taking the father's place in case of his death. The second is that of raising up a large family; for no man is so honored throughout the state as such a " family-father." He is granted a charter containing many privileges and exemptions; and the medal presented by the king bears the inscription, " To ——, our well beloved friend and creditor," a title proper only in this case; " for they say a king is debtor to no man, but for the propagation of his subjects." [1] In this feast they pray to Adam, Noah, and Abraham, whereof the former two peopled the world, and the latter was the father of the faithful.

Now, just these features are made emphatic in the *Christianopolis*. Family and table prayers and hymns are the daily rule. Contrary to conditions in all earlier utopias, there are no common tables, except for pupils in the boarding schools; but the family meets daily around its private board. The government deals out food and provisions each week to *families*,[2] a family consisting of father, mother, and

[1] *New Atlantis*, p. 149.   [2] Chap. xv.

younger children—the older sons and daughters being in boarding school or at college. And as to the importance of family increase, the quotation already suggested in the preceding chapter will suffice, " The crown of woman is motherhood." [1]

The second question asked of the guide in the *New Atlantis* is one relating to marriage: " Because propagation of families proceedeth from nuptial copulation, what laws have you concerning marriage; and do you keep marriage well; and are you tied to one wife? For where population is so much affected, such as with you it seems to be, there is commonly permission of plurality of wives." [2] The answer to this question is given with a considerable amount of pride, and shows the following facts: there is not under heaven so chaste a nation as that of Bensalem, so free from pollution and foulness. It is the virgin of the world. If the spirit of fornication be represented by a " foul and ugly Ethiop " then the spirit of the chastity of Bensalem would appear in the likeness of a fair, beautiful cherubim. There are no dissolute women, courtesans, and the like. These the people of Bensalem detest and they are surprised that Europeans countenance and permit a nuisance that is so detrimental to the lives and health of the inhabitants. Purity in married life even is observed. " For whosoever is unchaste, cannot reverence himself. And the reverence of man's self is, next to religion, the chiefest bridle of all vices." [3] The marriage relation is the most sacred in life. Polygamy is not practiced—that would be out of harmony with the spirit of the family. Consent of parents is necessary for legal marriage.

It will be remembered that the *Christianopolis* expresses

[1] Chap. xc.   [2] *New Atlantis*, pp. 151 and 152.
                   [3] *New Atlantis*, p. 153.

views almost identical with these.[1] "The glory of a conquest over the passions . . ." Purity of personal life, in the single as in the married state, consent of parents on the part of the contracting parties, permanency and seriousness of marriage—these are the chief points in both cases. Only in one respect does Bacon's ideal differ from that of Andreae, and here we must admit (as in the case of More and Campanella) that the latter stands infinitely higher in the ethical scale. " I have read," says the speaker in the *New Atlantis,* " in a book of one of your men (evidently More) of a feigned commonwealth, where the married couples are permitted, before they contract, to see one another naked. This the inhabitants of Bensalem dislike, for they think it a scorn to give a refusal after so familiar knowledge. But because of many hidden defects in men's and women's bodies, they have a more civil way; for they have near every town a couple of pools, which they call Adam's and Eve's pools, where it is permitted to one of the friends of the man, and another of the friends of the woman, to see them severally bathe naked." [2] This was for Bacon a desirable mean, or a compromise between the strictly " eugenic " conceptions of More, and his own notions of propriety.

A few other minor points of similarity will be mentioned before passing to the chief matter, that of the founding of a college.

Both governments are particular about health regulations and sanitary conditions. In the *New Atlantis* the ship's crew is disinfected (not very thoroughly, it is true) before landing.[3] The city is provided with baths [4] for health and cleanliness. Christianopolis has not only baths but an

---

[1] Chap. xviii.
[2] *New Atlantis,* p. 154.
[3] *New Atlantis,* p. 132.
[4] *New Atlantis,* p. 157.

elaborate sewer system as well;[1] and the authorities are very careful lest *contagion come to the citizens through guests.*[2]

Similar expressions occur in connection with the rules of hospitality to strangers. At his first meeting with the inhabitants of Christianopolis the shipwrecked sailor gives us the following information: " He led me to the city where he said I would be well taken up, according to the usual charitable kindliness shown in his country toward unfortunate strangers. I could answer nothing but ' Thanks and praise to God.' "[3] In the *New Atlantis,* in the rehearsal of the past history of the state, the visitors are told: " For first he (the king) hath preserved all points of humanity in taking order and making provision for the relief of strangers distressed, whereof you have tasted."—" At which," we are told, " as reason was we all arose and bowed." [4]

But the *New Atlantis* is important primarily and has become famous chiefly because of the picture drawn and the description given of a " college," a group of learned and capable men endowed, and working together toward a common end—the attainment of knowledge by experiment, the enriching of the world's store of information by the process of investigation into nature, and discovering in her the truths and principles that have existed from all time. Bacon is ordinarily credited with having originated the entire scheme and as being alone responsible for the founding of such colleges, academies, and societies in England. It is not alone his plan of a college that has been so much praised, nor yet the individual experiments or lines of investigation that he suggests. For of the latter some have proved to be visionary, impracticable, and not altogether desirable; and others were not original, but taken from More, Roger Bacon,

[1] Chap. xcv.
[2] Chap. xcvii.
[3] Chap. iii.
[4] *New Atlantis,* p. 144.

and other earlier investigators in England and elsewhere. It is rather the mere suggestion that such an institution would be desirable and would lead to good results which is of importance.

As in the case of the other utopias which have been discussed, and perhaps even to a much higher degree, this one represents the author's favorite work. There can be no doubt but that Bacon considered the *New Atlantis*, as far as completed, one of his most important productions, as embodying the principles which he had developed in years of experience. Yet the *New Atlantis*, aside from being a fragment, is not a complete description of a well-balanced city in the same sense as the *Christianopolis* is. In the former, certain features not always essentials are given very great importance, as for instance the history of the great Atlantis, while other factors more necessary for an ideal state are entirely omitted. Little or no mention is made of education of the children and youth, occupation of the citizens, and matters of daily life. This difficulty would not likely have been remedied even if the work had been finished according to the plans of the author. Rawley tells us on the title page, " His lordship thought also in the present fable to have composed a frame of laws, of the best state or mold of a commonwealth." [1] And it seems probable that the code of laws would have completed the work. This fits in well with Bacon's own life and interests. The account of his life in the autobiographical statement already quoted [2] shows the two objects of his life, benefit to humanity by founding a new system of experimental philosophy, and by a study of all legal conditions. In the *New Atlantis,* if completed, the

---

[1] *New Atlantis,* p. 127, p. 44 of this chapter.
[2] P. 42 of this chapter.

second object would have been fulfilled in the code of laws, while the prominence of the first is clear from the estimation in which the college is held, and the purpose which is ascribed to it:[1] "The knowledge of our foundation is the knowledge of causes and secret motions of things, and the enlarging of the bounds of human empire, to the effecting of all things possible."[2] "It so fell out that there was in one of the boats one of the wise men of the society of Salomon's House, which house or college *is the very eye of the kingdom.*"[3] "Ye shall understand that amongst the excellent acts of that king, one above all hath the preeminence. It was the erection and institution of an order or society which we call Salomon's House, the noblest foundation as we think that ever was upon the earth, and the *lantern* of this kingdom. It is dedicated to the study of the works and creatures of God."

This object of the college, the direction in which investigations are to be made, and the methods by which results are to be obtained are stated more in detail in succeeding pages of the *New Atlantis.* But only those matters which have become practical since Bacon's time will be considered here.

The organization of Salomon's House,[4] the College of Six Days' Work, is not complicated. The work is divided. Certain members of the staff, so-called fellows, are sent out into the world at definite intervals of time. It is their duty to visit the countries to which they are delegated, examine the conditions that exist, note the improvements and changes, especially in the " sciences, arts, manufactures, and inventions," and bring back books, patterns, and instruments of all kinds. They are well provided with

[1] *New Atlantis,* p. 137.
[2] *New Atlantis,* p. 145.
[3] *New Atlantis,* p. 145.
[4] *New Atlantis,* pp. 146-156.

money, so that everything of value is obtainable by them. Their reports and purchases are examined into by other members of the college at home. Of these, some read the books and test the value of experiments; some try new experiments based on the results of the former; some collect and tabulate the results, and so forth. The material actually dealt with covers a broad field. Observation of wind, weather, and heavenly bodies; analysis of soils and their use in forcing the growth of plants; study of trees and shrubs for their own improvement and the utilization of the fruit; study of the habits of bees and silkworms; preparation of drinks—wine, ale, and so forth, also of medicines and concoctions for the restoration of health; dissecting of bodies of animals with a view toward obtaining knowledge of the human body. In mechanics there are experiments dealing with motions in air and water, forces and projectiles, even perpetual motions.[1] There is the study of sound, light, and smell, resulting respectively in new scales, colors, and odors. For the performing of these investigations, large and elaborate rooms have been fitted up. Deep caves and high towers, laboratories, sound houses, perfume houses, perspective houses, engine houses, and so forth,—each equipped according to the latest models.

Concerning the contribution which Andreae made in this direction, Guhrauer says the following: " Here then (in the *Christianopolis*) principles of genuine natural science based upon observation and experiment, founded at the same time by Bacon, are applied to different faculties. And what is surprising, we see the plan of an academy or college of natural science, and the sciences and arts connected therewith, with collections of specimens, gardens,

---

[1] This was a favorite attempt among all experimenters. Comenius devoted considerable time to the matter.

and like establishments represented in clear outlines long before the famous fragment of Bacon of Verulam, which dressed in like costume pursues like purposes, namely the *New Atlantis,* was published, which latter is usually looked upon as the first impetus for the founding of natural science academies and colleges." [1]

Now it is perfectly true that Bacon and Andreae were men of somewhat similar type and that their interests followed similar lines. Both, one as a lawyer, the other as a preacher, came in touch with humanity and civilization. Both were led to see the conditions of society and, being of sympathetic and at the same time aggressive temperament, desired to make improvement. Both were men of letters, university-trained, insatiable students, and alive to all the ideas that were being promulgated. Both, though born and living in different countries, were breathing the same atmosphere and moving in the same realms of thought. And it is especially true that in their studies, their attention had been repeatedly drawn to the insurmountable difficulties in attaining knowledge through the means thus far placed at their disposal. Hence one might well see how they would arrive at somewhat similar results, though working quite independently of each other. But the very striking agreement between the plans and outlines, even in some of the details of the institutions which they advocated, makes one wonder whether the facts do not justify the assumption of more than a coincidence. In comparison with the views of Bacon regarding his college as quoted earlier,[2] there is the following from Andreae.

Speaking of the location of the college: " It is time that we go into the very innermost part of the city, which is as

[1] Quoted in Gussmann's article, p. 467.
[2] Pp. 65, 66 of this chapter.

it were the *soul of the city,* and imparts to the latter, life and inspiration." [1]   Bacon calls his college the " eye " and the " lantern " of Bensalem. Again, " Never have I seen the like —so much human perfection united in one place." [2]   And as for the directions in which advanced education branches out, things actually done and experiments carried out, very much in the *New Atlantis* has its counterpart in the *Christianopolis.* Andreae's chapter on astronomy [3] outlines the study of the heavenly bodies, their sizes and distances, courses of planets, and eclipses. Agriculture and cattle raising [4] are not only practiced but made a systematic study. The department is presided over by a man " exceptionally well versed in the science of agriculture, pasturing, and cattle breeding." The use of fertilizer is well understood and the times when it may be best applied to the cultivated fields. In addition to the garden plot behind every dwelling house,[5] which serves to beautify and decorate the lot, as well as to promote the health of those who take care of it, there are gardens [6] in connection *with the college* containing " over a thousand varieties of plants, as might be called a living botany text." Some of these are for decorative purposes only, others are to be used as food, while still others are carried to the drug shops to be prepared as medicines. The *New Atlantis* says of the plants and herbs, " Many of them we so order as they become of medicinal use," [7] and " We have dispensatories and medicine shops, wherein you may easily think, if we have such variety of plants and living creatures more than you have in Europe, the simples, drugs, and ingredients of medicines must likewise be in so much greater variety." [8]

---

[1] Chap. xxvi.
[2] Chap. xxvi.
[3] Chap. lxvii.
[4] Chap. viii.

[5] Chap. xxiii.
[6] Chap. xciv.
[7] *New Atlantis,* p. 158.
[8] *New Atlantis,* p. 160.

To return to the *Christianopolis,* the gardens are well ordered, each class of plants having its own proper place. And it is especially plain that these plots are all for experimental purposes; for *large* gardens are without the city walls where food materials are raised in proper amounts to supply the town. In the college gardens also are found birds and bees " which are tended with great care." [1] The practice of dissection is pursued and the principles of anatomy studied in an especially equipped apartment.[2] As in the *New Atlantis* the bodies of animals are made the subjects, and the information thus obtained is used to increase the knowledge of anatomy, " there being nothing in the world as wonderful as the workshop of the human body, which they call a miniature of the universe." It is stated: " They have a place especially dedicated to the dissection of animals. No one could find fault with this practice of finding the seat of bodily ailments and striving to assist nature, except such a one as, along with barbarians, thinks it unnecessary to know one's self. There are even among persons who consider themselves scholars, some who know nothing about where they live, breathe, digest, or discharge, except that it is somewhere within their skins. But the teachers of Christianopolis show the youth the operations of life from the organs of animals; and sometimes they dissect a human body, though this is rare." [3]

The mechanics are given their proper attention, as are also the crafts. Laboratories, physical and chemical, serve as workshops for trying out newly invented instruments. Minerals and metals are worked. " In the eastern quarter of the city are the seven shops fitted out for melting, forging, casting, and molding of metals. . . . Here, if anywhere, is seen the examination of nature, since whatever the

[1] Chap. xciv.   [2] Chap. xlvi.   [3] Chap. xlvi.

earth contains in its bowels is brought under the influence of the laws and instruments of art; the men are not impelled to their work without knowledge, like beasts, but have been long ago inspired by careful knowledge (*cognitio*) of the things of natural science, and thence take their delight in the bowels of nature. Unless you listen to the reasons and look into the anatomy of the macrocosmos, they think they have told and taught you nothing. Unless you determine by experiments, and make corrections with better instruments for the improvement of the arts and sciences, you are of no value. Take my word for it, if sophistry should wish to be considered here, it would be a mockery; to such an extent do they prefer activity (*res*) over words. For here one can greet true and genuine chemistry, and can listen to her freely and diligently. . . . In a word, *here natural science (physica) is active.*" [1]

As one more important similarity, the conception of the obtainment of knowledge by inspiration, the dawning of " light " must be mentioned. The *Christianopolis* is full of references to it, sometimes used purely in a religious sense and again with reference to an inner light, the flashes of genius. A few instances may be cited: in the introduction, " For the return of light." [2]   " That God permitted darkness to fall upon the minds of the godless." [3]   " The light of new religion dawned within us again." [4]   " The deceiver cannot withstand those who have a higher light within." [5] " They recognize their mistake, or the lack of light in their souls." [6]   " They try to remind themselves of the eternal light." [7]   " We believe in an everlasting life in which we will possess perfect light, contentment, quiet, wisdom, and joy." [8]

[1] Chap. xi.
[2] P. 2.
[3] P. 3.
[4] P. 4.
[5] P. 5.
[6] P. 10.
[7] Chap. xxv.
[8] Chap. xxviii.

" Those who know not what they want, and so, blind guides, who pride themselves with having much light, draw others into the abyss who are still blinder than they." [1]   " To promote the light of truth." [2]   " They will never repent that they have come from darkness into light." [3]

From the *New Atlantis* three instances only will be cited, but these are important. The one object in sending men out from the college and having them visit foreign lands, is knowledge. " Thus we maintain a trade, not for gold, silver or jewels, nor for silks, nor for spices, nor for any other commodity of matter; but only for God's first creation, which was light, to have light, I say, of the growth of all parts of the world." [4]   The twelve men who go out into the world are called " merchants of light "; and " Then after diverse meetings and consults of our whole number, to consider the former labors and collections, we have three men that take care out of them to direct new experiments of a higher light, more penetrating into nature than the former. These we call ' lamps.' " [5]

It is not necessary to rely solely upon the *Christianopolis* in support of this opinion. An even more striking similarity between the ideas of Bacon and Andreae is to be found in the *Fama*, which was written nine years earlier, and in several intermediate works where the same plan is found. The " *Fraternitas* " is a body of men banded together for the very same purpose as that suggested in the *New Atlantis*—" to institute a general reformation " [6] and " a general reformation *divini et humani*," [7] " to discover the mysteries of nature " [8] and " to study men all over the earth." [9] This brotherhood, beginning with only four mem-

[1] Chap. xviii.
[2] Chap. xxix.
[3] Chap. xxxiv.
[4] *New Atlantis,* p. 147.
[5] *New Atlantis,* p. 164.
[6] Pp. 3, 12.
[7] P. 30.
[8] P. 4.
[9] P. 1.

bers, later increased its membership to include eight, " all free men through whom a volume of knowledge might be collected of all that man could hope for." [1] The college is called that of the Holy Spirit. *Its members travel abroad and learn what they can in foreign countries, but return upon a set date each year to the college to report, or give a satisfactory reason if unable to come.*[2] These are the essentials of the *Fama,* and, it would appear, also the elements of Bacon's College of Six Days.

A few matters of importance might be spoken of in which the *Christianopolis* and the *New Atlantis* seem to differ considerably, or which are looked upon from a different point of view by the two writers. The idea of freedom, so oft recurring and so much emphasized in the *Christianopolis,* does not play so important a part in the *New Atlantis.* Even the political conception of the state is not quite so democratic as might have been expected. The plan of government in the latter is monarchical and rather centralized. This is not surprising in view of the fact that Bacon had been and was on the closest terms of friendship with the King of England and might expect assistance or hindrance according as his works met with the latter's approval or disapproval. Nor were the Stuarts, with their ideas of divine right, a type to be pleased with the picture of an ideal state in which freedom and democracy were too prominent.[3]

In the foregoing pages an effort has been made to point

[1] P. 13.   [2] Pp. 15 f.
[3] In the *New Atlantis* (pp. 154, 155) we have a lengthy description of the history, early prominence, and decay of the civilization of America, the large Atlantis. This is a matter which, naturally wanting in the *Christianopolis,* can be easily accounted for from the close relations existing between America and England in Bacon's time. The description of the clothes and costumes worn on state occasions corresponds well with the elaborateness and gaudy colors

out that, contrary to the opinion of most commentators on Bacon, his was not the first utopia which definitely outlined an ideal state built upon the basis of modern philosophy ; and that his college of scientific research based upon an experimental method of reasoning was preceded several years by another, just as carefully outlined and completely detailed as his own ; that the elements of the college were present in the *Fama,* which was *published* a decade before the *New Atlantis* was composed, and was circulated as early as 1610.[1] Moreover, it is not at all impossible both from his close association with continental scholars and from the intimate and international character of the learning of the time that Bacon knew these very works either directly or indirectly. A careful comparison of the two utopias definitely eliminates any suggestion of mere coincidence and makes the mental kinship of Bacon and Andreae almost indubitable.

of dress in the 16th and 17th centuries at the English court. The *Christianopolis* is simpler in this respect, and on like occasions when great and good men are to be described, speaks of the face and bearing rather than of the dress. On the other hand, Andreae's interest in music and art, the fact that he was himself musical and a critic of art, explain the prominence given in his utopia to these features. Such evidences of the personality and environment of the two authors are noticeable in other parts of their ideal states, which need not be mentioned.

[1] A Latin translation of the *Fama* appeared as early as 1614, and it is quite probable that through this version Bacon became acquainted with Andreae's ideas.

CHAPTER IV

THE *CHRISTIANOPOLIS* AND *NOVA SOLYMA*

THE immediate effect of the *Christianopolis* in Germany was not so great as might have been expected; it did not become the pattern for other works of a similar nature, nor was its publication received with startling enthusiasm. This will not seem so strange, however, when we remember that Andreae was as yet not very well known as a writer and had only local reputation as a man of ability and knowledge of social and religious conditions. His chief works previous to this time had been published anonymously and he himself stood decidedly in the background. An additional explanation for the fact that the *Christianopolis* met with seemingly little success, will be found in the horrors of the Thirty Years' War, with its wholesale slaughter of citizens, destruction of property, devastation of whole sections of countries, and dissipation of the vital strength of the German states. Such conditions were not conducive to the composing of "ideal states," nor encouraging even to the studying of works that were calculated to reform church, state, and school system. Germany had first to recover sufficiently from the effects of the war to be able to plan calmly for future improvement. Thus we find that while the production of More, a man of national fame, had been enthusiastically received by his own countrymen, read, re-edited, and even committed to memory,[1] Andreae's *Chris-*

[1] Morley: *Ideal Commonwealths,* Introduction, p. 7.

tianopolis, the work of a private citizen, pastor, and teacher in a small community, was covered up and all but lost and forgotten.

In England social and political conditions were not in the same state of actual turmoil either at the time when the *Christianopolis* was published or during the decades immediately following. While the country was politically unsettled and almost on the verge of civil rupture, it was not actually being devastated by war. On the contrary, the national mind was occupied with just such problems of educational and social improvement. The elements of reform took root sufficiently to survive the shock of civil war when it did come. It will become evident that Andreae's ideas on education and science, as contained in the *Christianopolis,* were carried over to England by some of his friends and admirers at home; and that the atmosphere there proved more conducive than in Germany to their further development and ultimate practical application. It is a remarkable fact that seventeenth-century England produced a number of utopias. Whether this is due to an exceptional inclination of the English mind toward the utopia, or whether it is to be explained by the state of religious agitation of this period and widely spread chiliastic hopes of the religious sects, it is difficult to decide.

Among the half-dozen utopias, then, that were produced on English soil, one in particular has an especial claim upon our consideration—first, because it shows some new features in the development of utopias as yet little noticed by those who have concerned themselves with this subject; and secondly, because it bears a close relation to the work which forms the center of the present discussion.

Nova Solyma appeared anonymously in 1648. It was

written in Latin, consisted of six books, and bore on the title page only the words:

Novae Solymae Libri Sex.
Londoni Typis Joannis Legati MDCXLVIII

The following year a second edition was issued in which the title was supplemented by the words " *Sive Institutio Christiani*," followed by a heading for each of the six books. It is also noted that the work was printed for Thomas Underhill, among whose books it is catalogued in the British Museum. No further notice seems to have been taken of *Nova Solyma*. At least we find no reference to it in the literature of the period. In 1902, however, the entire work appeared, translated into English, accompanied by a long introduction and with elaborate notes. The editor of this publication was the Reverend Walter Begley. In his commentaries Mr. Begley makes a very thorough comparison of *Nova Solyma* with the various works of John Milton, and cites innumerable detailed examples of construction, style, vocabulary, phraseology and thought, to prove that Milton was the author of this work. Begley divides his argument into a series of proofs—proofs from music, poetry, pedagogy, and so forth, and finally proof by elimination. Then in his conclusion he states: " The authorship of this romance must clearly be confined to a very small class of men. Neither Shakespeare nor Bacon could by any possibility have produced such a book as this even if the date allowed the supposition. No one but a first-rate Latinist could have written our romance. . . . As a matter of fact the book could not have been written by any then-living Englishman except such men as Alexander Ross, Phineas Fletcher, Dr. Duport, Thomas May, Thomas Farnaby, Andrew Marvell, Cleveland, Cowley, Crashaw, and men of that stamp of erudition.

Now let any scholar try this list of names severally, by the contents of *Nova Solyma*—by its tone, its sentiment, its opinions, its sublimities both in prose and verse, its maintained seriousness, its religious principles, and its independent theories,—then I think these names will disappear from the list of probable candidates, and they will be weeded out one by one till all are gone." Milton, therefore, he concludes, *must* be the author of the book.

Quite by accident it has become known that, while Milton may have influenced the work to some degree, the real author was quite another person—a man of whom Begley probably never heard. Stephen K. Jones [1] states that while collating Baxter's *Holy Commonwealth* he happened to notice among the books printed for Thomas Underhill, a list of three, whose author was Samuel Gott. The first one of these was the *Nova Solyma*.

Samuel Gott is a man almost entirely unknown to-day, and mentioned in none of the encyclopedias or histories of literature. He was born in 1613. His father, also Samuel Gott, was a dealer in iron, and seems to have been a man of some means, for in 1640 his name is mentioned among those merchants from whom the king hoped to borrow money. The younger Gott completed the Merchants' Tailors' School and continued his education at St. Catherine's College, Cambridge. Here he took the bachelor's degree in 1632. The following year he became a member of the Society of Gray's Inn and in 1640 was admitted to the bar. There is no evidence that he ever practiced law. After his father's death in 1642, he married, retired to a country estate, and lived privately until shortly before the time of the return of the Stuarts. After a few years' residence in London, during which time he was elected an

[1] *The Library*, July, 1910, p. 225.

" Ancient," he again withdrew to his home at Battle, where in all probability he stayed until his death, which occurred in 1671.

Begley in his argument for Milton's authorship of *Nova Solyma* speaks [1] of the prominent part which was being played at this time in England by four men, all close friends and associates of Milton. These men, John Dury, Samuel Hartlib, Theodore Haacke, and William Petty, will be considered more closely in the following chapter. They were all vitally interested in the general subject of education; they were the ones who kept agitating the subject of the founding of a society for the study of the natural sciences. It was Hartlib to whom Milton addressed his *Tractate on Education* in 1644. It was Hartlib who became more and more interested in the idea of a " reformation work " and in 1647 presented to the High Court of Parliament certain considerations on reformed education and the redressing of public evils for the advancement of God's " Universal Kingdom " and the general communion of His saints. These are phrases that occur in *Nova Solyma* [2] and are, as Begley points out, favorite expressions with Hartlib and Dury in their doctrine of unity in churches. In 1649, the year after the first issue of *Nova Solyma,* Hartlib edited a work by Dury, in which the latter begins by saying: " We (referring to his group of investigators) are upon the design of a public reformation; herein everybody is one way or another, if not engaged yet concerned, some more, some less, some in private, some in a public way." [3] Now, as has been stated, Gott took his degree from Cambridge in 1632. This was also the year in which John Milton completed his course at the same institu-

[1] Begley, *op. cit.,* I, pp. 311 ff.   [2] I, p. 86.
[3] *Nova Solyma,* I, p. 313.

tion. There can hardly be any doubt that Gott was acquainted and closely associated during the succeeding years with the same group of men as was Milton, especially since he was constantly at work on the same problems, as his authorship of *Nova Solyma* proves, which were occupying their minds. But these very men were the warmest admirers of Comenius, the friend and co-worker of Andreae, and even corresponded with Andreae himself.[1] Hence all the arguments brought out by Begley (and they are many) to prove that Milton must have written *Nova Solyma*, because he knew Hartlib, Dury, and the others well, and because so many of the ideas contained in the work are clearly theirs—this argument and testimony have now double effect in proving the connection between *Nova Solyma* and Andreae, since Gott, through these men, had direct relations to Andreae and his group.

The utopia now to be considered shows a number of differences from all those that have preceded. It is not a brief summary of laws, education, religion, and customs—a description of conditions in an ideal city, with the evident and one purpose of making these known. But in *Nova Solyma* we have a long romance, with various characters and incidents—love, rivalry, robbery, bloodshed, pageants, and feasts, with scenes shifting to different countries, even continents—all interwoven and combined in a novel of somewhat modern type. Yet it is didactic throughout, and built up on a system of education—a moral and a religious code which are always discernible. That Gott meant to teach certain truths, and merely clothed them in the dress of romance to make the whole easy and interesting reading, is plain from the titles of the six books which are given on the first page of the second (1649) issue. For the au-

[1] *M. C. G.,* II, p. 236.

thor, the important facts are summed up: 1) Boys. 2) The creation of the world. 3) Youth. 4) Sin. 5) The age of the adult. 6) The redemption of man. And in fact these single words contain the kernel of the respective books.

Two young men, students at Cambridge, have heard of the famous republic in the East, and being filled with a desire to learn of the place first-hand, they set out without the consent of their parents and arrive at Nova Solyma, after having on the way taken into their services a young man who proves to be the son of the chief ruler of the city, and the hero of the story. It might be noted here that Nova Solyma is evidently on the site of the biblical Jerusalem. This statement is not made definitely, but several references would strongly imply it. The young Cambridge students [1] (and later their father also),[2] on leaving Dover, take ship for Joppa. In the second instance, the journey is made from Joppa to Nova Solyma on horses, and requires a considerable part of one day. Now as Joppa is the nearest seaport to Jerusalem and as the distance is thirty or thirty-five miles, the locations of Jerusalem and Nova Solyma might well be the same. The description of the place corresponds with that of Jerusalem, Nova Solyma being built on a hill (possibly on hills).[3] The walls " stand four square " and there are twelve gates named after the twelve tribes, as in the biblical account.[4] It is stated that " not a vestige of the old Solyma remains, but its glories are renewed on a larger scale." [5] Furthermore, the return of the Jews after their conversion was to be to the city of Jerusalem, and this was the indication of the Millennium.[6]

To continue the narrative, these young men are hos-

[1] I, p. 98.
[2] II, p. 181.
[3] I, p. 78.
[4] Ezekiel xlviii, 31, and Revelation xxi, 12.
[5] Cf. Luke xix, 44.
[6] Jeremiah xxxi, 8 ff.

pitably taken up and taught the principles by which the inhabitants of Nova Solyma govern their lives. The visitors make many mistakes and at such times are kindly corrected by their host. In the course of their stay they visit the schools and are given information as to the system of education—elementary and advanced—by which the youth is trained. They also attend festivities and celebrations, witness death-bed scenes and funerals, and become acquainted with a representative number of persons in the city. A love affair, whose beginning dates from the first day they spend in Nova Solyma, continues throughout the story, and culminates in the marriage of the two young men to the daughters of their friend and host—the chief ruler.

This is in very brief the romance—occupying in time exactly one year, the annual pageant following immediately upon the general election being used to introduce as well as to conclude the story. The events themselves, by no means uninterestingly told, are interspersed, sometimes even interrupted, by lectures, religious teachings, moral discourses, recitations of poetry, by hymns and songs. Individuals tell the outward events of their lives, as well as their inner experiences. It is thus that the reader becomes acquainted with the history of the state, and those facts and principles which the author wishes to make known—the proper relation which should exist between man and man, the object of education, and the relation of the individual to the state—the extreme importance of a clean, religious life. It will be the purpose of this chapter to summarize the teachings of *Nova Solyma*, and compare them in essentials with those of the *Christianopolis*, with which they have so much in common, and upon which they seem to be based.

It might well be supposed that Gott, living in the same

country with Francis Bacon, whose *New Atlantis* had been published some twenty years earlier and had been welcomed with such great enthusiasm at home and in other countries, would model his novel upon the utopia of his already famous fellow-countryman. And it is not the purpose here to deny that Bacon's ideal state did have its influence upon, and help to furnish material and ideas for Gott. There are numerous traces of such an influence in the form and in the content of *Nova Solyma*. But in the main, Gott's object was an entirely different one from that of Bacon, and in this main object Gott has followed quite a different model. The most important points in Gott's mind were neither law (to which Bacon intended to devote the second half of his work, had he been able to complete it) nor yet scientific discovery and invention as such, to which, however, he does pay some attention as an element in his chief general scheme. Gott's highest aim is the plan of a system of *education,* beginning with children, and continuing through life, resulting in a broad, full, and complete development for the individual, in the field and the directions for which he is best adapted by natural talents; and thus furnishing capable and energetic citizens for the community, able and willing to discharge their proper obligations to neighbor, state, and God. While it is true that no specific statement is made regarding the education of girls, the implication is very strong that they are not neglected. For the two sisters of the hero are well-bred, well-developed, physically and mentally, and entirely fit to associate with the men of the family and their guests. Furthermore, the two boys of the family are, until their tenth year, under the partial charge and tutorage of a matron,[1] whose experience is thought beneficial to their

[1] I, pp. 109-128.

early years. In the pages just referred to, she tells the boys a long story—a fairy tale—to impress upon them lessons of right and wrong, and to instruct how to distinguish between them "by the critical faculty." It is hardly likely that boys, the importance of the education of whose early years is mentioned several times, would be left in the care of ignorant and untrained individuals. One cannot agree entirely, then, with Begley's statement [1] when he says, that throughout the whole work, as also in preceding writings of the sort, "girls are entirely ignored," even though the reference to their education is only by implication.

Gott's system of education begins with the children. The two sons of the chief man in the city are taken as examples, because the visitors are staying at the home of the latter, while in the city, and naturally come into contact with the members of his family circle. These boys are respectively nine and ten years of age. They have been in the care of women as well as men, that they might get advantages of the kindness of the one and the firmness of the other sex. "As soon as children can stand on their feet and begin to walk, they are taught to do so, gracefully and firmly" . . . "after that we practice running. . . . Dancing, swimming, archery and such like pursuits receive attention." [2] . . . "And thus we do not, like the Europeans, regard culture as consisting mainly in the accomplishments and training of the mind, and take hardly any account of the body; nor yet like the barbarians do we dispense with all mental training and book learning because we share their high opinion of a strong and enduring frame. We follow the glorious examples of the Greeks and Romans and pay our regard to both mind and body." [3] "Our highest endeavor is to kindle into flame the *spark*

---

[1] I, p. 94; note.   [2] I, p. 91.   [3] I, p. 91.

of genius that may be latent in each; for we cannot hope that those who only follow the trite and vulgar pursuits of the mob, can ever be so fired with enthusiasm as to dare, I will not say to do, any truly great and noble act. Meanwhile we season their minds with the salt of soberness and self-restraint, lest by want of it they should fall into the splendid sins of the pagan world." [1]

Grammar and mathematics are taught early, as these sciences have close connection with daily life; and they are taught as much as may be objectively. They also "attach importance to the proper exercise of faith and imagination." [2] Impurity and dishonesty are rooted out, or rather prevented by anticipation. So the children are brought up to worship God and love their country, reverence parents and elders, and treat each other with consideration. And an effort is made that this form of education be made available to as many children as possible. " Our plan is to have prudent men of experience who can be questioned and consulted—who are, so to speak, inspectors and directors of education. And besides these we have public discourses held frequently in all parts of the land, not only of a religious nature, but on ethics, the family life, and such topics. And so you see our education gives an entrance to the family circle; and although it cannot be successful everywhere, still if anyone is gifted with abilities out of the common, it looks after him and looks after his career. No one with natural endowments of a higher order is allowed to remain unnoticed and neglected from the obscurity of his birth, as is so often the case elsewhere. Nor are the less gifted despised on that account and reckoned unworthy of such educational care. Indeed we use especial endeavors in their case that

[1] I, p. 93.   [2] I, p. 94.

they may be able at least to rise to the full height of their capacity." [1]

Thus far the matter has been one of the preliminary education at home. The second stage in the education of the youth is the entrance into the public academy.[2] The reader is introduced to this, by accompanying the older brother and his two visiting friends as they take the ten-year-old boy to enter the institution. After some mutual greetings and introductory remarks, the head tutor at the request of the visitors, outlines their method and courses. He begins, "The founders of our republic, in their zealous inquiry how best to establish it on a sound basis, put the education of the rising generation in the very forefront of all means to that end. They held the opinion that good laws, an effective army, and all the other defenses of a state, were of comparatively no avail if obedience and benevolence and the other virtues which tend to the well-being of mankind were not early planted in the minds of the young. . . . Therefore they spared neither skill nor labor nor expense in properly preparing the ground at this critical period of youth. Especially did they bestow every care on this great public school, or academy, intended for the flower of the age, and to be an example for all other teaching institutions in the land." [3] " The first and chief care is to induce the religious habit of mind, the next to inculcate the ethical duties, and the last care (which others make their first) is a liberal education, both literary and scientific. Our religious training is mainly directed to the feelings of a spiritual character." [4]

When a boy enters the school, the tutors spend as much time with him as possible to learn his personality—the faults

[1] I, p. 96.
[2] I, p. 129.
[3] I, p. 235.
[4] I, p. 239, pp. 93, 94 of this chapter.

and the vices, the accomplishments and the virtues, as also the preferences in subjects. By a psychological process of directing the energies, the evil tendencies can be and are diverted into different channels, without retarding development and growth. Each pupil is considered separately and treated peculiarly according to his own special needs. He is trained for that position and occupation in life which will best suit him, at which he will be able to make greatest success and be most contented, and which will therefore make him fit to render the highest possible services to the community in which he is to live.

In order that one may know the essentials of statecraft and government, and the duties toward the same, it is necessary to have studied the history of the peoples of past times. And that this may be done most successfully, it should be in the language of the peoples themselves. Hence general instruction is given [1] in Greek, Latin, and Hebrew, the last named being of course in this city the native tongue. All are used in daily conversation, sometimes the one and then the other; for only thus can the real soul of the language be mastered. Furthermore, the foreign contemporary languages are taught, especially those of the countries with which Nova Solyma comes into commercial contact. They are not satisfied with a mere makeshift knowledge; but exact pronunciation, use of idioms, and the " genius of the tongue " [2] are carefully sought after. Thus they not only can carry on all correspondence and conversation with their trade countries, but are not " subject to ridicule nor exposed to loss of dignity " [3] when using the foreign tongue; in reading the works of an author it is not the exact translation of a word that counts, but " the

[1] I, pp. 245, 246.   [2] I, p. 246.   [3] I, p. 246.

' genius ' of the work is revealed and the book, so to speak, becomes alive—not a mere dead letter." [1]

Specialization takes place in the education of each individual when he becomes ready for it; and such specialization is in the direction in which the greatest talent, interest, and ability have been shown. In the school of letters and art,[2] prizes are offered for proficiency in style of writing, rhetoric (by which are to be understood oratory and debate), poetry, drama, and the novel. " Rhetoric within the bounds of prudent restraints is a most powerful weapon, and can be turned to the highest use." [3] This is the opening sentence of a long eulogy upon rhetoric in which the tutor mentions its many practical applications. The artificial flourishes of the haranguer are scorned, as well as bombast and " logical puzzles " in writing. Poetry is one of the highest forms of literature, and it is taught to all students. For though only few become expert, yet the training in it gives a touch of refinement which is not to be attained in any other way.[4] The poetry of *Nova Solyma* is entirely of a religious nature, and excellent examples of adaptations of the psalms, as well as original themes, epic and dramatic, are to be found in the records of the school. In his discussion of the novel, the author permits to be seen his objections to the cheap love-stories that at the time were being circulated—to a considerable extent imported from Spain or built upon the picaresque model. The ideal of the novel in *Nova Solyma* is that of a book (the name of book and author being concealed) whose argument is the

[1] I, p. 247.
[2] I, p. 250.
[3] I, p. 253.
[4] Poetry plays the same part in Gott's system of education that painting does in Andreae's (cf. p. 36, above, and *Christianopolis*, chap. xlviii).

history of a life that is free, that has received a liberal education and has been well and religiously brought up. The story keeps within the limits of human possibility, and deals as a rule with those in the middle ranks of life " who are the best and certainly not the least numerous." It is, then, a biographical, realistic production in the " Bürger " life that Gott would recommend.   There are certain pupils who, after reasonable effort, show that they are not adapted to a literary career.   These are trained to some craft, or find useful employment in farming.

The beginning of all education is nature.   This is true whether the matter in hand be a subject like public speaking (where, as has already been seen, naturalness is the first requirement) or whether it be in the line of scientific research.   " Human ingenuity produces certain extras, but from no other source than nature do they come.   For what, I pray, can a cook or a physician or a chemist produce except the preparation or the distillation of natural products?   Nay more, the most peculiar and admirable results of art, if we thoroughly look into them, we shall find to be commonplace and inconsiderable; for indeed, the very best of them, have been discovered rather than invented." [1]   " And religion too has its original foundation in the very bosom of nature." [2]

In answer to the question " Do you then wish us all to become philosophers and adepts in the chemistry of nature?" the tutor informs his visitor, " Yes I do, if you are such adepts as to be able to extract the meaning of the divine goodness, and such philosophers as to look at common things with no common views.   Philosophers have been wont to let their studies end in the desire for knowledge and fame only, and have not used them as they ought,

[1] I, p. 165.   [2] I, p. 225.

to God's praise and glory. Now the special advantage of natural science is to rise from nature to nature's God, tracing His footsteps everywhere therein."[1] And nature furnishes a spectacle worthy of the deeper consideration of the inward eye.

The physical development of the boys at academy or college is not neglected. There is a gymnasium, in and near which all kinds of "exercises and games are practiced—running, leaping, games of ball and the quoit, swimming in the baths, riding, drilling, marching,"[2] and so on; in these the students are not only encouraged, but obliged to take part. At all such regular athletic sports masters are present to assist and coach, as well as to check any improper behavior; "for nowhere is a boy's natural disposition more clearly discovered than when in excited play."[3]

As advanced work for students[4] who have already obtained their degree in arts, two lecture halls are provided—the one in which lectures are heard in philosophy and civil prudence, the other which is fitted up and equipped for theology, medicine, and jurisprudence. Only the very best professors and lecturers are engaged, and at the highest salaries, to superintend the work here; and students are given more liberty than in their previous years. A word should be said here also concerning the type of teachers employed in all the grades of the schools, and the standing of such men. The following description is given by the visitors who are being conducted through the school by the head master: "The tutor was well advanced in years, of grave and commanding appearance; but his kind eyes, pleasant voice, and sweet expression all pointed to the best of dispositions. The inhabitants of Nova Solyma do not

[1] I, p. 171.
[2] I, p. 304.

[3] I, p. 304.
[4] II, p. 7.

hold schoolmasters in contempt, as so many other nations do, nor do they class them simply as superior servants, who have to see chiefly that the children are kept safe and do not get into mischief. On the contrary, they are classed with the chief magistrates of the nation; and especially are those schoolmasters held in honor who have charge of the young and untrained, for they are invested with the Order of the Sun, appropriately enough too; for the sun is the dispeller of all darkness, and renders possible the active duties of life." [1]

Closely identified with the educational system, is the religious training; and hand in hand with the latter goes the use of music. Nova Solyma [2] is a city of christianized Jews. After a long, wandering, and unsettled life, caused by "that most awful deed of crime committed by the fore-fathers," the chosen people again find themselves under one government. For a "sudden flash of divine light" re-moved the "stubborn mental darkness" that had existed. And it is now fifty years since the nation has been restored to prosperity and contentment. Here appears the chiliastic character of the utopia.

The highest ideal in life is the religious ideal. "Even as knowledge is the servant of morality, so both are true servants of religion." [3] One of the chief themes of the story is the enlightenment and complete conversion of the two young men who have sought out the republic from a desire to know its inner life. Apollos, Joseph, and Jacob—the three chief religious teachers mentioned—take every occa-sion to turn the thoughts of the young men to a realization of the importance of the future life. Two death-bed scenes are used for this purpose also. Here are shown the agony of a sinful soul near the moment of its departure from the

[1] I, p. 234.   [2] I, p. 88.   [3] I, p. 306.

earth;[1] and the contentment and peacefulness of one at the time of death whose life has been an attempt to coincide with the Divine Will.[2]

"Inner light," "inner feeling," and "revelation" are expressions often used. "Flashes of light,"[3] "Excess of heavenly light,"[4] "Dark places made plain as it were by the light of heaven,"[5] "true renewed life of the soul, and a lively exercise and warm experience of faith,"[6] "that inner life of the soul,"[7] "the fierce light of all sciences,"[8] "the sweetness and light of the intellectual life,"[9] "We believe every good gift cometh from the same source of divine light,"[10] "'Tis true, I see sometimes a slight ray of omnipotent grace flitting across the darkness of my night, with frequent flashes as from some tiny crevice,"[11] "The light of divine favor seemed to beam on his soul,"[12] "The only authority in all cases is divine truth,"[13] "like rays of heavenly light breaking through their former gloom,"[14] "Clear light of heaven into my poor dark soul,"[15] "And each glorified saint shall give forth, as doth a lantern, its own inner light,"[16] are a few of the very frequent references to the subject.

There are long discourses, lectures, and private talks on religious and philosophical subjects—the origin of the world,[17] origin of evil in the world,[18] discourse on the sabbath,[19] prayer,[20] conception of God.[21] And all point to one conclusion: The true religion is that of Jesus Christ; real happiness consists in adapting of the will to that of God.

[1] II, p. 180.
[2] II, p. 67.
[3] I, p. 88.
[4] I, p. 195.
[5] I, p. 222.
[6] I, p. 223.
[7] I, p. 225.
[8] I, p. 227.
[9] I, p. 238.
[10] I, p. 245.
[11] II, p. 168.
[12] II, p. 196.
[13] II, p. 196.
[14] II, p. 207.
[15] II, p. 217.
[16] II, pp. 219 and 220.
[17] I, p. 178, and II, p. 9.
[18] II, p. 26.
[19] II, p. 190.
[20] II, p. 193.
[21] II, p. 149.

A pure, active, and unselfish life is the outward evidence of Christianity within.

"The people of Nova Solyma take great delight in the art of music."[1] "It has indeed a subtle influence, yet so elevating and vehement that it seems to throw an enchantment on the mind, nor has God failed to include this natural and suitable instrument among the adjuncts of worship. . . . The human voice is the fittest instrument wherewith to praise God."[2] In Nova Solyma the singing of psalms stands next to prayer in religious devotion.

The educational system, the religious views, and the proper use of music have now been outlined as they exist in Nova Solyma. A comparison of these with the views held by the inhabitants of Christianopolis will show likenesses that cannot fail to point to a knowledge on the part of Gott of the "Christian state" of Andreae. Though involving some slight repetition of the material of a preceding chapter, it will be necessary to cite a few references from the *Christianopolis*. Where a subject has been discussed in previous chapters, a page reference merely will be given.

The most striking similarity is found in the very kernel of the educational systems of the two utopias. In the *Nova Solyma* the essence of the system is twice mentioned, once in detail[3] and once in substance.[4] The *Christianopolis* gives the same thought exactly, and almost the identical words and phraseology.[5] "The most important duty is to reverence God with a pure and worshipful soul; next, to cultivate pious and unsullied morals, and finally to train the mind." *In both instances* there is added in parentheses as

[1] I, p. 103.
[2] II, p. 195.
[3] I, p. 239, and p. 86 of this chapter.
[4] I, p. 88, and p. 91 of this chapter.
[5] Chap. liv.

an afterthought: "*This order is regularly inverted in the world.*" It would not be surprising that these two men, religious in their make-up, should put religion first in importance in their utopias; nor need it be startling even, that the other two items should follow in the same order. But inasmuch as in both utopias this particular matter is taken as the basis for all the rest, the prominence given to the statements and the exact similarity of the means of expression cease to appear as a mere coincidence.

Up to the age of six in the *Christianopolis*, ten in the *Nova Solyma*, children are educated at home. At this period they are given over by their parents to the public boarding school, but with earnest prayer.[1] So also the *Christianopolis:* "Youth the most valuable treasure of the republic,"[2] and "Not without fervent prayer."[3] And in *Nova Solyma:* "Youth the most important item in the state."[4]

As in Nova Solyma[5] so in Christianopolis, the instructors are men of the highest talent and ability, and the description tallies remarkably. In the latter, instructors are of "mature years, virtuous, upright, industrious;" they develop the pupils, are held in high esteem, and are capable in their departments.[6] Here as there, the pupils are kept under close observation and taught as individuals.

In the study of languages, the same principles and purposes exactly are mentioned. In the *Christianopolis*,[7] as has already been seen in *Nova Solyma*,[8] the classics and the

---

[1] *Nova Solyma*, I, p. 239; p. 86 of this chapter.
[2] Chap. lxxix.
[3] Chap. liii.
[4] I, p. 235; p. 86 of this chapter.
[5] I, p. 234; pp. 90, 91 of this chapter.
[6] Chaps. lii, liii, and liv.
[7] Chap. lvii.
[8] I, pp. 245 f.; p. 87 of this chapter.

modern languages are taught—the former, to prepare men to understand ancient civilization, the latter that intercourse with other states may be facilitated. *They* also learn the languages rapidly; and are surprised that Europeans waste years in acquiring one language. And here again, the essence and concrete meaning of the language is considered more important than the abstract grammar.

Rhetoric [1] is emphasized—but not the unnatural application of it. "Without the natural gift (*natura*) the accomplishment is tasteless, and shows rather something forced, than ingenious." Poetry and music are in Christianopolis, as in Nova Solyma, auxiliary forces to religion. "Choral singing, and singing and chanting of psalms play an important part in private as in public worship." With them [2] music is no small part of the worship. "They praise God especially with words (that is, singing), then also with harps . . . and all kinds of instruments." [3]

In both cities the colleges of theology, medicine, and law [4] are located closely together and are so treated. They are for the advanced students. Students in the *Christianopolis* have courses in physical training [5] as in *Nova Solyma*. The same forms of exercise are employed, and under strict superintendency.[6]

The similarities in religious matters as such, the sacraments, baptism and the Lord's Supper,[7] prayer, worship forms, and so forth, have been sufficiently discussed and

[1] Chap. lvi; cf. also p. 32, above.
[2] Chap. lxxxv.
[3] Cf. *Nova Solyma*, II, p. 195; p. 93 of this chapter.
[4] *Christianopolis*, chaps. lxxvii, lxxviii, and lxxix; *Nova Solyma*, II, p. 7.
[5] *Christianopolis*, chap. liv.
[6] *Nova Solyma*, I, p. 304; p. 84 of this chapter.
[7] *Christianopolis*, chap. lxxxvi; *Nova Solyma*, II, p. 198; pp. 91, 92 of this chapter.

require no further comparisons. Politics, society, family relations, and so forth, are wonderfully alike in both states. The governments are democratic, built up on principles of liberty; and the note of freedom is loudly sounded throughout. So in *Nova Solyma,* "If any humanly authorized power denies this principle (that is, of liberty and religion), it is the people's duty to resist and death itself is to be chosen in preference to such an unjust and monstrous tyranny."[1] "Liberty of judgment is conceded to us, and recommended."[2] "We have indeed liberty of will."[3] In the *Christianopolis* "Christian freedom, therefore, cannot tolerate even restrictions, much less threats."[4] Yet this feeling of freedom does not in any way lean toward license, is not at all anarchistic. It is the inner freedom that regulates the individual will, and makes it voluntarily obedient to a just, higher authority. Hence also patriotism is strongly developed. Of this there are numerous suggestions. In *Nova Solyma* "That he must needs relieve his mind in a joyous song of home and fatherland."[5] Again, "The affairs of the state should have a special call upon us."[6] "We are joined in family and state by the closest ties." And in the *Christianopolis* "Those who have deserved well of their native country have here an enviable reputation."[7]

The home life in *Nova Solyma* follows the same principle as in the *Christianopolis.* Filial obedience is the rule. Children are polite and respectful.[8] The disrespect shown by the two Cambridge students in leaving Europe for the East without the knowledge of their parents, is severely rebuked by Jacob—the chief ruler of Nova Solyma. Again

[1] I, p. 224.
[2] II, p. 196.
[3] II, p. 170.
[4] Chap. xix.
[5] I, p. 175.
[6] I, p. 243.
[7] Chap. xli.
[8] I, p. 99.

the parting of father and son [1] when the ten-year-old boy leaves for academy, is indicative of the closest ties between the two. Even after the children grow up they are expected to look to parents for advice and suggestion. So Joseph, the grown son of Jacob, says, " that he is not yet independent of paternal authority, and is simply a member of the family council." [2] And at the time of marriage, the consent of the parents of both parties is necessary. " Now since marriage is in a way the granting of freedom to one's children, and sending them forth into a new colony or home, it not only requires the consent of the parents, but before that, it requires that they should be *consulted*. . . . Certainly it can scarcely be expected, that God will approve of that marriage of which the parents disapprove." [3] These ideas of filial obedience and marriage have been brought out in the *Christianopolis* already. Marriage is then a sacred institution sanctioned and approved by parents and by God ; and patience must be exercised to make it happy. So in the *Christianopolis*, " Their friends recommend to the newly married couple, unity, work, moderation, but primarily piety and *patience*." [4] In *Nova Solyma* " Discords can be smoothed out by care and *patience*." [5] Self-control and patience are urged in all matters, as the chief virtue. " Nothing is more worthy than to control oneself," [6] " The man who can rule himself is the greatest of all commanders." [7] " To acquire the position of a ruler among men, one must begin by ruling himself—that is the first great requisite." [8] In the *Christianopolis*, " The glory of conquest over one's passions," [9] " make effort to control our

[1] I, p. 231.
[2] I, p. 207.
[3] II, p. 205.
[4] Chap. lxxxviii.
[5] II, p. 208.
[6] *Nova Solyma*, II, p. 130.
[7] *Nova Solyma*, II, p. 125.
[8] *Nova Solyma*, II, p. 120.
[9] Chap. xlviii.

anger," [1] " to be patient in distasteful affairs." [2] The scenes around the death-bed are similarly described [3]—exhortation, prayer and encouragement, and contentment, if the departing one is at peace with God.

Several minor and unrelated points will be but hastily mentioned: The library and the armory are adjacent. In both cases the visitors are led through (or past) the one, to get to the other.[4] " Mars and Pallas," says *Nova Solyma,* " should not be too far separated." But in both Christianopolis and Nova Solyma " the pest of war " is a necessary evil. " Nor is it only that one man becomes a pest to another, but vast multitudes of men, sworn in under a deadly compact, fitted out with all the weapons of destruction, . . . are led forth to lay waste a country, to burn its cities, and to slaughter its principal people; and the more terror they cause, and the greater ravages they commit, so much the more do they boast and triumph in such deeds; and their names are handed down to posterity loaded with honor, this glorious condition being kept up, perhaps to cover the vile atrocities of our ancestors from the researches of later generations, or to encourage posterity to rise to like wicked barbarity." [5] And in the *Christianopolis,* " When other nations are accustomed to pride themselves with their cannon and war equipment, these people look upon all their heaps of murderous weapons with horror." [6]

As in keeping with the other customs of home life, the families of Nova Solyma, as has already been noticed in

---

[1] Chap. xxix.
[2] Chap. xliii.
[3] *Nova Solyma,* II, pp. 67, 180; cf. p. 91 of this chapter, and *Christianopolis,* chap. xcix.
[4] *Christianopolis,* chaps. xxxix, xl; *Nova Solyma,* I, p. 243.
[5] *Nova Solyma,* II, p. 38.
[6] Chap. xl.

the case of Christianopolis, take their meals in their private houses and at a family table.

The description of the gardens and the various hues and colors of flowers therein [1] is almost identical, indeed whole sections in this connection are very similar.

It would be possible to carry on the process of likenesses to a much further degree, but this would be tedious and entirely unnecessary. The general plan of the two works has undoubtedly been shown to be one; the system of education and the ethics of life—the important points in the minds of both authors—must surely be recognized as the same. (In the former especially, Bacon's *New Atlantis could not* have been the pattern for *Nova Solyma*.) And enough parallels have been cited to show direct relation between the two. When it is remembered that Gott himself was in all probability in the circle of Andreae's best friends and warmest admirers—Dury, Hartlib, Comenius, and others—and that he was interested in exactly the same sort of a reformation of society as was Andreae, and hence would eagerly make inquiry of his friends regarding all possible writings along the line of his work—the evidence that Gott actually knew Andreae's *Christianopolis* becomes too strong to deny.

[1] *Christianopolis,* chap. xciv; *Nova Solyma,* I, p. 162.

V

ANDREAE, THE ROYAL SOCIETY OF LONDON, AND EDUCATIONAL REFORM

IN tracing the probable effect of Andreae's teachings upon the development of education, and especially the agitation which resulted in the foundation of societies for the investigation of the experimental sciences in England, it will be necessary first of all to consider his relations to certain prominent contemporary educators in Germany and abroad.[1] Among these, Johann Amos Comenius will occupy an important place. He was born in 1592 in Nivnitz, Hungary, but received his education for the most part in Germany. Having completed his preparatory work at the Latin school in Herborn, Nassau, he entered the University of Heidelberg, and after a brief stay in the Netherlands, returned home, taking up a position as instructor in 1614.

[1] G. Waterhouse, in a recent publication (see bibliography), discusses the literary relation of England and Germany in the seventeenth century. After asserting the superiority of German literature over English in the sixteenth century, and stating that England paid back the debt in the eighteenth, he continues (Introduction, xii, xiii) that "German literature of the seventeenth century is not worth reading for its own sake"; that "vernacular literature is practically unknown," that "the beginning of the century is for Germany a period of absolute stagnation." This is speaking somewhat extremely, as none of these statements is quite true. That certain works of Comenius, for instance, were considered important even in England will be shown later in this chapter; also that he as well as Andreae wrote in German and advocated the use of the vernacular at the same time that Bacon was having his English works translated into Latin so that they might better survive the effects of time.

He was later (after he attained the required age) ordained at Fulnek. During the years of the invasion of the Spanish armies, hundreds of prominent Bohemians were driven out of the country; and in 1627 Comenius, accompanied by a part of his congregation, withdrew to Poland. He took up his abode in Lissa, having added to his ministerial duties, that of director of the local " Gymnasium." In 1613 appeared his first work of importance, *Janua Linguarum Reserata*—which made him famous throughout Europe. This deals entirely with a reform for contemporary education. His next publication, the *Didactica Magna*, shows his interest also in the rebuilding of the whole system of scientific research and secured for him a call from Sweden to superintend a reform of the school system. But he was more attracted by an invitation extended by the British Parliament to come to England. The invitation had been procured through the activity of Samuel Hartlib, who had opened a correspondence with Comenius, and had caused to be published the latter's *Prodromus Pansophiae.* In 1641, then, Comenius came to London. While political conditions in England did not at the time admit of the forming of any permanent organization according to Comenius's

Waterhouse states that the influence of English literature on Weckherlin, Morhof, and Schupp was great. This is undoubtedly true (Weckherlin lived in England more than thirty years!), but that there was also a powerful current in the other direction, through the same and other individuals, is not mentioned. Only three lines are devoted to Hartlib, whose great activity in many fields cannot be overestimated. While Waterhouse records the English translations of Jakob Boehme's works he seems to have no knowledge of the remarkable and widespread influence which German mysticism had upon seventeenth-century England, and the names of men such as Sebastian Franck, Kaspar von Schwenckfeld, Valentin Weigel, and Andreae are not even mentioned in his book. See Margaret L. Bailey: *Milton and Jakob Boehme,* New York, Oxford University Press, 1914.

plans, his visit brought him into association with some of the most learned men of the time. Among these are to be counted Hartlib himself, John Dury, and perhaps Milton. At any rate, the latter's *Tractate on Education*, published in 1644 and dedicated to Hartlib, shows a strong tendency toward Comenius's views on this subject. Choosing between an invitation to France and a second one to Sweden, Comenius took up his abode at Elbing in 1642, which had at that time been given over to Sweden. Here he stayed most of the following eight years, under the patronage of Oxenstierna, the chancellor. These years, besides being spent in practical teaching activity, produced the *Novissima Linguarum Methodus* which, with his earlier mentioned works, presents his method in education. The following six years were spent in various parts of Germany and Hungary. In 1656 he took up his abode in Amsterdam, where his death took place in 1671. These years were spent in work upon his *Pansophia* (which he did not succeed in completing); and the collection of *Opera Didactica* was published in 1657.

Comenius's acquaintance with Andreae's productions began early. As early as 1628 he wrote Andreae of his interest in the latter's work, and expressed the hope that "Andreae will not scorn to consider him in the number of his admirers, disciples, and pupils."[1] The answer was favorable, and was probably accompanied by a copy of the laws of *Societas Christiana*. Comenius's next letter requests Andreae, "That he should not leave the field of battle before he had trained up successors; advanced age should not hinder the veteran general from giving the recruits a start. . . ."[2] The letters exchanged between the two were neither regular nor numerous. Until 1647 there was no further corre-

[1] Möhrke, p. 21.　　　　　[2] Möhrke, p. 21.

spondence. In that year a long letter from Comenius to Andreae acknowledges favorable comment on the part of the latter upon Comenius's *Pansophia;* and refers in turn with great praise to Andreae's *Theophilus,* which Comenius must have seen at least fifteen years earlier. The friendly relations between the two were kept up to a great extent by Hesenthaler, a young friend of both men; and [1] a regular exchange of their later works took place. The request for correspondence, and so forth, was invariably on the side of Comenius; and Andreae was always offering excuses for his neglect. At Andreae's death in 1657, Comenius showed his further respect for him by the use of a motto of Andreae's in the publishing of *Didactica Magna.*

Just to what extent Comenius is dependent upon Andreae for his views on education is hard to say. Being contemporaries and in direct communication with each other's works, their effect was in all probability to a considerable extent a mutual one. Furthermore, as Möhrke very rightly says,[2] conditions very often cause like ideas to rise simultaneously in the minds of isolated thinkers. Especially was this true in this century when the scholars of Italy, Germany, England, and France were working under a common world-impulse, developing solutions to the same great scientific problems.

If we can believe Comenius's words, he was certainly indebted to Andreae for his most fundamental ideas. He speaks of Andreae always in the highest terms, and ranks him among the first of those from whom he received incentive and inspiration for his own work. This he mentions again and again early in his career, and as late as 1656 in a letter to Hesenthaler he says incidentally while speaking of Andreae, ". . . for from him I obtained almost the

[1] Möhrke, pp. 23, 32. [2] P. 138.

very elements of my pansophic thoughts,"[1] and he begs Hesenthaler that he make an effort to secure for him at any cost all available works of Andreae, many of which (including the *Christianopolis*) he had once not merely read, but possessed and had lost in the burning of Lissa by the Poles in 1656. Hüllemann[2] and Hossbach[3] accept Comenius's statement of the case, as supplemented by an analysis of the productions of the two men. Brügel also concludes his argument on this point with, " Andreae laid the foundation upon which Comenius completed the admirable structure of his didactic."[4] On the other hand, there are those who deny any debt of Comenius to Andreae, and attribute the similarity in their methods and plans merely to the general spirit of reform and investigation which conditions had brought forth.

A comparison of the views of the two would certainly seem to support the conclusion of Hossbach and the others who take stand with him, and would justify Comenius himself in the frank statement he makes regarding his position with reference to Andreae. Only a few striking instances will be cited. The different realms in which education should be carried on are for Comenius, as stated in his *Didactica,* three: *sapientia* or *eruditio, virtus,* and *religio*—corresponding to the three so-called divisions of the activity of the soul, *intellectus, voluntas, conscientia.* These are also the elementary principles in the *Theophilus* and have already been cited from the *Christianopolis.*[5] The principle of happiness and prosperity of the succeeding generation provided by a proper care of the youth of to-day, is developed by both in exactly the same way— public schools for all children, of both sexes, and of

---

[1] Möhrke, p. 34.
[2] I, p. 1.
[3] Pp. 163 f.
[4] Möhrke, p. 14.
[5] Chap. liv, and pp. 93, 94, above.

all ranks in life;[1] instructors of the highest possible type and ability; not merely lecturing, but actual activity and effort on the part of the pupils. Languages, ancient and modern, are to be taught, as in the *Christianopolis* the former to acquaint the present with ancient civilization, the latter for convenience in intercourse with other nations. Möhrke[2] gives Comenius the advantage in his insistence upon proficiency in the vernacular. Instances will be found, however, where Andreae advocates this just as strongly. "Those are credulous people who would attribute to Latin that it gives greater wisdom than German."[3] "What is not clear in Latin or a foreign modern language, must be explained in the vernacular. It is foolish to try to learn the former before one is expert in the latter."[4] In the chapter relating to schools,[5] the word "*vernacula*" occurs three or four times. Again, the oft-repeated refrain of Comenius and the essence of his method, "Everything back to nature, and nothing without nature," is according to Möhrke[6] not to be found in Andreae, however closely one may search for it. This cannot be conceded; for such expressions as[7] (where the advantage of efficiency in rhetoric is the theme), "They look more upon *nature* than upon art," are to be found throughout his works.

Comenius insists upon exercise for the pupils and cleanliness in their quarters. He recommends the same outdoor sports as does Andreae and in the same manner bars all games that require no physical motion, as cards, dice, and so forth. He emphasizes the necessity of guarding against

---

[1] *Christianopolis,* chap. liii.
[2] P. 45.
[3] Chap. lvii.
[4] *Christianopolis,* chap. lv.
[5] Chap. lv.
[6] P. 72.
[7] *Christianopolis,* chap. lvi.

disease, and requires "large, roomy, and pleasant halls and apartments for the pupils." Andreae is just as particular in these points,[1] and by advocating individual attention to pupils, lays the basis for the Montessori system of education, so popular to-day. Comenius accepts Andreae's views on astronomy, astrology, and mystic numbers directly. Their objective instruction and scientific research coincide, as do also their methods of learning a foreign language. Finally and most important of all is Andreae's scheme for the organization of a college, that is, a body of men, educated, equipped and desirous of improving human affairs, "working together" to fulfill a common purpose. For it was this point in Andreae's plans which first attracted the attention of Comenius and caused him to seek a closer acquaintance with the former.

Leaving Comenius for the moment, we will briefly survey the lives and activities of Samuel Hartlib and John Dury. The former was born at Elbing, Germany, near the close of the sixteenth century. His early years are not well known, and most of the information at hand comes from some casual remarks of his own. His father was a Polish merchant and his mother the daughter of an Englishman. Hartlib came to England about 1628 and was himself a merchant. It is impossible to over-emphasize the enthusiasm of this very interesting man, as also the power and spirit he lent to the movement of better education in England. He felt that the era of democracy was well adapted for the improvement of all religious and educational conditions, and he devoted his life to the faithful performance of the mission of realizing such results. His aim was not only the cultural progress of England or of Germany; but the thought that he had early imbibed from Andreae—that of a

[1] Chap. liii.

general reformation of the whole world, was ever present in his mind. National and world growth by means of the education of the youth, was his ambitious purpose. The fact that parliament appointed him—a foreign-born man—as " agent for the advancement of universal learning " shows in what esteem he was held by his contemporaries. He introduced the writings of Comenius into England. In 1644 Milton addressed to him his *Tractate on Education.* Hartlib published pamphlets on educational and industrial matters and gave encouragement to all undertakings of this nature. In 1646 a pension was conferred upon him in return for his valuable works on husbandry; for, his essay on *The Erection of a College of Husbandry* is the first attempt on record for the founding of an agricultural school.[1] All the time he was carrying on an extensive correspondence with literary men at home and abroad. The latter part of his life he spent at Oxford, and he was intimately associated with the group of men who later became a part of the Royal Society. His idealistic interests are shown also in *The Description of the Famous Kingdom of Macaria,* a utopia published in 1641. He made numerous translations of works into English, especially of the Latin writings of Comenius. His death took place about 1670.

It was in 1633 that Hartlib first heard of Comenius through the latter's *Janua.* He seems to have been naturally an enthusiast for the subject, and from his first acquaintance with Comenius's theories was completely captivated. Comenius already had conceived the idea of an *Enzyklopädie der Pansophie,* and in 1634, in answer to Hartlib's request, sent him a brief of his plan under the title, *Praeludia.* The *Pansophie* was Comenius's favorite work and idea, though his plans for the whole were not

[1] Friedrich Althaus, in *Historisches Taschenbuch,* 1884, p. 244.

quite clear in his own mind and in the nature of the case it was a work he could not hope to complete. It was to be [1] fundamentally a " universal science " containing a résumé of all human knowledge, both resting upon a religious basis and leading toward a religious enlightenment. As has already been seen, he attributes the incentive for the idea to Andreae. And no one can read Andreae's works—especially the *Christianopolis*—without discovering in every chapter just this same thought, " God and nature are the beginning of all man's knowledge; and all scientific researches have in view the betterment of mankind and the glorification as well as the ' defense ' of God "—religion being the basis and the ultimate purpose of the whole; knowledge and science, the means. In order to enlarge the means and insure a more rapid and successful outcome of results, he advocates schools, study of the languages, and most important of all, the society or college of learned men, founded to collect information from all countries, to work out conclusions experimentally therefrom, and to share the results with the world at large. Comenius's plan is a *Pansophie* and includes the world in its scope.

These were the ideas which attracted Hartlib to Comenius and kept him in correspondence with the latter. Hartlib was in close touch with men of learning in several countries and with all new scientific developments in England; and he saw in Comenius's plan, elements which he felt would advance the common cause materially. Hence, he made every effort to bring Comenius to England, that the latter's mental picture of his work might be personally outlined.

In the meantime Comenius had been close to other enthusiasts in London and in the university towns, chiefly

[1] Möhrke, p. 32.

through Hartlib's efforts and activity in the cause. One of these, who took the matter up with almost equal energy and enthusiasm, was John Dury. He was born at Edinburgh in 1596, in a Presbyterian home. His father, a minister, was banished in 1606 and the son was educated at Leyden. After completing his university course, he was made pastor of an English congregation at Elbing (then under the dominion of Gustavus Adolphus). The English ambassador to the place, Sir Thomas Roe, took an interest in Dury's plans of religious unity between the Presbyterian and Lutheran churches, and gave him recommendations to Sweden and to men in England. To England Dury went in 1630. From this time on for practically the rest of his life, he wandered from place to place visiting Germany, France, Sweden, Switzerland, and the Netherlands, trying to bring about unity in the church. In 1661 he went to Cassel, where he died in 1680.[1] It was at Elbing in all probability that Dury and Hartlib met, although Hartlib left about 1628, very shortly after the former arrived to take up his pastorate in the English settlement there. It has been suggested [2] that Hartlib's departure for England at this time was partly caused by his willingness to prepare the way for Dury's mission. The latter was primarily a preacher, interested in bringing about unity in the Christian church. He also had very decided views on education; and Hartlib here, as in the case of Comenius, furnished the inspiration and enthusiasm to make the pedagogical theories practical. During the years that followed, Dury wrote (and Hartlib published with a preface) a number of religious and educational tracts at the suggestion of a " Christian *brotherhood* whose members wished to be of service to one another and to humanity."

[1] *M. C. G.*, VI, p. 65.   [2] *M. C. G.*, Massons, VI.

Dury's system of education shows, again, a very noticeable similarity to the educative principles of Andreae.[1]
Girls and boys are educated [2] in separate halls—the former
have governesses, and the latter, tutors (the "masters" of
Christianopolis). The schools are supervised by an inspec-
tor. Girls are trained to the duties of mothers and house-
wives—boys are instructed particularly in agriculture, commerce, and political science; but all study the languages.
Good methods and excellent instructors save pupils much
trouble and unnecessary difficulty.[3] The chief objects are
exactly as in Andreae, and even his accepted order—
1) education to piety, 2) decency in morals, 3) growth in
sciences—is followed. He inserts also "preserving of
health." Under the first head we find all the relations for
daily prayer and worship, as we saw in the *Christianopolis,*
though these are elaborated and developed according to
Dury's own personal views. His training in manners, and
so forth, is based upon strict morality. The pupils are
closely watched and corrected in their daily behavior.
Character building must begin with the early years. As far
as concerns mental training elsewhere, he complains, pupils
are taught very poorly, and trained in the least important
matters. They are given words, rules, and sections to commit before they understand the meaning.[4] These blunders
are eliminated by teaching nothing that the pupil cannot
grasp and understand. So education becomes experimental,

[1] *M. C. G.,* XVI, pp. 191 ff.
[2] See *Christianopolis,* especially chaps. xxxviii, xlviii, lii, liii, liv.
[3] Recall here the description of the excellent methods in use at
Christianopolis and the wail of the visitor when he recalls his own
early grapplings with languages.
[4] It will be remembered how often Andreae complains of the
"dead letters of Aristotle" as compared with the living "genius"
of the subject.

and is successful in proportion as it promotes knowledge of nature and the application of her creatures!

The work of the pupils is graded. This is very carefully done in the *Christianopolis*, though the whole is less definitely outlined. For Dury's third or advanced grade there are exact equivalents in the *Christianopolis*. The subjects are even in like groups: medicine, pharmacy, chemistry; logic, rhetoric, poetry; theory of music with mathematics. A comparison of the indices of the two works will show surprising likenesses. It will not be necessary to note them here. The practical applications of science to daily life recall the many workshops and so forth, in the *Christianopolis*, where the rules and theories are tested and worked out. Precautions for health—an open location for the school, plenty of air, absolute cleanliness of the rooms, frequent baths, physical exercise, regular and informal recreation—all have been noted before.

Such is the system of Dury, the comrade in arms, as it were, of Hartlib, and it shows at every turn exact marks of coincidence with the utopia of 1619. That Dury was well acquainted with Andreae's works cannot be doubted. First of all, he was introduced by Hartlib to Comenius's works and became, like Hartlib, an admirer of them. It will be remembered that Comenius in his educational productions made frank and open use of Andreae. Moreover there is evidence [1] of direct correspondence between Andreae and Dury on the subject that lay near the hearts of both men— education of the youth to insure betterment of society, church, and state.

The intellectual relationships that had been growing up for several years between England and Germany were strengthened and made more definite in 1636 by two young

[1] *M. C. G.*, II, p. 233, and *Vita*, pp. 126, 166.

men, Peter Figulus and Joachim Hübner. The former, an orphan, had been adopted into the home of Comenius, and now entered the service of Dury, who was at the time visiting his friend Matthie in Sweden, and endeavoring to get a letter of recommendation from Oxenstierna (chancellor of Sweden) to the University of Upsala, with a view toward introducing his doctrines of unity. The other, Hübner, was a friend of Hartlib, through whom the arrangements had been made at Oxford in 1634 for the publishing of Comenius's *Praeludia*. Hübner's interest in this work was acknowledged by Comenius, when the latter wrote him a few years later and sent along a copy of his *Didactica*. From this time on, regular correspondence was carried on, and frank mutual criticism was indulged in which fortunately did not lead to serious differences. The next edition of the *Praeludia* (1639), now called the *Prodromus Pansophiae,* with Hartlib's preface, gave additional impetus to the ever increasing longing for the " society " outlined by Dury. It was clear that if the principles of the *Pansophia* were to become of practical value and the work completed, a company of organized co-workers would be necessary. Hence in 1640 definite plans were undertaken to make the theory a reality. Comenius was asked to map out the details for a society of scholars and finally urgently invited to come to England and describe the whole in assembly. This finally resulted (after an address to parliament by Bishop Gaudentius, in which he speaks of Comenius and Dury as furnishing peace on the foundation of " truth ") in the official invitation, already mentioned, extended to Comenius and Dury, and in their subsequent visit and consultation with parliament. These meetings of 1641 and 1642, twenty years before the founding of the Royal Society, half a decade before the

Oxford and London gatherings of Robert Boyle and his comrades, were undoubtedly the forerunners in England of the organization as realized under Charles II.

In the early correspondence of Hartlib and Hübner on the subject of education and scientific research, a number of men are discussed and their views. The chief one mentioned by Hübner is Andreae, with especial reference to his *Dextra Amoris Porrecta.*. In the meantime conditions in England had arrived at a point where national assistance to educational schemes was not to be immediately looked for. The king and the parliament were otherwise engaged, the factions at war; and the group of scholars and enthusiasts became scattered. Comenius, after some hesitation, went to Sweden, Hübner to Paris, to treat in the place of Comenius with Cardinal Richelieu. Dury remained in England until 1654.

During the few years immediately succeeding, unavoidable circumstances prevented regularity of meetings and attendance. But interest was still kept up and to a considerable extent through the influence of Robert Boyle, the chemist and natural philosopher. Boyle was younger than the men thus far discussed and was not in England at the time of the early meetings of the society in 1641 and 1642. He was born in 1627, and sent to Eton, where his father's intimate friend, Sir Henry Wotton, was provost at the time. In 1638 he left England for the Continent, staying at Paris, Lyons, and Geneva. Later he spent some time in Italy, studying at Florence with Galileo. The latter died (1642) while Boyle was at the place. In 1644 he returned to England and after some years spent in Ireland, where he had been called on private business, he settled in Oxford, 1654. Here he met often with Christopher Wren, Goddard, and others. A laboratory was fitted up and experiments of importance were performed which were written up and published several years later. While still in London in 1645 he had met with those who remained of the associates of the preceding years, and these gatherings were a little later referred to as the " Invisible College." During these years Boyle corresponded with Newton, John Evelyn,[1] Henry Oldenburg,[2] and Hartlib.[3] It was not until after some time that he could be persuaded to read Bacon or Descartes because he wanted to work out his own views without prejudice from others. In Ireland, where he spent

---

[1] John Evelyn (1620-1706) was born at Wotton and received most of his education from private tutors. He spent much time on the Continent and corresponded with Boyle on the subject of founding a college. He became very much interested in the Royal Society and held the offices of secretary and president. In a letter to Boyle, dated September third, 1659 (found in Boyle's *Works*, edition 1772, VI, p. 288), he urges the banding together of " gentlemen who have the common interest of preserving science and cultivating themselves," to form a society. His works, like those of Hartlib, deal with a great variety of subjects.

[2] Henry Oldenburg, natural philosopher and man of letters, was born at Bremen in 1615, the son of a " Gymnasium " tutor. His education was received in his native city, and he went to England in 1640, where he made the acquaintance of a number of learned men in parliament. Returning to Germany, he was for years engaged in diplomatic service, though in private he devoted his time to scientific research. In 1654 he met Milton, having gone back to England, and entered into closer relations with the English educators than before. He lived at Oxford, was much with Boyle and Petty, and was a part of the early movements, described before, for the foundation of the Royal Society. He spent the latter part of his life in England and was the first secretary of the Royal Society.

[3] In the correspondence of Boyle and Hartlib (Boyle's *Works*, VI, pp. 76-136), covering a period of ten or fifteen years, there are numerous references to Haacke, Dury, Petty, and also to German experimenters and men of letters. Hartlib mentions receiving letters urging and furnishing plans for " a real reformation and advancement in all manner of literature " from a man of the greatest importance " whose name would be known to those traveling on the Continent."

years without chemical equipment, he devoted much of his time to experiments in anatomy and dissection. The Invisible College is mentioned several times in his correspondence of the years 1646 and 1647. In one of his letters he urges a former tutor of his to bring along to London " good receipts or choice books on any of these subjects (natural philosophy, mechanics, or husbandry) which you can procure; which will make you extremely welcome to the Invisible College." Later on " The corner stones of the Invisible College, or as they call themselves, the Philosophical College, do now and then honor me with their company." [1]

The meetings during these years at London (1645 and following) were entirely informal and not as hopeful of ultimate and permanent organization even as those of a few years earlier. But they were a desperate attempt to persevere and win in spite of the unfavorable conditions.

At some of the meetings Dr. John Wallis was present as lecturer on mathematics. In his account of one of them he tells of the subjects discussed and also of the most prominent members who attended. Among the latter was Theodore Haacke, as Wallis says: " A German of the Palatinate and then resident in London, who, I think gave the first occasion, and first suggested these meetings." Haacke was a Calvinist, born in 1605 at Neuhausen near Worms. He received his earlier education at home, but in 1625 came to England and studied at Oxford and Cambridge. For a year after visiting continental universities, he returned to Oxford in 1629, remaining three years. Having been ordained deacon and having accepted a charge, he was appointed to raise money by subscription for benevolences in Germany, during the war. In 1648 parliament granted

[1] Boyle's *Works*, I, pp. 17, 20, 24.

him sole right in the translation into English of *The Dutch Annotations on the Bible*. He was often employed by the government as translator and counsel, and received a pension. About 1645 he gave fresh impetus to the "meetings of learned men" and in 1663 was elected one of the original fellows of the established Royal Society. His work as translator was notable, and shortly before his death he had ready for print some three thousand German proverbs, translated into English.

In 1648 several of the company in London moved to Oxford, among them William Petty.[1] Here also was Boyle after his return from his Irish estates. A society similar to that in London was at once formed. This company became in 1651 the Philosophical Society of Oxford and met for a generation. Those who remained in London, including John Evelyn, continued to meet regularly until 1658, when the meetings were interrupted by the wars, " For then, the place of their meeting was made a quarter for soldiers." [2] At the time of the restoration the meetings were resumed with renewed zeal and finally the permanent organization was formed. Sprat [3] states that "the wonderful pacific year 1660" marked the real beginning of the Royal Society and that while the prospective members were arranging their platform, "the contrivance of it was much hastened by a certain treatise, and that was a proposal by Master

---

[1] William Petty (1623-1687) was born at Romsey in Hampshire. From his early childhood he showed a taste for mechanics. He studied abroad, in France and Holland chiefly, making medicine his specialty at Leyden. Returning to England in 1646, he devoted himself to mechanical inventions and scientific studies. This brought him into touch with educators, and he moved to Oxford. From this time his interests are the same as those of the other founders of the Royal Society.

[2] Thomas Sprat, *History Royal Society of London*, p. 58.

[3] Pp. 58, 59.

Cowley[1] of erecting a philosophical college. The intent of it was that in some place near London there should liberal salaries be bestowed on a competent number of men, to whom should be committed the operations of natural experiments." Charles II finally permitted his name to be enrolled among those of the members, and issued a royal charter in 1662.

The aims and purposes of the Royal Society, as given by Sprat in his history, and the directions in which investigations were made, cover a narrower field than was planned in the programmes of either Andreae, Hartlib, or Comenius. For centuries education had been merely a matter of scholarship in rhetoric, logic, languages, and subjects of like nature; but now the Royal Society, the earlier academy of Telesius in Italy, and the later societies on the Continent showed a tendency toward narrowness in the other direction. With Andreae, and this shows the usual breadth and thoroughness of the man, it was a matter of the proper balance of *all* faculties and the development of *all* phases of education. It is just in this respect that his utopia is so much superior, for instance, to that of Bacon. His successor, Comenius, and the latter's associates, Dury and Hartlib, were true disciples of his in this respect. As a matter of fact, after the founding of the Royal Society in England, Comenius wrote to a number of its members on this very point, warning them against one-sidedness in the organization, and recommending attention to reform in literary education also.

For this reason a section in Sprat[2] is interesting, in which he digresses from his theme and rather apologetically inserts a recommendation for the founding of an academy in language and cultural subjects. After congratulating the Italians

[1] Abraham Cowley, the poet.   [2] Pp. 39 ff.

on the number of their academies for the study of " language, style, and so forth," and speaking in the highest terms of the French Academy at Paris, " composed of the noblest authors of the nation " and boasting of the " Great Cardinal Richelieu " as its founder, Sprat continues: " I hope now it will not be thought a vain digression, if I step a little aside to recommend the forming of such an assembly, to the gentlemen of our nation. . . . I shall not stick to say that such a project is now seasonable to be set on foot, and may make a great reformation in the manner of our speaking and writing. The thing itself is no way contemptible. For the purity of speech, and greatness of empire have in all countries still met together. Besides, if we observe the English language, we shall find that it seems at this time more than others, to require some such aid, to bring it to its last perfection. The truth is, it has been hitherto a little too carelessly handled; and I think has had less labor spent about its polishing than it deserves."

The suggestion of Cowley, as quoted from Sprat,[1] was " every way practicable; unless perhaps in two things: he did more consult the generosity of his own mind than of other men. The one was the largeness of revenue with which he would have his college at first endowed; the other, that he imposed on his operators a second task of great pains, the education of the youth. The last of these is indeed a matter of great weight, the reformation of which ought to be seriously examined by prudent men. For it is an undeniable truth, which is commonly said, that there would be need of fewer laws, and less force to govern men, if their minds were rightly informed and set straight while they were young and pliable."[2] This last statement of Sprat coincides exactly with several passages

[1] P. 116 of this chapter.   [2] P. 59.

in the *Christianopolis* as will be remembered, and also with the views of Comenius. Sprat is thoroughly in sympathy with this feature of a college and regrets that it is as yet unfeasible. " It was not the excellent author's fault," he adds, " that he thought better of the age than it deserved."

The Royal Society [1] is a general body, the membership of which is unrestricted by religious belief, nationality, or language. Andreae's views were also broad, and his " reformation " as described in the *Fama,* the *Christianopolis,* and *Theophilus* was a general one of the whole world. His " fellows " also travel into all countries and gather information everywhere. In the *Fama* one " fellow " died in England and " his name is well known in that country." [2] In the *Christianopolis* the religious requirement was necessarily narrower. In the Royal Society the fellows must be chiefly " gentlemen, free and unconfined." In the *Fama* exactly the same qualification is demanded.

Innumerable are the parallels in ideals between Andreae and the Royal Society. In many cases it is merely a matter of the development of a planted seed. The *Christianopolis* is never elaborate in description, rather suggestive. But in the more extended plan of the Royal Society the germs of the *Christianopolis* are often discoverable. Sprat complains that heretofore " the seats of knowledge have been not laboratories, but only schools, where some have taught, and all the rest have subscribed." [2] The *Christianopolis* lays like stress on experimental learning. [4] Instruments are to be made, and even new ones invented, especially those for mathematics. [5] So also *Frater R. C.* in the *Fama* on his

[1] Sprat, p. 63.
[2] P. 17.
[2] P. 68.
[4] Chap. lxxx.
[5] Sprat, p. 246.

return from the East spends his last years "making and inventing new instruments in mathematics."[1]

The subject-matter to be investigated by the Royal Society is included [2] under three heads—God, man, and nature. " As for the first, they meddle not otherwise with divine things than only as the power and wisdom and goodness of the Creator is displayed in the admirable order and workmanship of the creatures." In the *Christianopolis* it is stated that "What goes beyond natural experiment is accepted as coming from God."[3] The second head deals with the " faculties, the constitution of their bodies, and the works of their hands." And the third, investigation of nature—the experimental sciences as often mentioned. Here as in the *Christianopolis* the latter are related, " and so there will be a mutual communication of the light of one science to another."[4]

In discourse, plain speech is to be preferred to involved.[5] " In a few words I dare say, that of all the studies of men, nothing may be sooner obtained than this vicious abundance of phrases, this trick of metaphors, this volubility of tongue which makes so great a noise in the world. But I spend words in vain; for the evil is now so inveterate, that it is hard to know whom to blame or where to begin the reform." This scorn of artificial application of rhetoric has already been brought out in a preceding chapter of this discussion of the *Christianopolis*.

The astronomical observations,[6] the library,[7] the courses of education,[8] references to crafts and men working in metals, the care and study of bees, the gardens and parks, and scores of other details, all have corresponding factors in

[1] *Fama*, p. 12.   [4] Sprat, p. 85.   [7] Sprat, p. 25
[2] Sprat, p. 81.   [5] Sprat, p. 112.   [8] Sprat, p. 32
[3] Chap. lxiii.   [6] Sprat, p. 241.

the *Christianopolis*. The rules for the members [1] have close similarity with those in the *Fama*. Fellows pay their expenses, meet at regular intervals—*in secret* (except as the society votes to admit others to the meetings). Their programmes, as they are carried out at the meetings, are alike.

In speaking of Andreae, the criticism is often made that he leaned too strongly toward astrology, alchemy, and the supernatural.[2] Now in the plan of the Royal Society among the investigations to be made and at that time not as yet well understood, are mentioned some that, in addition to being rather absurd, border on the alchemistic and supernatural as well: "What river turns wood into stone," [3] "Turning water into earth," [4] "growth of pebbles in water," [5] "Springs that petrify," [6] "gold into silver," [7] "feeding of a carp in air," [8] "making insects of cheese and sack," [9] "As to whether spiders are enchanted by a circle of unicorns' horns or Irish earth roundabout them." [10] It might be noted here that Boyle had some faith in transmutation and alchemy, for he was instrumental in repealing the statute against "multiplying gold." [11] And even Bacon was at times, especially early in his career, not quite ready to give up all the contentions in favor of the magical.[12]

[1] Sprat, p. 145.

[2] Nothing could be plainer than Andreae's position with respect to this question. He takes every occasion to distinguish between real and false science, as in chaps. iv, xi, and xliv of the *Christianopolis* and in the introduction of the *Fama* (already quoted, p. 39). In the introduction to his edition of *Die Christenburg* (p. 246), Grüneisen summarizes Andreae's purpose in this respect as indisputably "to contrast the true secret, the basis and kernel of genuine science, and the deep spirit of the wonders in the realm of nature . . . with vain secrets and valueless brooding, quibbling, and trifling with nature."

[3] Sprat, p. 159.   [6] Sprat, p. 191.   [9] Sprat, p. 223.
[4] Sprat, p. 191.   [7] Sprat, p. 221.   [10] Sprat, p. 223.
[5] Sprat, p. 191.   [8] Sprat, p. 223.   [11] *Dict. Nat. Biog.*
[12] *Works*, III, pp. 289, 331.

As to the relations existing between the Royal Society of London and the Continent, Sprat himself, one of the original fellows of the society, acknowledges in his history a close connection. Yet it must be confessed that he is more inclined to attribute help to the rest of Europe from England than to admit the existence of influence in the opposite direction; and he gives Germany credit for a very small share of the results attained. " It is evident," he says, " that this searching spirit and this affection to sensible knowledge, does prevail in most countries round about us. 'Tis true, the conveniences for such labors are not equal in all places. Some want the assistance of other's hands; some the contribution of other's purses; some the benefit of excellent instruments from the patronage of the civil magistrates. But yet according to their several powers, they are everywhere intent upon such practical studies. And the most considerable effects of such attempts throughout Europe, have been still recommended to this society by their authors to be examined, approved, or corrected." [1]

Sprat then explains at some length the relations existing between the Royal Society of London and similar groups of men on the Continent; the following paragraphs are quoted therefrom:

" In France, the Royal Society has maintained a perpetual intercourse, with the most eminent men of art of all conditions; and has obtained from them, all the help which might justly be hoped for, from the vigor and activity, and readiness of mind, which is natural to that people. . . . And, to instance once for all, it has been affectionately invited to a mutual correspondence by the French Academy of Paris."

" In Italy the Royal Society has an excellent privilege of

[1] Sprat, p. 125.

receiving and imparting experiments, by the help of one of their own fellows, who has the opportunity of being resident there for them, as well as for the king. . . . This application to the Royal Society I have mentioned, because it comes from that country which is seldom wont to have any great regard to the arts of these nations that lie on this side of their mountains."

Speaking of the Low Countries, he says:

" And this learned correspondence with him and many others is still continued, even at this present time, in the breach between our countries; their great founder and patron still permitting them to maintain the traffic of sciences, when all other commerce is intercepted. Whence we may guess what may be expected from the peaceful part of our king's reign, when his very wars are managed, without injury to the arts of civil knowledge."

" In Germany, and its neighboring kingdoms, the Royal Society has met with great veneration as appears by several testimonies in their late printed books which have been submitted to its censure; by many curiosities of mechanical instruments that have been transmitted to it; and by the addresses which have been sent from their philosophical inquirers. For which kinds of enterprises the temper of the German nation is admirably fit, both in respect of their peculiar dexterity in all sorts of manual arts, and also in regard of the plain and unaffected sincerity of their manners; wherein they so much resemble the English, that we seem to have derived from them the composition of our minds, as well as to have descended from their race."

In the foregoing pages an attempt has been made to establish the following points: Andreae, himself influenced somewhat by the spirit of research and the idea of an academy of science in Italy, developed a system of education and a definite plan for a college. His ideas in both matters were accepted and further elaborated by Comenius, who, through his friend Hartlib and by a personal visit, introduced them into England. In this, Hartlib was assisted by John Dury, whose acquaintance with Andreae was not only through Comenius, but also by direct correspondence. Peter Figulus and Joachim Hübner were both also means of intercommunication—the one between Comenius and Dury, the other between Comenius and Andreae on the one hand, and between Comenius and England on the other. The meetings of these men at London as early as 1641, with and also separate from a commission appointed by parliament, were responsible for the first agitation toward not only a better educational system, but also the founding of a college of science. Political conditions interfered with further developments. Had this not been the case, the Royal Society might well have been founded nearly two decades earlier than it was. The members of the group scattered and later founded societies in London and Oxford. The moving factors of this second attempt, Boyle, Haacke, and others, were also acquainted with and inspired by the Andreae-Comenius system.[1] These meetings were the direct forerunners of the Royal Society, which was incorporated in 1662. Furthermore, Bacon, to whom is usually accorded exclusive credit for giving incentive to the Royal Society through his *New Atlantis* and other works, also bears the

---

[1] It may be of interest to mention here that as a result of Andreae's plans for a college, a society, similar in purpose and scope to the later Royal Society of London, was founded as early as 1622, under the name *Societas Ereunetica,* at the University of Rostock, by Joachim Jungius, one of the foremost scholars of the time and an ardent admirer of Andreae. See G. E. Guhrauer, *Joachim Jungius und sein Zeitalter,* pp. 69 ff.

stamp of Andreae, and helps to further the latter's views. The *Nova Solyma* shows clear traces of the ideas of Andreae, some of which could not well have come through Bacon,—traces in organization, purpose, and results attained.

BIBLIOGRAPHY

AIKEN, LUCY.
Memoirs of the Court of King James I. London 1822, I.
(After Ernst Höpfner's *Georg Rodolf Weckherlins Oden und
Gesänge.*)

Allgemeine deutsche Biographie.

ALTHAUS, FRIEDRICH.
Samuel Hartlib, ein deutsch-englisches Characterbild. (In *Historisches Taschenbuch,* 1884.)

ANDREAE, JOHANN VALENTIN.
Fama Fraternitatis, Confessio, Allgemeine Reformation. 1616.

ANDREAE, JOHANN VALENTIN.
Mythologiae Christianae Libri Tres: 1) *Apologorum Christianorum Manipuli Sex et Alethea Exul.* 2) *Reipublicae Christianopolitanae Descriptio.* 3) *Peregrini in patria Errores.*

ANDREAE, JOHANN VALENTIN.
Reise nach der Insul Caphar Salama. (*Christianopolis,* translated into German by D. S. Georgi. 1741.)

ANDREAE, JOHANN VALENTIN.
Vita ab ipso conscripta. (F. H. Rheinwald. Berlin 1849.)

ANONYMOUS (A. von Kirchenheim).
Schlaraffia Politica. Leipzig 1892.

BACON, FRANCIS.
Life, Letters, and Works. Spedding, Heath, and Ellis. 1858-
1868. (References are made to this edition. *The Fable of the
New Atlantis,* III, pp. 118 ff.)

BEGLEY, WALTER.
Nova Solyma. Samuel Gott. (Translated into English, with
Introduction, Notes, and Bibliography. London 1902.)

BOYLE, ROBERT.
Complete Works. J. & F. Rivington. 1772.

BRÜGEL, JULIUS.
Johann Valentin Andreae. (Schmidt, *Geschichte der Erziehung.*)

BRÜGGEMANN, FRITZ.
Utopie und Robinsonade. (*Forschungen zur neueren Literatur-
geschichte* No. 46.)

CARRIÈRE, MORIZ.
Die Philosophische Weltanschauung der Reformationzeit. Leipzig, 1887.

COMENIUS, JOHANN AMOS.
Selections from his various works as found in Kvačala, Möhrke, and *Monatshefte der Comenius Gesellschaft.*
Dictionary of National Biography.
GOEDEKE, KARL.
Gedichte von Georg Rodolf Weckherlin. Leipzig 1873.
GLÖCKLER, JOHANN PHILIPP.
Johann Valentin Andreae, ein Lebensbild. Stuttgart 1886.
GRÜNEISEN, CARL.
Die Christenburg von Johann Valentin Andreae. (*Zeitschrift für die historische Theologie.* Bd. 6, S. 231.)
GUHRAUER, G. E.
Der erste deutsche Staatsroman.
GUHRAUER, G. E.
Joachim Jungius und sein Zeitalter. Stuttgart 1850.
GUSSMANN, W.
Reipublicae Christianopolitanae Descriptio. (In der ZkWL. Jahrg. 1886, S. 326 ff.)
HERDER, JOHANN GOTTFRIED.
Vorrede zu Johann Valentin Andreae. Dichtung zur Beherzigung unseres Zeitalters. (In Suphan's edition.)
HÖLDERLINS *Gesammelte Dichtungen.* Berthold Litzmann. Stuttgart.
HÖPFNER, ERNST.
Georg Rodolf Weckherlins Oden und Gesänge. Berlin 1865.
HOSSBACH, WILHELM.
Johann Valentin Andreae und sein Zeitalter. Berlin 1819.
HÜLLEMANN, CARL.
Valentin Andreae als Pädagog. I Teil, 1884; II Teil, 1893.
JONES, STEPHEN K.
The Authorship of "Nova Solyma." (*The Library,* July, 1910, p. 225.)
KIPPENBERG, AUGUST.
Robinson in Deutschland bis zur Insel Felsenburg. Hannover 1892.
KLEINWÄCHTER, FR.
Die Staatsromane.
KVAČALA, IVAN.
J. A. Comenius. Berlin 1914.
LOPES, FRANCISCO.
Istoria de las Indias. (After G. C. Moore Smith's edition of the *New Atlantis,* Introduction, p. 19.)
MAACK, FERDINAND.
Geheime Wissenschaften. I Band. Berlin 1913.

MÖHRKE, MAX.
Johann Amos Komenius und Johann Valentin Andreae, ihre Pädagogik und ihr Verhältnis zu einander. Leipzig 1904.

MOHL, ROBERT VON.
Geschichte und Literatur der Staatswissenschaft.
Monatshefte der Comenius Gesellschaft.

MORLEY, HENRY.
Ideal Commonwealths. New York and London 1901.

PRYS, JOSEPH.
Der Staatsroman des 16. und 17. Jahrhunderts und sein Erziehungsideal. Würzburg 1913.

RAWLEY, WILLIAM.
Life of Francis Bacon. (In Spedding's *Works,* I.)
Realenzyklopädie für protestantische Theologie.
Record of the Royal Society of London. 1912.

SCHMIDT, K. A.
Geschichte der Erziehung.

SIGWART, CHRISTOPH.
Kleine Schriften. Freiburg und Tübingen 1881.

SMITH, G. C. MOORE.
Francis Bacon's " New Atlantis." Cambridge Press 1909.

SMITH, G. C. MOORE.
The Date of the New Atlantis. (In the *Athenæum,* Feb. 1900.)

SPRAT, THOMAS.
History of the Royal Society of London. 1667.

ULLRICH, HERMANN.
Robinson und Robinsonaden. Bibliographie, Geschichte, Kritik.
Teil I. Weimar 1898.

VOGT, CARL.
Johann Balthasar Schupp. (*Euphorion,* 1910, pp. 38-48.)

VOIGT, ANDREAS.
Die Sozialen Utopien. Leipzig.

WACKWITZ, FR.
Entstehungsgeschichte von D. Defoes " Robinson Crusoe." Berlin 1909.

WATERHOUSE, G.
The Literary Relations of England and Germany in the 17th Century. Cambridge, 1914.

WESSELY, IGNAZ EMANUEL.
Thomas Campanellas " Der Sonnenstaat." (Trans. into German.)

WINDELBAND, W.
Lehrbuch der Geschichte der Philosophie.

WOLFF, EMIL.
Francis Bacon und seine Quellen.

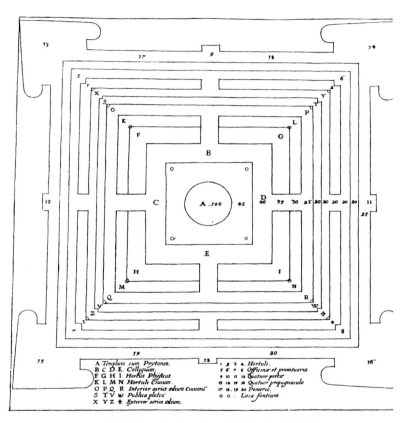

GROUND PLAN OF CHRISTIANOPOLIS

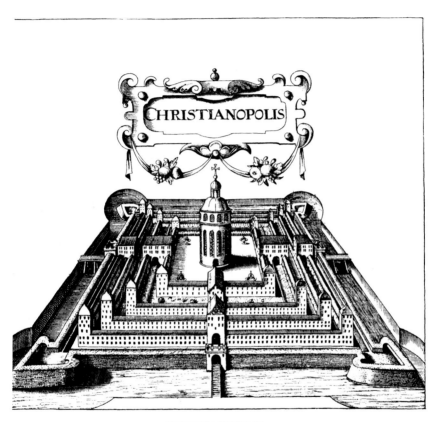

CHRISTIANOPOLIS

CHRISTIANOPOLIS

By

JOHANN VALENTIN ANDREAE

Thou Most Noble and Worthy Man, John Arndt, Reverend Father in Christ.

This our new state recognizes and respects thee; for inasmuch as this colony has its source in that Jerusalem which thou didst build with mighty spirit, against the wishes of the sophists, it is impossible not to refer all things to thee, to give thee thanks for the institutions and laws, to beseech thee at the same time not to think it beneath thee to communicate out of thy kindness what in thine opinion should be added or changed. So may God grant to thy most honored old age that thou mayest see as many as possible heeding thine interpretation of loyalty, uprightness, and scholarship. Farewell, reverend father in Christ, and continue thou to commend me to God as I give heed to thee.

Jan. 1, 1619. R.D.T.

Most faithfully,

JOH. VALENTIN ANDREAE.

HAIL, CHRISTIAN READER.

I see two classes of men in the commonwealth. A class of those who do not so much approve of those things over which they are set or under which they are placed, as they admire them and defend them to the teeth. The other class, men who endure human affairs, but in such a way, it is true, that they do not hesitate to wish for better things and to obey moderate changes. But as the latter class never readily causes disturbance, because of backwardness and sense, but rather as far as possible gives way, is silent and tolerant; so also the former, because of blind madness and lack of self-control, attack, torment, and not rarely drag those into the conflict who merely grumble at them though they may not at all desire it. Of this, Antichrist gave us the clearest example when he oppressed the church of Christ with wicked burdens. And it is surprising that there were people who, though perhaps they may not have approved of such baseness, at least tolerated it. Be that as it may, it was admitted and done so disgustingly that when some sought a correction of such terrible disgraces in the most temperate way, they were given over to punishment, proscribed from the protection of law, and torn by God knows what curses; until, as men's minds became enraged with the indignity of the thing, an impulse was given to restore light and dispel the darkness. What now may be the cause of this, since it opposes all reason, is not very clear. For whether it be a spirit of ambition, which will suffer correction from no one, or whether it be greed, which does so flourish among men; whether it be a mental dullness which makes no choice or distinction between good and evil, or whether people foolishly become accustomed to things in a way that lessens all ugliness—all this does not at all compare with the great boldness with which we ourselves oppose the most evident truth and the most hoped for good. And so many believe, and not without reason, that this cloud was sent by God upon the minds of the wicked, lest they should conform to the modesty of the good, which can be done with moderate and tolerable means; that, once convicted of their impudent wickedness and regarded as unworthy of being yielded to farther, they may be compelled to do greater things, and thus, when the mask is removed, lose their influence among the people.

It was thus that our hero Doctor Luther proceeded; when men would not heed his prayers and tears, he began to breathe threats out of the Word of God. Accomplishing nothing by submissiveness, he began to rise up. When he had carried on siege for a long time, he began to storm the opposing power, and with such success, that WE REJOICE though they gnash their teeth. I am rather inclined to think that this very drama may be played again in our own day. The light of a purer religion has dawned upon us; in accordance with it, the administration of public affairs has been regulated, and the brilliancy of letters and arts has been restored; we may be able entirely to triumph over many conquered enemies—superstition, dissoluteness, and rudeness.

But the secret snares of the Devil give us trouble, as a result of which our rejoicing is made less firm, and a mere name without the substance is left us. For though all our doings should be patterned after our Christ, whose name we bear and confess, yet it happens on account of our weak indulgence that Christians differ in no respect from men of the world. For whether we look at the churches, the courts, or the universities—nowhere is there a lack of unscrupulous ambition, greed, gluttony, license, jealousy, idleness, and other mastering vices at which Christ violently shuddered, but in which we chiefly delight. From this may very easily be imagined the joy of the Devil, who when he has secretly stolen from us the kernel, gladly allows us to glory in the shells and rinds, and it is easy to notice our simpleness in that we are content with the bare shadow of anything, though we listen like religious, polished, and educated men. And yet that impostor does not deceive all, and least of all those who have a higher light within.

Very many of these, men of most fervent spirit, have lifted their voices loudly even before us, and will continue to do so very zealously in the future also. From their number I will mention only Doctor John Gerhard, Doctor John Arndt, and Doctor Mart. Moller, as especially deserving it of me, most upright theological scholars, although the last named is a little disturbed on the subject of the Lord's Supper. When these men noticed that the whole world was resounding with disputations, so that the spirit of Christ could hardly be heard through them, they desired greatly to procure intermittent silence, which should be devoted to piety and should permit a breathing space after the heat of disputing, and thus unite scholarship with uprightness in such a way that each might add splendor to the other. This was asked for very modestly, and allowed with the greatest ill will. Since the bishops of the churches would acknowledge the presence of no simony, the political leaders no dishonesty, the university no lack of education, being warned against devotedness, uprightness, and letters, they were accused of treason. If we put faith in those who answer the argument, it will appear that the whole church is full of windows, into which anyone may fly whenever it pleases him, and where he may whisper to his liking; the republic, a market place where vices may be bought and sold; the academy, a labyrinth in which it is a game and an art to wander about; and whatever is squandered upon these is pure gain. Defenders arose who were willing to be betrayed; good people would have taken oath upon their innocence, while now the evil ones detest the public testimony of their evil deeds. For the erring world would much prefer to have its acts concealed than to have them praised in public.

Those who perform sacrifice in the church have grown incensed because the security or rather the nothingness of their calling, the carelessness of their sermons, their culture, smacking all too much of the world, are not approved. And yet the churchmen forbid all this. The greedy ones of the world roared because the harshness of their law, the license of their morals, the accumulation of their riches, their contempt of eternity were not praised. And yet even their own civil authority prohibits these. Teachers of letters babbled on behalf of their lack of knowledge of the arts, lack of languages, cheapness of their academic degrees, the insatiable depth of their expenses, and even against the direct wishes of scholarship; and so, as ignorance was willing or rather required it, hypocrisy has undertaken and violently usurped the protection of religion, tyranny that of civil authority, quibbling that of letters, it is true, with many and diverse judgments; but the champions of God, or the servants of a good cause, remained unafraid. For though particularly of some they might have hoped for and expected greater fairness, learning, and especially greater moderation, who were thought to be well versed in the affairs of the state, and of great merit; yet anyone who has once examined the world more closely, has clearly noticed that nothing is more intolerable to impostors, than truth and uprightness; and they hate these so thoroughly that, in the impotency of their wrath and forgetful of themselves, they throw off their masks, covers, and wrappings, rush forth bare, and thus give way the secret of their wickedness. No sensible man can see without repulsion how basely gluttony in the midst of the church, moral looseness in the very public square and in the schools, empty titles without stability, and prodigality without limit are overlooked—nay, even commended and brought before the public. This is just the reason why these persons, from whom one would least expect it, give way and yield to truth more readily, since when once convicted of their own mistakes they find nothing left except infamous impudence and low banter; and with these they try in vain to exonerate themselves. And so with their innate politeness they hear and bear reproofs; they confess their faults or their mental darkness, the inventions of the Devil, the force of habits, credulity, and other shackles of the same sort; and wish that they were faultless again.

A certain FRATERNITY, in my opinion a joke, but according to theologians a serious matter, has brought forth evident proof of this very thing. As soon as it promised, instead of the taste of the curious public, the greatest and most unusual things, even those things which men generally want, it added also the exceptional hope of the correction of the present corrupted state of affairs, and even further, the imitation of the acts of Christ. What a confusion among men followed the report of this thing, what a conflict among the learned, what an unrest and commotion of impostors and swindlers, it is entirely needless to say. There is just this one thing which we would like to add, that there were some who in this blind terror wished to have their old, out-of-date, and falsified affairs entirely retained and defended with force. Some hastened to surrender the strength of their opinions; and, after they had made accusation against the severest yoke of their servitude, hastened to reach out after freedom. And then, to get closer to the matter in hand, there were some who made accusation against the principles of Christian life as heresy and fanaticism. Others even embraced this with a whole heart. While these people quarreled among themselves, and crowded the shops, they gave many others leisure to look into and judge these questions. Of this now we have this benefit, that, as it seems to us, the world is not so sure of its affairs as it would like to seem, nor is it so steadfast in its views that it cannot be turned aside; nor yet (and this is the chief point) are all so far from Christ that no one would be willing to admit His rules of life and then regulate his own life according to them, if the opportunity were given. Moreover I am prone to praise the judgment of a man of the most noble qualities in piety, ethics, and nature who, when he saw that men were undecided and for the most part deceived by the report of that BROTHERHOOD, answered, "If these reforms seem proper, why do we not try them ourselves? Let us not wait for them to do it.",—meaning that there was nothing to hinder us from learning these things from the Gospels and making the attempt from the praiseworthy examples of devoted Christians, if we really wished to imitate the life of Christ and improve our daily lives. For we certainly would not commit such an injury against Christ and His Word, as to prefer to learn the way of salvation and emulate it, from some society (if there really is such a one)—hazy, omniscient only in the eyes of its own boastfulness, with a sewn shield for an emblem and marred with many foolish ceremonies, than from Him who is Himself the Way, the Truth, and the Life, whose precepts are so in evidence and so easily located that we have to make use of the greatest subterfuges and evasions to avoid them. For if our conscience urges us that we have ground for complaint against the too great security of religion, the impurity of life, and the mockeries of learning, what shall hinder us from driving out of ourselves at least (if others do not desire it) the vices of life, from planting virtues instead, and from joining closer to our Christ whom we fear is farthest removed from our affairs?

It is quite certain that nothing gives this permission to us or to Christ except the fear of the judgments of men, which attempts to preserve us from our own friends and the usual customs of life, and to keep for us the good will of men; yet which none the less a little later hurls us through the difficulties of this age, to groan and grieve when it is too late, naturally, because we have given faith to the world and denied it to Christ. And this is to be considered the best determination, which, when the Word of God has been heard and accepted, does not look to men or to any society or assembly for approval, but stands at the command of God and of the human conscience, walks zealously under the direction of the Holy Spirit, and bears unjust criticism no more unwillingly than the croaking of frogs; since altogether it is evident that only a very few people dare to attack piety, uprightness, and character in the open, but by circumlocutions rather trifle, lie, or try to devise something at which after a while they can bark. And so you will hear first of all the words " fanatic," " turbulent," and " a danger to literature "; then you will be accused and will have to look at the wounds of a chimæra and the conflicts of blind gladiators. But if you quietly put your faith in a clear conscience, you will yet take the greatest joy with you.

Now, my excellent reader, you see as an evident example of this Christian security, this new REPUBLIC which it seems best to call CHRISTIANOPOLIS. For inasmuch as other people (and I myself also) do not like to be corrected, I have built this city for myself where I may exercise the dictatorship. And if you should call my own insignificant body by this name, perhaps you would not be so far from the truth. But even as the laws almost everywhere are good and yet the morals of the people loose, so I fear you will suspect that the case is the same with the citizens of my state. However that may be, I have determined not to praise my citizens, but to describe them; and to reveal and communicate to you according to what statutes we are commanded to live. I could not speak to you about different things more frankly or freely, I could not give you the facts with less restriction, nor draw forth your opinion more unreservedly than in this manner. Whether you approve or disapprove of this matter I shall praise you, provided you give answer with like candor. But if you answer me with some sophism, nothing will be easier for me than to bear your unfavorable criticisms and ignore you. If you find our state at all attractive, nothing shall be denied you; if you decline it, nothing shall be thrust upon you. My citizens do neither waste their own substance nor do they covet yours. Furthermore they are willing to accept whatever you care to give them, and they are glad to give you whatever you desire. Our laws compel or constrain no one; they do persuade—standing forth with the Word of God and not giving way to Satan. Moreover, they admit every good man as an adviser. The structure has no art, but abundant simplicity.

We have not told everything. Perhaps we have said more than the wicked can stand—less than we offer to the good, however often they may wish it mentioned.

Finally let me say, it is a public show, a thing which has not been said to the disadvantage of the famous Thomas More. As far as concerns my own work, it ought to be more easily laid aside as not being as serious or as clever as his. I have written to my friends, since one can joke with them; I should not dare to write to eminent men, even if I wished to do so; I should not be able to if I dared; and I should not want to if they permitted it. So great is my respect for them, such the knowledge and confession of my inexperience. At any rate, those may read who wish to, and let them remember that among friends many imperfections are overlooked which would not stand the critical test of evil wishers. If anyone doubts the truth of my story, let him put off passing judgment until all reports of wanderings and sea travels have been made. But the safest way will be (provided Heaven permits, the land does not interfere, and the sea is calm, with Christ the guide of your voyage, and your comrades all desirous of a just life), for you to embark upon your vessel which has the sign of the Cancer for its distinctive mark, sail for Christianopolis yourself with favorable conditions, and there investigate everything very accurately in the fear of God. So farewell, my Christian reader, and gird you on the road to heaven.

CONCERNING THE STATE OF CHRISTIANOPOLIS.

I.

THE REASON FOR THE JOURNEY, AND THE SHIPWRECK.

WHILE wandering as a stranger on the earth, suffering much in patience from tyranny, sophistry, and hypocrisy, seeking a man, and not finding what I so anxiously sought, I decided to launch out once more upon the Academic Sea though the latter had very often been hurtful to me. And so ascending the good ship, Phantasy, I left the port together with many others and exposed my life and person to the thousand dangers that go with desire for knowledge. For a short space of time conditions favored our voyage; then adverse storms of envy and calumny stirred up the Ethiopian Sea [1] against us and removed all hope of calm weather. The efforts of the skipper and the oarsmen were exerted to the limit, our own stubborn love of life would not give up, and even the vessel resisted the rocks; but the force of the sea always proved stronger. Finally when all hope was lost and we, rather of necessity than on account of bravery of soul, had prepared to die, the ship collapsed and we sank. Some were swallowed up by the sea, some were scattered to great distances, while some who could swim or who found planks to float upon, were carried to different islands scattered throughout this sea.

[1] Mare Aethiopicum. Probably intended to imply " Sea of Stupidity."

REIPUBLICÆ

CHRISTIA-
NOPOLITANÆ
DESCRIPTIO,

PSALM. LXXXIII.

stat dies unus in DEI atrijs quàm alibi mille: malim in DEI mei domo ad limen esse quàm in impiorum tabernaculis habitare. Non Sol & propugnaculum: ich Va DEVS; Iehova gratiam, gloriamq́, confert ijs, qui se gerunt innocentes, eis bona non denegans.

SCIENTIA IMMVTA BILIS.

ARGENTORATI,

Sumptibus hæredum LAZARI ZETZNERI,

Anno M. DC. XIX.

TITLE PAGE OF THE ORIGINAL EDITION
OF THE "CHRISTIANOPOLIS"

Very few escaped death, and I alone, without a single comrade, was at length driven to a very minute islet, a mere piece of turf, as it seemed.

II.

DRIVEN TO THE ISLAND, CAPHAR SALAMA.

EVERYTHING here pleased me, except I did not please myself. The island, moreover, small though it had appeared, had a great abundance of all things, and there was not a foot of soil to be seen which was not under cultivation or in some way put to use for mankind. The site of the island, such as I found it to be a little later, I will not refuse to explain. It is in the Antarctic zone, 10° of the south pole, 20° of the equinoctial circle, and about 12° under the point of the bull.[1] To trifling minutiae I will never answer. The form is that of a triangle, whose perimeter is about 30 miles. This island is rich in grain and pasture fields, watered with rivers and brooks, adorned with woods and vineyards, full of animals, just as if it were a whole world in miniature. One might think that here the heavens and the earth had been married and were living together in everlasting peace.

While I was drying my undershirt, the only garment I had saved, in the rays of the morning sun, an inhabitant of the island, some one of the many watchmen of the place, came upon me suddenly. He inquired into my mischance with all kindness, and while sympathizing with my misfortune, bade me trust him and accompany

[1] Andreae seems purposely to locate his utopia in an impossible place.

him to the city, where, with their usual consideration toward strangers and exiles, the citizens would supply my needs; and he added: " Happy are you whose lot it has been, after so severe a shipwreck, to be thrown on land at this place." And I answered only, " Thank God! Glory to God!"

III.

THE ORIGIN OF CHRISTIANOPOLIS.

MEANTIME the sight and the beauty of the city as we approached it surprised me greatly, for all the rest of the world does not hold anything like it or to be compared with it. So turning to my guide I said: " What happiness has established her abode here?" And he answered: " The one that in this world is generally very unhappy. For when the world raged against the good and drove them out of her boundaries, religion, an exile, gathering about her the comrades whom she regarded the most faithful, after crossing the sea and examining various places, finally chose this land in which to establish her followers. Later she built a city which we call Christianopolis, and desired that it should be the home, or, if you prefer, the stronghold of honesty and excellence. The generosity of this our republic to all in want, you are about to experience. So if you desire to traverse the city (but you must do it with dispassionate eyes, guarded tongue, and decent behavior) the opportunity will not be denied you; nay, the city lies open to you in its individual parts." Then I answered: " Oh, blessed hour when after so many monstrous sights seen with dread and exertion, I shall be granted the privilege of observing something really elegant and beautiful. I shall evade neither the bath, the razor, nor the brush, that, being washed, scraped, and cleansed, I may be admitted to the pure abodes of truth and goodness. For how unfortunate my mistakes and evasions have been, has become known to many, a long time ago. Oh, may I some time see better, truer, more fixed, and more stable conditions—in brief, those which the world promises, but never and nowhere produces!"

IV.

EXAMINATION OF THE STRANGER, FIRST, AS TO HIS IDEAS OF LIFE AND HIS MORALS.

Now we had approached the eastern gate, when my companion introduced me to the prefect of the day's guard. He received me pleasantly and asked me what I desired. "Very many things," said I, "for as you see I have been cast up from land and sea. But now since I seem to have met God Himself here, why should I not seek largely of that which I have lacked all my life?" The prefect of the guard smiled and kindly advised me, inasmuch as this island had nothing indecorous, not to prove to be one of those whom the citizens of the community would not tolerate among them but would send back to the place from which they had come, such persons as: beggars, quacks, stage-players who have too much leisure, busybodies who worry unnecessarily in the details of unusual affairs, fanatics who however have no real feeling of piety, drug-mixers who ruin the science of chemistry, impostors who falsely call themselves the BROTHERS OF THE ROSICRUCIANS, and other like blemishes of literature and true culture, whom this city has never ceased to suspect. Then when I had purged myself by a testimony of my inmost conscience, and had with many words vowed the service of my whole powers to truth and to integrity, he said: "There is no reason now why you should not have the benefit of our goods, and what is much more important, of ourselves." So saying, he grasped me by the hand, took me into the home of some watchmen or guards near by, and refreshed me with very savory food and drink.

V.

EXAMINATION, SECONDLY, AS TO HIS PERSON.

Now when I had put on different clothing, not at all extravagant, but easily procured and comfortable, he gave me over to some attendants who took me to my second examiner. This man appeared as one born for the purpose of drawing forth from a man his innermost and most private thoughts. He returned my greetings very kindly and put several friendly questions to me, meanwhile watching my bearing and the lineaments of my face very critically. With a smile rather than with serious expression he inquired as to my native land, my age, my manner of life, all, as it were, incidentally. After a few courtesies had been exchanged, he said: "My friend, you have undoubtedly come here under the leadership of God that you might learn whether it is always necessary to do evil and to live according to the custom of barbarians. That this is not the case we will give you proof this very day as we ought to all persons. And all the more gladly will we do this since neither nature nor your fortune seem indisposed, but rather you possess a heart favorable to the influences of both. And if God indeed rule you, so that you be free from the attractions of the flesh, then we do not doubt that you are already ours, and that you will be forever." While thus speaking (as I seemed to notice) he was studying the calmness of my being, the modesty of my countenance, the closeness of my speech, the quiet of my eyes, my personal bearing, with such thoroughness that it seemed to me he could scrutinize my very thoughts, with such affability that I could conceal nothing from him, with such respect that I felt I owed everything to him. And so, when my mind had been laid bare all around and he had at length touched somewhat on the subject of letters, he said: "My friend, you will grant me your indulgence when I discourse in so unscholarly a way as I have done. Be not discouraged, for in this community of ours you will find no lack of men who are fairly steeped in learning and culture." At the same time he issued a command to an attendant that he should accompany me to a third examiner. And so he shook my hand and bade me farewell, urging me to have confidence. But I thought to myself: "Heaven help me! If they call this 'discoursing in an unscholarly way,' what shall become of me?"

VI.

EXAMINATION, THIRDLY, AS TO HIS PERSONAL CULTURE.

Now when I came to him, I found no less kindness than in the former case; for let me say once for all, all haughtiness and pride are banished from this place. But when I heard this man speak, I felt more ashamed than ever before. I had to "know nothing" with Socrates, but in an entirely

different sense. How I regretted having spoken of literature! He asked me, in most pleasant terms it is true, to
what extent I had learned to control myself and to be of
service to my brother; to fight off the world, to be in harmony with death, to follow the Spirit; what progress I
had made in the observation of the heavens and the earth,
in the close examination of nature, in instruments of the
arts, in the history and origin of languages, the harmony
of all the world; what relation I bore toward the society
of the church, toward a compendium of the Scriptures, the
kingdom of heaven, the school of the Spirit, the brotherhood of Christ, the household of God. I was amazed when
I understood that so very little had been made a part of
myself, of the many things which are so freely and in such
generous amounts given to man. And so, doing all that I
could under the circumstances, I turned to frank confes-
sional and said: "Most honored sir, all these things I am
entirely unacquainted with and I have never had instruction in them. But of this much I assure you on my word,
that within me I have very often wrestled with them, desired
to know them, and have dared to attack them." Whereupon
he almost shouted out aloud. "You are ours," he said,
"you who bring to us an unsullied slate, washed clean, as
it were, by the sea itself. It but remains that we pray God
that He inscribe upon your heart with His holy stylus the
things which will seem, in His wisdom and goodness, salu-
tary to you. And now truly you shall see our city in its
individual parts. And after you have returned we will
listen to whatever you may further desire of us, in so far
as we are mentally prepared and provided." And he gave
me three men, Beeram, Eram, and Neariam, worthy individuals as was evident from their countenances; and they
were to show me around everywhere.

VII.

DESCRIPTION OF THE CITY.

I⸱f I describe to you the appearance of the city first of all, I will not be making a mistake. Its shape is a square, whose side is seven hundred feet, well fortified with four towers and a wall. It looks, therefore, toward the four quarters of the earth. Eight other very strong towers, distributed throughout the city, intensify the strength; and there are sixteen other smaller ones that are not to be despised; and the citadel in the midst of the city is well-nigh impregnable. Of buildings there are two rows, or if you count the seat of government and the storehouses, four; there is only one public street, and only one market-place, but this one is of a very high order. If you measure the buildings, you will find that from the innermost street, being twenty feet in width, the numbers increase by fives even up to one hundred. At this point there is a circular temple, a hundred feet in diameter. As you go forth from the buildings, the intervals, storehouses, and the rows of houses are each twenty feet wide and the wall is twenty-five feet. All buildings are in three stories, and public balconies lead to these. All this can, however, be better understood from the accompanying plate.[1] All buildings are made of burnt stone and are separated by fireproof walls so that a fire could not do very severe damage. Spring water and flowing water are here in great abundance, supplied partly by artificial means, and partly by nature. Things look much the same all around, not extravagant nor

[1] For this and future references to the plan of the city, see diagram following p. 128.

yet unclean; fresh air and ventilation are provided throughout. About four hundred citizens live here in religious faith and peace of the highest order. We shall have something to say about each individual one. Outside the walls is a moat stocked with fish, that even in times of peace it may have its uses. The open and otherwise unused spaces contain wild animals, kept, however, not for purposes of entertainment but for practical use. The whole city is divided into three parts, one to supply food, one for drill and exercise, and one for looks. The remainder of the island serves purposes of agriculture and for workshops. These I have noted down in some way or another in the plan. And next we must take a trip through the city.

VIII.

AGRICULTURE AND ANIMAL HUSBANDRY.

IN the farthermost section of the corporation which faces east is the farm quarter. It is divided into two parts, the agriculture proper on the one side, and the animal husbandry department on the other. For all the grain, vegetables, and greens which the state can get from the island, and all the pack-animals, beef-cattle, and flocks of which they have need, are kept in fourteen buildings, so constructed that they will shelter the guards and care-takers also. For, since the buildings rise in three stories, as I have shown, they hold more than one would suppose. Whatever waste materials accumulate, are taken through the gateways in the corner towers and carried to the edge of the walls, until the time arrives for distributing them over the fields and meadows. Directly opposite these buildings is a rather large tower, thirty by forty-five feet, which connects the farm buildings with the city buildings; it also incloses a space of land, so that under the tower a rather broad vaulted entrance into the city is open, and smaller doors lead to the individual houses.   This tower can be so fortified on both sides at the gates that there can be no passing back and forth through the walls to the town when once the gates are closed.   A hall with windows all around, is built under the dome of this tower.   Here the citizens of that side of the town may come together, as often as the ordinances require, and act on sacred as well as on civil matters.   Uriel, a man very expert in agriculture, soil fertility, and breeding and care of animals, lives above in this tower.   Kapzeel and Simea, subordinate to Uriel, are the prefects of the towers, and they assist him in his work whenever it is possible.   Here there is no rusticity, but the agriculture of the patriarchs is reproduced, the results being the more satisfactory, the closer the work is to God and the more attentive to natural simplicity.

IX.

MILLS AND BAKERIES.

SEVEN mills and as many bake shops adjoin these two public storehouses which face south; while seven meat shops and as many provision chambers are on the side that faces north.   Larger towers divide the two sides as in the former case; and likewise, towers very much like those smaller ones, inclose them.   The mills do not only grind the grain and have it stored on the upper floors, but whatever is to be done with machinery apart from fire, is done here; and as this is a place for originality to work its way, there is a great variety of such for devising pleasure and wonder on the part of the spectator. Here paper is made, trees are sawed into beams, and arms and tools are polished. All the bread which is necessary to supply the island is baked in these bake shops, and all flour is kept here. Between these are tanks for oil, and underneath, cellars are dug out for receiving wine. And the men in charge of the storing and packing away, are expert tasters. Neria, who lives in the middle tower, has charge of these, and Simea and Gadiel, prefects of the small towers, assist. The arrangement is that each prefect is responsible to two of the four men. You will be surprised how a supply of provisions, not at all very great, can be made to suffice for temperate habits in everything. For though no one in the whole island ever goes hungry, yet by the grace of God or the generosity of nature, there is always abundance, since gluttony and drunkenness are entirely unknown. Of the distribution of food I will speak later; let me add just one thing now, that everything is done neatly and with proper appreciation of the gifts of God. Men that have to do the heavy work do not become wild and rough, but remain kindly; the guards are not gluttons, but are temperate, not evil-smelling but cleanly washed. And to conclude, the government is administered in a way so advantageous in all respects, that the people can enjoy all these privileges with a pleasure that is decent and need not be concealed.

X.

THE MEAT SHOP AND THE SUPPLY HOUSE.

A DISTRICT on the north is devoted to the slaughter houses and to fourteen other buildings which have to do with the same. This part has no suggestion of the bestial about it. And yet in other places I have seen men become coarse from the daily custom of shedding blood, or the handling of meats, fat, hides, and the like. Here also there are kitchens intended for the roasting, boiling, and cleansing of animals; but which know no delicacies or dainties. And inasmuch as they praise neatness and sanitation, there are wash houses for washing the clothes and linen.

The provision chamber is divided into several rooms; it has butter, lard, suet, grease, tallow, and other supplies of this kind; but also fish, dried and fresh, and all kinds of fowl, not only for the inhabitants but also for strangers and traveling merchants. For there is the greatest opportunity for commerce in this island, though the inhabitants of the place, individually, have nothing to do with it. Such matters are left to those selected to attend to them. And here the real value of exchange appears, which looks not so much at the gain, as at the variety of things; so that we may see the peculiar production of each land, and so communicate with each other that we may seem to have the advantages of the universe in one place, as it were. From this, the recognition of this little point, our earth, and also the generosity of God, the Giver of all, becomes manifest; and finally, that which is the gift of all men, is rendered that of every individual. I will not say more along this line now, for in the first place there is need of too much else, and then the subject will recur often in the rehearsal of other parts. Thirhena and his comrades, Kapzeel and Zarphat, have charge of this part of the work, and they regulate the daily life and the work of the subordinates.

XI.

METALS AND MINERALS.

THERE remains the section on the west which is given over to the forge. For here on the one side are seven workshops fitted out for heating, hammering, melting, and molding metals; while on the other side are seven others assigned to the buildings of those workmen who make salt, glass, brick, earthenware, and to all industries which require constant fire. Here in truth you see a testing of nature herself; everything that the earth contains in her bowels is subjected to the laws and instruments of science. The men are not driven to a work with which they are unfamiliar, like pack-animals to their task, but they have been trained long before in an accurate knowledge of scientific matters, and find their delight in the inner parts of nature. If a person does not here listen to the reason and look into the most minute elements of the macrocosm, they think that nothing has been proved. Unless you analyze matter by experiment, unless you improve the deficiencies of knowledge by more capable instruments, you are worthless. Take my word for it, if sophistry should undertake to prattle here, it would be a mockery—to such an extent do they prefer deeds to words. Here one may welcome and listen to true and genuine chemistry, free and active; whereas in other places false chemistry steals upon and imposes on one behind one's back. For true chemistry is accustomed to examine the work, to assist with all sorts of tests, and to make use of experiments. Or, to be brief, here is practical science. Sesbazar with his two assistants, Zarphat and Gadiel, have charge and seem to require not so much the labor itself as a fit exercise for the human body. For while among us one is worn out by the fatigue of an effort, with them the powers are reinforced by a perfect balance of work and leisure so that they never approach a piece of work without alacrity. Moreover, as I looked on the work, this self-reproach kept coming into my mind, that, urged by so long a time, employed at so much expense, assisted by books, I had learned nothing of all these things, which it is altogether fitting one should know, and that by my inexcusable folly I had neglected the countenance of nature, which is after all the most attractive.

XII.

DWELLINGS.

WHEN then I had examined the inclosure containing the shops and the storehouses, I entered through the east tower and saw the city proper, square and with two rows of buildings facing each other. The street which separates these rows of houses is twenty feet wide, and is of sufficient width, when you stop to consider that horses and wagons are not used upon it. The buildings on the outer side are fifteen, those on the inner side twenty-five feet wide; they are thirty-three feet high and most of them forty feet long on the side facing the street. The walks are arched and supported by columns five feet wide and twelve high, that rainy weather may do no damage. Where the walls face each other, a walk is formed by the balconies on the second and third stories, all of which it has been deemed wise to represent in the diagrams. The larger side of the city, if you stop to count the towers, has thirteen buildings, the smaller side, eleven, making eighty-eight in all;[1] and, if this is multiplied by three, they constitute two hundred and sixty-four homes. The distribution of these is shown on the sketch. No one need be surprised at the rather cramped quarters; for there being only a very few persons, there is also need for only a very little furniture. Other people who house vanity, extravagance, and a family of that sort, and who heap up baggage of iniquity, can never live spaciously enough. They burden others and are burdened themselves, and no one measures their necessities, nay even their comforts, easily otherwise than by an unbearable and unmovable mass. Oh, only those persons are rich who have all of which they have real need, who admit nothing else, merely because it is possible to have it in abundance! For as often as I have seen wealth on this earth I have also always noticed dissatisfaction standing by; but in only the one condition, which we call "lack," has contentment appeared.

XIII.

MECHANICS.

IN walking around the city, I could easily notice what the distribution of the craftsmen was. For even as the

---

[1] Probably a typographical error in the original.

city is four-cornered, so also its inhabitants deal with four
materials: metals, stones, woods, and the things that are
needed for weaving; but with this difference, that the occupations which require more skill and innate ability are assigned to the inner square, while those which admit of more
ease in working, to the outer or greater square. And
they, furthermore, regard clock-makers and organ-makers,
cabinet-makers, sculptors, and masons on the same basis.
This feature, moreover, is entirely peculiar to them, namely,
that their artisans are almost entirely educated men. For
that which other people think is the proper characteristic
of a few (and yet, if you consider the stuffing of inexperience as learning, the characteristic of too many men already) this the inhabitants argue should be attained by
all individuals. They say neither the subtleness of letters
is such, nor yet the difficulty of work, that one man, if given
enough, cannot master both. And yet there are some who
incline more to this or to that occupation, who, if they prefer to make a craft a specialty, are made masters over their
fellows, that they may in turn train up others and still others.
I saw what mechanics I thought were workers in brass, tin,
iron; knife-makers, turners, makers of jewel cases, of
statuary, workers in gypsum, fullers, weavers, furriers, cob-
blers; and among the nobler crafts, sculptors, clock-makers,
goldsmiths, organ-makers, engravers, goldleaf-beaters,
ring-makers, and innumerable other like trades not to be
despised. Tanners, harness-makers, blacksmiths, wagon-
makers, trunk-makers, stonecutters, glass-makers, all these
you will find here. Now that we have named those that
follow the trades it might be said that patching, sewing, and
embroidery are all done by the women. All these things are
done not always because necessity demands, but for the
purpose of a competition among the mechanics, in order

that the human soul may have some means by which it and the highest prerogative of the mind may unfold themselves through different sorts of machinery, or by which, rather, the little spark of divinity remaining in us, may shine brightly in any material offered. Of the overseeing and incentives, as also of the hours of leisure and of work, we will speak later.

XIV.

PUBLIC PRAYERS.

BEFORE I proceed, something should be said regarding their public worship. Three prayers are offered each day, morning, noon, and in the evening, when thanks are given to God for blessings received; and on bended knee and with folded hands, a continuation of His aid and a worthy death are implored in a solemn formula. No one may be absent from these prayers, except for the most urgent reason; parents bring all their children hither that they may learn even in infants' prattle to praise God. Then a reading from the Holy Scriptures is listened to, and the meeting, of about half an hour, is dismissed with a hymn. If the day be a special day, on which some remarkable instance of God's grace is to be commemorated, somewhat more time is expended in the devotions. These meetings are held in the larger halls of the towers, and each one has his assigned place. And nothing is more worthy of Christians than this observance. For though we owe secret prayers to God, our best ones, and very frequent, yet this communion of spirits and prayers has a distinctly pleasant sound in the ears of God, and an especial efficacy. Those who neglect this are perhaps a little bit too sure of their salvation, while those who are expecting at some time a communion of saints, even as they plan all things in this world with a view toward the heavenly fatherland, so they are occupied in divine praise more diligently and more eagerly than in any other thing. On this account, happy and very wise are those who anticipate here on earth the firstlings of a life which they hope will be everlasting; and most unfortunately foolish are those who close their life with this most grievous mortality.

XV.

FOOD.

THEIR meals are private to all, but the food is obtained from the public storehouse. And because it is almost impossible to avoid unpleasantness and confusion when the number of those partaking of a meal is so great, they prefer that individuals shall eat together privately in their own homes. Even as the food is distributed according to the nature of the year, so also it is apportioned weekly according to the number of families. But provision of wine is made for a half year, or if conditions admit, of still longer period. They get their fresh meat from the meat shop, and they take away as much as is assigned to them. Fish, as also game, and all sorts of birds are distributed to them according to each one's proportion, the time and age being taken into consideration. There are ordinarily four dishes, and these after being carefully washed are prepared by the women, and are seasoned with wise and pious words. Whoever wishes to have a guest may do so, and the parties concerned, join their dishes accordingly; or if it be a foreigner, they ask from the public supplies what may be necessary. For the kitchen, which I have mentioned above, serves this purpose, that whatever decency requires beyond the regular measure may be obtained from it. Since grown children are brought up elsewhere, in most instances a family consists of four or five, less frequently six individuals, father, mother, and one or two children. Servingmen and serving-women are a rare thing, nor very noticeable, except in the case of those attending the sick, those in confinement, or babies. The husband and wife perform together the ordinary duties of the home, and the rest is taken care of in the public workshop. Matters relating to boys and girls just arriving at adolescence, we shall hear of later. Let us just consider for a minute what an enormous burden we would be freed from, if the multiplex difficulty of providing food and drink, and the perplexity and daily care of stuffing our stomachs were taken from us.

XVI.

OCCUPATIONS.

THEIR work, or as they prefer to hear it called, "the employment of their hands," is conducted in a certain prescribed way, and all the things made are brought into a public booth. From here every workman receives out of the store on hand, whatever is necessary for the work of the coming week. For the whole city is, as it were, one single workshop, but of all different sorts of crafts. The ones in charge of these duties are stationed in the smaller towers at the corners of the wall; they know ahead of time what is to be made, in what quantity, and of what form, and they inform the mechanics of these items. If the supply of material in the work booth is sufficient, the workmen are permitted to indulge and give play to their inventive genius. No one has any money, nor is there any use for any private money; yet the republic has its own treasury. And in this respect the inhabitants are especially blessed because no one can be superior to the other in the amount of riches owned, since the advantage is rather one of power and genius, and the highest respect, that of morals and piety. They have very few working hours, yet no less is accomplished than in other places as it is considered disgraceful by all that one should take more rest and leisure time than is allowed. Since in other places it is true that ten working men with difficulty support one idler, it will not be difficult to believe that with all these men working there is some time of leisure left for the individuals. And yet they all together attend to their labors in such a way that they seem to benefit rather than harm their physical bodies. Where there is no slavery, there is nothing irksome in the human body which weighs down or weakens. And who will doubt that where God is favorable, all things are done with greater force and zeal, more easily and more accurately than where, against the wishes and favor of God, a mass of useless buildings is heaped up?

XVII.

VACATION PERIODS.

IT will not be unprofitable for us to see how the inhabĭ-
tants of Christianopolis spend their leisure time, or to name
it more properly, the breathing spell which is allowed one.
When they have cheerfully done enough to fill the requirements of piety, patriotism, and literature, and have exercised their bodies in the mechanical arts according as
the season admits, they take longer or shorter periods of
quiet. This vacation, they say, they owe not so much to
the flesh as to the spirit, not less to the soul than to the
body. There is the greatest need that we return to ourselves as often as possible and shake off the dust of the
earth; that we may restock our minds with generous reso-
lutions and attack vice, it is necessary to take a fresh
start; that we may revive the wearied faculties of the soul
and sharpen our wits, we must stand near or even sit
down upon a whetstone. Thus you will not expect to find
the sporting of fools nor the noise of aimless wandering, the
result of this national rest; but a relaxation of the mind,
intent upon some subject, and especially a recollecting of
things that pertain to a care of the future life, lest anything at all dearer or higher than God be brought back to
us. So during these free hours it is common to see the
greatest calmness among the citizens, many devoting themselves to some special service to God, or to some neighbor
bearing a cross, or especially instructing each other mutually
in Christian conversations. But alas how different among
those who struggle in the world and whom Satan harasses,
who weary the spirit and relax the flesh, who are occupied

in the mud and rest in filth! They are never less with themselves than when alone. How therefore should they hear the Lord speaking among us! How should they attempt to do manly deeds of valor! How should they give birth to new offspring of genius or discover new inventions when between the tumults of others and themselves they grow deaf and stiff!

XVIII.

REWARDS.

And now, I judge, you will want to know of what advantage it is for one of regular morals and excelling talent to live in this city when you hear nothing of rewards. Well, he of the Christian City solves this difficulty very easily; for it is glory and gain enough for him to please God. And yet incentives of the Holy Spirit are not lacking. For really deeds of the children of God are of such weight with these citizens, so often are they praised, and in so many ways are they impressed upon the minds of the youth, that every generous nature burns with a desire to imitate. Besides, the pleasure of the consciousness of having done right, the dignity of a nature that has overcome darkness, the greatness of dominion over the passions, and above all, the unspeakable joy of the companionship of the saints, take possession of a refined soul far too deeply than that the renouncing of worldly pleasure should be feared. Even if anything makes it worth while on the part of a Christian to be preferred to others, here there is no prerogative except of virtue, in this order that the greatest worth is that of devotion to God, then of moderation, after that of a subdued nature, and finally of human strength; and as far as each one is nearer the will of God, that much the more fitted is he thought to be for governing others. And since the world changes this around, understands but little the experience of a good life, and pricks up its ears to hear the pipe of vanity, it subjects the mind and body to the poorest guide. It is not surprising for one not to know what he wishes or does not wish, and for blind leaders, though promising light, to follow a far blinder one into the abysses of darkness.

XIX.

PENALTIES.

In the same way we may say of penalties, there is no use of these in a place that contains the very sanctuary of God and a chosen state, in which Christian liberty can bear not even commands, much less threats, but is borne voluntarily toward Christ. Yet it must be confessed that human flesh cannot be completely conquered anywhere. And so if it does not profit by repeated warnings (and in case of need, serious corrections) severer scourges must be used to subdue it. For this purpose fit remedies are on hand, not of one sort only, but chosen to suit different individuals. For truly, if one withdraws the sustenance from one's carnal appetites, or substitutes the cudgel for the tickle of lust, much may be remedied. It is the art of arts to guard against permitting sin to become easy for anyone. On the other hand, how wicked it is to vent one's wrath against those toward whose ruin you hurl stones. At any rate, the judges of the Christian City observe this custom especially, that they punish most severely those misdeeds which are directed straight against God, less severely those which injure men, and lightest of all those which harm only property. How differently the world does, punishing a petty thief much more harshly than a blasphemer or an adulterer. As the Christian citizens are always chary of spilling blood, they do not willingly agree upon the death sentence as a form of punishment; whereas the world, ever prodigal even of a brother's blood, pronounces wantonly the first sentence which occurs to it, feeling safe in this subterfuge that it has not personally employed sword, rope, wheel, and fire, but only through a servant of the law. Christ be my witness, it is certainly handsome logic on the part of a government to make thieves of dissolute characters, adulterers of the intemperate, homicides of loafers, witches of courtesans, in order that it may have someone with whose blood to make expiation to God! It is far more humane to tear out the first elements and roots of vice than to lop off the mature stalks. For anyone can destroy a man, but only the best one can reform.

XX.

NOBILITY.

In this republic no value is set on either succession of title or blood apart from virtue. For while it is true that those who deserve well are given the highest rank and are decked with medals, yet the advantage of this to their children, as in advance of others, is that they are admonished more frequently of this family example, and thus the heredity of virtue is inculcated. For if they possess this, they are easily moved to the laudable memory of their parents, in such a way however, that a free choice may not be detrimental to the new virtue. For those who rise in life by the help of God, which is the first moving factor of all virtues, are to be honored in the worship of God, and employed in conducting the state business. But this is always evident, that divine gifts rise here and sink there, thus showing that excelling is not a human attainment nor due to the distribution of a few men, but to the choice of heaven. It is not necessary to state what a mistake those make who so frequently take the license of sinning and the tinder of corruption out of the prerogative of family distinction, with the result that the offspring of heroes, who has not deteriorated, is an object of surprise. For as it is true that parents climb the lofty citadel of virtue over the difficult hills of work, so children often slide through the labyrinths of extravagant pleasure to the lowest engulfing depths of vice. If these should look back or around into the affairs of mortals, they would never admit that what might have commended them to God and men, did, by free rein to their pleasures and destruction of their flatterers, direct them into the readiest downward path of body and soul.

XXI.

OFFICIALS.

THIS central part of the state is governed by eight men, each of whom lives in one of the larger towers. Under them are eight other subordinates, distributed through the smaller towers. The spirit of all of these is rather parental than overbearing; and the fear of those intrusted to the authorities is not greater than their respect. For whatsoever they may order others to do, this they do also themselves. They do not lead any more with the voice than by their example. Nothing is easier than imitation under conditions of this kind, nothing more natural than following an example, where no one corrects except he be himself above criticism; where no one teaches except he be himself learned; and where the rule itself is the precept. He who first brought violence and disdain into the world had nothing divine about him. God approaches His own, and is approached of them. God is heard of them and hears. So far from mutual worship and contempt being permitted us, earthen vessels of the same clay, it is not even seemly. Since all things in the Christian Republic are referred to God, there is no need of secrets and councils of state, in which Satan in his kingdom rejoices. Here everything is open, giving opportunity, forsooth, to fear God and to love one's neighbor, which is the very crowning point of human society as well as of divine law. What answer then will they give, who convert religion, justice, and human intercourse into veritable chains, shackles, and prisons; and who with wrinkled brow, poisoned dress, and oily tongue, a hardened heart and a grasping hand, wish not merely to be in command of men, but to lord it over beasts and fill whole volumes with these monstrosities? Surely neither the law of God nor the Gospels of Christ admit confusion; and yet they never praise the human dominion in their followers, but always inculcate a common brotherly communion. And now because the church has renounced these principles, she has become richer and more formidable, but not at all holier, she who could not be influenced even in her last cleansing to lay aside arrogance and harshness and persuade her curators to use a more sensible government. And so the Christian grieves and is kept in the midst of Christianity neither giving orders nor yet sufficiently obeying.

XXII.

PUBLIC WORKS.

THERE are also public duties, to which all citizens have obligation, such as watching, guarding, harvesting of grain and wine, working roads, erecting buildings, draining ground; also certain duties of assisting in the factories, which are imposed on all in turn according to age and sex, but not very often nor for a long time. For even though certain experienced men are put in charge of all the duties, yet when men are asked for, no one refuses the state his services and strength. For what we are in our homes, they are in their city, which they not undeservedly think a home. And for this reason it is no disgrace to perform any public function, so long as it be not indecent. Hence all work, even that which seems rather irksome, is accomplished in good time and without much difficulty, since the promptness of the great number of workmen permits them easily to collect or distribute the greatest mass of things. Who does not believe, since we are willing, all of us, to rejoice in and enjoy privileges and conveniences of a community, that the care and the work are ordinarily imposed upon a few, while continual idleness and gluttony are made permissible to the many? On the contrary, who denies that every citizen, in his own place and order, owes his best efforts to the republic, not merely with his tongue but also with hand and shoulder? With an entirely mistaken sense of delicacy do the carnal-minded shrink from touching earth, water, stones, coal, and things of that sort; but they think it grand to have in their possession to delight them, horses, dogs, harlots, and similar creatures. Now the inhabitants of Christianopolis laugh at this and not unjustly, since painted on their coats of arms they show here and there, not implements of fierceness and pomp, but those of humanity and work; and against other people the former prove a confession of their vanity and brutality.

XXIII.

THE HOMES.

No one owns a private house; they are granted and assigned to individuals for their use; and, if the state desires, they easily change their abodes. Almost all the houses are built after one model; they are well kept and especially free from anything unclean. There are three rooms in the average house, a bathroom, a sleeping apartment, and a kitchen. And the latter two are generally separated by a board partition. The middle part within the towers has a little open space with a wide window, where wood and the heavier things are raised aloft by pulleys. The house has one door and the head of the house is responsible for it. This leads to the balcony from which one ascends either through the towers or by way of a spiral stairs. In this connection the plan should be examined carefully, for there is not leisure to recount details. At the rear of each building is a garden, kept with much care and nicety, inasmuch as the gardens are conducive to health and furnish fragrance. The roof serves a common purpose; for the walls, built up in steps and frequently constructed as a check for fire, separate and the gutters unite it. The buildings have double windows, one of glass and one of wood, inserted in the wall in such a way that each may be opened or closed as is desired. There are small, private cellars, for not a great deal need be stored in them. And so whatever extravagance and burdens there may be in the world, these people draw together into what you might call a very suitable shell, where nothing is lacking which should cover a man and contain his belongings. The houses are kept up at the expense of the state, and provision is made by the carefulness of inspectors that nothing is thoughtlessly destroyed or changed. Fire can hardly ever do any damage or break through and spread. They drive out cold with furnace heat, and counteract heat with shade. How unfortunate are those who believe that they have built lasting dwellings for themselves here and then discover too late that they have been working in the dark for others; meantime they have never been at home, not even in their own bodies. But even more unhappy, if Christ passes by their inauspicious palaces and enters the huts of the poor!

XXIV.

FURNITURE AND FURNISHINGS.

Now it will be easy to guess what the furnishings are. There are none except the most necessary, and even then scant. The beds for both family and stranger are comfortable, neat, and well arranged. The neatness of the women provides for clean bed- and table-linen as well as underwear and chaplets.   There are the necessary dishes for the table and enough cooking utensils.   For why should you want great numbers of things when all that you may reasonably desire can always be obtained at the public store-house?   They have only two suits of clothes, one for their work, one for the holidays ; and for all classes they are made alike.   Sex and age are shown by the form of the dress. The cloth is made of linen or wool, respectively for sum-mer or winter, and the color for all is white or ashen gray ; none have fancy, tailored goods.   Drinking goblets are for the most part of glass, yet some are tin and the rest brass. Of the arms and letters we will speak later.   It is quite evident that all this furniture requires no care except that incident upon cleaning, no guarding except the simplest, no expenses except the most insignificant; yet they are not less effective than the heaps, caves, chests, and like prisons of the riches of this world.   If you need any in-strument other than what is in daily use, you may get it at the supply house.   For there are enough implements on hand, both private and public, since the whole state is one of artisans.   Moreover, they ought to be ashamed of them-selves who are inactive in the great multitude, but in the meantime pride themselves with all sorts of vessels and in-struments, while they do absolutely nothing except with other people's hands, eyes, and ears, and in the same way accumulate wealth with useless solicitude ; wretched they are in the midst of such a laborious and manifold group of props, with which they hope to be raised from the ground on stilts and appear sublime.   They are made fools equally for their attempt to wander over the earth and to fly toward the sky.

XXV.

NIGHT LIGHTS.

THEY do not allow the night to be dark, but brighten it up with lighted lanterns, the object being to provide for the safety of the city and to put a stop to useless wandering about, but also to render the night watches less unpleasant. They would strive in this way to resist the dark kingdom of Satan and his questionable pastimes; and they wish to remind themselves of the everlasting light. What Antichrist expects from the great number of wax candles, let him see for himself; but let us not shrink back from any system which lessens the fear of a man working at night in the darkness, and which removes the veil which our flesh is so anxious to draw over license and dissoluteness. And there is no reason why we should consider expense here, when in other matters these citizens are exceptionally economical and when in other places there is the greatest extravagance in most all affairs. Oh, if we would but turn more to the light, there would not be such an opportunity for every sort of meanness, nor such great numbers of swindlers! Would that the light of our hearts were burning more frequently, and that we would not so often endeavor to deceive the all-seeing eye of God! Now that the darkness serves as excuse for the world and opens it for all sorts of baseness, while it spreads blindness over those things of which it is ashamed, what will be the situation when at the return of Christ, the Sun, every fog will be dispelled and the world's corruptness which it guards with so many covers, shall appear, when the wantonness of the heart, the hypocrisy of the lips, the deceitful deeds of the hands, and its much other filth shall be a disgrace to itself and a mockery to the blessed?

XXVI.

THE COLLEGE.

Now is the time when we approach the innermost shrine of the city which you would rightly call the center of activity of the state. It is square, two hundred and seventy feet on the outside, a hundred and ninety feet on the inside, bounded by four corner towers and intersected by as many others, opposite each other and inclosed by a double line of gardens. There are in the whole building four stories, rising respectively to a height of twelve, eleven, ten, and nine feet; and the towers extend eight feet more even above these. Toward the market-place, on the inside, there is an open porch, very attractive with its seventy-two columns. Here religion, justice, and learning have their abode, and theirs is the control of the city; and eloquence has been given them as an interpreter. Never have I seen so great an amount of human perfection collected into one place, and you will confess the same when you shall have heard a description of the sights. And yet I often wonder what people mean who separate and disjoin their best powers, the joining of which might render them blessed as far as this may be on earth. There are those who would be considered religious, who throw off all things human; there are some who are pleased to rule, though without any religion at all; learning makes a great noise, flattering now this one, now that, yet applauding itself most. What finally may the tongue do except provoke God, confuse men, and destroy itself? So there would seem to be a need of co-operation which only Christianity can give—Christianity which conciliates God with men and unites men together, so that they have pious thoughts, do good deeds, know the truth, and finally die happily to live eternally. Let us then cooperate once lest we be separated for eternity.

XXVII.

THE TRIUMVIRATE.

Now let us consider why they prefer an aristocracy to a monarchy. For though a monarchy has many advantages yet they prefer to preserve this dignity for Christ, and they distrust, not without cause, the self-control of human beings. Christ does not tolerate too absolute a representative, nor does a man raised too high look up at the sky; he looks down upon the earth. One's own experiences are the nearest, and they are worse, the more one is given to tyranny and weakness of character. In such an instance, at least, the triumvirate is the safest form of government, when it admits only the best in the state and those most experienced in public affairs, since one must work up through all steps of virtue to it. Each one of the leaders does his own duty, yet not without the knowledge of the others; all consult together in matters that concern the safety of the state. Each has a senate, but on fixed days they all meet together that decision in the most important matters may be reached with common consent. As is fitting, all these men must be loyal, prudent, and wise; yet some are designated for these ranks, or distinguished as being more exact. The chancellor announces all the decrees of the senators, repeats them, and makes them public. This man must be one of greatest tact and trustworthiness. No litigation is adjusted here; for the citizens have no controversies too great to be settled by the arbitration of the tribunes. But questions of the truth of the Christian religion, the cultivation of virtues, the methods of improving the mind; also the need of treaties, war, negotiations, buildings, and supplies are deliberated upon, with great, yet modest freedom and with a proper appreciation of the gifts of God. So it comes that they act upon serious matters calmly while other peoples become disturbed and anxious over trivial things, a very evident witness of their vanity, who roll up and impose troubles upon themselves, or if there are none, trump up some in order that they may torture themselves in bearing up under them.

XXVIII.

RELIGION.

LOOKING all these things over, I might have suspected this place of being some fanatical city, since, in the world whatever seeks the skies is heretical. But a double plate on which stood the sum of their confession and profession inscribed in letters of gold, soon freed me from error. The words of this tablet, as I wrote them down, have the following import:

I. We believe with our whole heart in one triune God, very good, very wise, great, and everlasting: the Father, who created the world out of nothing, preserves, moves, and directs the same, whose ministers are good angels, against whom the condemned Satan is rebellious, whose delight is man, once the divine image and prince of the world, to whom sin is hateful, whose interpreter of all wisdom and summary of all uprightness is the Scriptures, and whose love, through the giving of His Son, is most open and kind.

II. We believe with a whole heart in Jesus Christ, the Son of God and Mary, coequal with the Father yet like us, our Redeemer, united as to personality in two natures and communicating in both, our Prophet, King, and Priest, whose law is grace, whose scepter is that of peace, whose sacrifice, that of the cross.

III. We believe in the same regeneration of the Spirit, the admission of sin, even the brotherhood of our flesh with Him and in Him, and the restoring to dignity, lost by the fall of Adam.

IV. We believe that by His life, suffering, and death He has given satisfaction to the justice of God, that mercy has been merited, the same has been brought to us through the Gospels, given over to our faith, intrusted to the purity of life, and that thence the dominion of sin was crucified, destroyed, and buried.

V. We believe that the kingdom of hell and the poison of death have been destroyed, and that in the victory of the resurrection, security has been restored to us under the care of God.

VI. We believe the kingdom of Christ is infinite and eternal, where He is present to His church at the right hand of the Father Omnipotent, Omnipresent, and that He feeds, keeps, and quickens her spiritually with His Word, even as He does literally with flesh and blood.

VII. We believe His supreme judgment, which He shall pronounce upon all men, good and evil, with highest majesty, and shall distinguish the just from the unjust most critically.

VIII. We believe with our whole heart in the Holy Spirit, our Comforter and Teacher, by whom we are sanctified, enlivened, and equipped, after we go from freedom to doing good, by whom we are made wise beyond nature, armed against nature, and put at peace with her; by whom we grow warm, are united and divided into languages; by whom we see and hear the past, present, and future properly correlated; by whom we look into the Word of God.

IX. We believe in a holy, universal church, purified by the water of baptism from infancy, and fed by the communion of the eucharist, thus guarded with the seals of the new covenant, taught in the ministry of the Word, disciplined with the cross, ready to serve in prayers, active in charity, generous in communion, powerful in excommunication, which though distributed over the earth, the unity of faith joins, the diversity of gifts strengthens, Christ, the

Bridegroom and Head, renders invincible, and which the standing of the different classes and the purity of marriage embellish.

X. We believe in a free forgiveness of all sins through the ministry of the Word, and in the obligation of our gratitude and obedience on account of this.

XI. We believe in the general resurrection of the human flesh, so much desired by the faithful that on account of it they particularly love a natural death; so formidable to the wicked that on account of it they consider the natural life to be especially cursed.

XII. We believe in an eternal life by which we shall obtain perfect light, ability, quiet, knowledge, plenty, and joy; by which also the malice of Satan, the impurity of the world, the corruption of men shall be checked; by which it shall be well with the good, and evil with evil-doers, and the visible glory of the Holy Trinity shall be ours forever.

XXIX.

ADMINISTRATION OF THE STATE.

THUS far it has been permitted us to hear about the religion; the other tablet prescribes the rules of daily life, and the words read as follows:

I. We strive with all our strength to submit ourselves in all reverence and adoration to God, the one Founder and Ruler of the human race, and to prefer nothing in heaven or on earth to Him; to refer our life and all our actions to His glory and to succeed with His aid.

II. We strive never to provoke the holy name of God with any form of blasphemy, never to alienate it by grumbling, dishonor it by frivolity, neglect it on account of laziness; and we strive to regard reverently the most holy mysteries of our salvation.

III. We strive to have leisure ever for our God, to rest from the confusion of cravings of the flesh, to provide a quiet shrine for the Trinity, a pure dwelling place for our neighbor, breathing-space for all creatures, to devote our time only to the Divine Word.

IV. We strive to preserve and practice love to parents, respect to our superiors, propriety to our equals, modesty toward those that have been trusted, labor for the republic, a good example to posterity, and to perform the duties of Christian love with mutual kindnesses.

V. We strive to bridle our wrath, to restrain our impatience, to value human blood, to forget revenge, to abhor jealousy, and carefully to imitate the very gentle heart of Christ.

VI. We strive to shield the innocence of youth, the virginity of maidens, the purity of matrimony, the unpolluted restraint of widowhood, and to overcome luxury and intoxication with the temperance and fasting of the flesh.

VII. We strive to enjoy the goods intrusted to us by God, as diligently as possible, peacefully, properly, and with giving of thanks; to exercise the duties of acquisition and distribution as justly as possible, of employment modestly and of conservation safely.

VIII. We strive to propagate the light of truth, the purity of conscience, the integrity of bearing testimony, freely and correctly, to reverence the presence of God at every time and place, to protect the innocent and to convict the guilty.

IX. We strive to disturb nothing of another, nor to confound divine with human things, to submit to our lot, to inhabit our dwellings peacefully, and to despise the sojourning place of the whole world.

X. We strive so to establish our intercourse that each one's property be given and preserved to him, and that no one would rather covet the affairs of another than to put his own in order and devote them to the glory of God and the public safety.

When I had read these tablets I was not a little more strengthened in the belief that here lived a people of Christ, whose religion agreed with that of the apostles and the state administration with the law of God. For although pseudo-Christians boast of these two characteristics, yet anyone who associates with them, even occasionally, will easily see that their words are sacred, but their secret acts unfeeling; though their confession is honorable, their confusion is distressing; it will be evident that their formula of peace is very frequently a thoroughfare of discord; meantime they accuse their flesh and yet will not accept the helping hand of God nor the corrections of the Spirit.

XXX.

THE MINISTER OR PRESBYTER.

Now when I was led away from this place, I was admitted into the presence of the chief priest, not by any means a Roman pontifex, but a Christian. His name was Abialdon, a man of revered old age and from whose countenance there shone real divinity. No one is more practiced in the Holy Word, no one more experienced in the same. When he was graciously and zealously speaking with me, I recognized the ambassador and mediator of God; he did not look at things of the earth at all. When I attempted according to our custom to recognize this man with titles, he, disdaining such earthly absurdities, would not tolerate it, saying he considered himself sufficiently well appreciated if I believed him to be the servant of God and my spiritual father. They say that he is very often inspired of God and that he then announces some unusual things, but with the greatest modesty of the spirit. Only once a week, and that on Sunday, he addresses the people and teaches them with divine eloquence; and they confess that they have never listened to him without receiving an inward impulse for good. He is ashamed to advise others to do a thing which he has not already done himself. Hence when standing before the people, though he be silent, he teaches. His whole time he spends in sacred meditations and especially in efforts to further Christianity, and he seeks no other refreshment than heavenly food. When he blessed me I felt something warm within me, and it permeated my whole being. Truly this genuine theology is more efficacious than the assertions of many among the worldly. I blushed when I remembered the pride, greed, jealousy, and wine-drinking of some, and the other sins of our sacred order. You would suppose that they did not themselves believe what they were persuading others to believe, granted that they have actually learned to persuade anyone. Under their good favor, I was well pleased with Abialdon, a man of fervent spirit, but temperate flesh, a lover of the heavens, but forgetful of the things of the world, always doing, rarely speaking, intoxicated with God, abstaining from voluptuousness, guarding the flock, neglecting himself, first in merit, last in boasting.

XXXI.

CONSCIENCE.

I DO not hesitate either to praise the wife of the preacher (for he is a married man). Her name is Senidis, a very excellent woman, observing to the last detail the rules of piety and moderation. She neglects nothing of which it is right that her husband should be advised. Being very sensible herself, she is not often deceived; and being upright she does not deceive others. She always bears an untroubled countenance and is of calm mind, being, as she well knows, most happily married. She has blessed her husband with a numerous and beautiful offspring; two of these children are daughters, Alethea and Parrhesia. She guards her own affairs carefully, takes greatest pride in her married state, and seeks nothing else. In order that nothing may go wrong, because of her negligence, she tends things carefully and aspires to cleanliness in everything. She speaks when there is reason. At other times she prefers to keep silent. When there is need of skill and diligence she has no equal; for this reason the hangings and coverings of the shrine were woven by her hands. When I remember her, I am disgusted with worldly women; for they either are superstitiously scrupulous, or altogether dull, or they rudely scold, or they admit anything however wicked, or they wrinkle up their faces, or they revel wantonly; finally they keep giving their husbands advice, and never in season; they never love them sincerely nor take care of them economically. Forsooth, such is the light-mindedness of the consciences of the world, that after the dances of human vanity, when the honey of vices has turned bitter, they do not turn to God with a timely change of heart; but they annoy one with their dog-like yelps and drive people to desperate, hasty acts. Happy is that holy matron who by her example has taught that it is possible to pay the closest attention to one's affairs, and yet be holy with a joyful countenance.

XXXII.

THE MINISTER'S ASSISTANT OR THE DIACONUS.

THE church of the Christian City has also a diaconus by the name of Achban. He is very closely associated with Abialdon, and his duty is to educate the youth, distribute the sacraments, perform marriage ceremonies, and give comfort to the sick. Not that this is not also the office of the presbyter himself, but less his than that of the diaconus. The superior does not despise his colleague, but rather the colleague has the greatest respect for his superior. The former does not burden and weigh down the latter with heavy tasks, but the latter supports the former. The one does not command, but the other is naturally obedient. Even as between father and son there should be a mutual affection, exactly such is the relation in this case, though there is little difference in their ages. No power commands more effectively and none serves more readily than love. The diaconus does not care to make any changes, nor does he ever forget himself so far as to boast. But he is glad to hear from his spiritual father what God commands, what is best for the church. He preaches one sermon before the people in the middle of the week. I do not know why they should meet in assembly less often than others, unless it be, as I suspect, that they prefer to have sermons well prepared, a thing impossible when there are too many in a given time; and they make up the difference generously with their daily prayers and readings. They receive from their theological seminary those who read in public the devout meditations of illustrious servants of God, a custom which they think far in advance of the juvenile efforts of others. And it did not displease me either when I heard a reading grounded on a firmer basis than mere doubtful memory. Truly one man is not sufficient to hearken unto the Holy Spirit, bridle his passions, tame the barbarians, bear his labors, take care of his family, and earn his daily bread; and yet the world asks this very thing of ministers twenty years of age; and, for fear they may have a lack of something to do, they are compelled to combat hunger. I marvel at two points truly, in the case of men who prevail upon mere boys to care for their souls, and who are prevailed upon to intrust their souls to them. Of course I would give way if there were many like Timothy, but since I see so few of these, and especially since I see so much wickedness, I grieve for the lot of the church which is vexed at the sluggishness and audacity of the world.

XXXIII.

THE JUDGE.

THEN I met the second of the triumvirs, Abiefer by name, a man born after such a pattern that he does to no one what he would not wish done to himself, and what he desires for himself, he tries to secure for all. Neither blood nor riches, which here amount to nothing, exalted him; but a calm and peace-loving soul. He does not make his responses, confined, as it were, and seated on a tripod; and a citizen does not tremble at his look; but like the rising sun, he shines upon all and clears up everything. To state it all briefly, he is the PATER FAMILIAS of the city, and he rejoices in being called the minister of Christ. It is his duty to keep close watch over the measures, weights, and numbers, and to administer the specific proportion of things. Whatever methods they exercise in taming their passions and in thoroughly overcoming Adam, these he considers his sphere and he regulates everything with a view toward life eternal. For he feels that the best plan for a republic is one which agrees as nearly as possible with heaven; and being very pious himself, he believes that a propitious God is the salvation of a city, the destruction of the same a wrathful God. So he strives that the Divinity become not offended by the sins of the citizens, that it rather be conciliated by adornments of faith. Hence the city is invincible, unless it yield first to its own vices. No evil however small is admitted into it, and the citizens do not fear Satan's influence, but overthrow it as soon as possible. Surely one could never wonder enough at the feeling of security of the world, which tolerates the public trading in vices and does not fear contagion; which offers abominations to God and is not sure of the latter's disgust; which deals with the greatest political schemes and yet boasts of a Christian society; which thinks it has provided enough for itself when it is sure that one is not lacking who will govern it with great pomp and with the greatest protection of all lusts. Even as the Christian City is august and most flourishing because of its watchfulness of justice, so worldly cities wither away from day to day under the weakness of wickedness.

XXXIV.

UNDERSTANDING.

Now I pray that you listen to some facts regarding his wife. I have never seen a woman less credulous, I have never heard conversation deeper or more considerate. But if she once believes a thing and repeats it, you may depend upon its being true. Hence she does not do anything without cause, a cause in which her husband agrees. She has the sight of an eagle, eyes that can bear the light of the sun and can see very far. She tolerates no empty rumors nor the unreliable reports of the crowd. She does not tolerate the concealment of virtue nor the advertisement of vice; she does not countenance the restriction of liberty nor the loosing of servitude; nor does she stand any overhastiness. Her husband is not ashamed to discuss difficult problems with her; he hears her freely, but reserves the decision for himself. If she gets a little too curious regarding matters of his sphere he holds her in check and admonishes her of heaven, and requires that she restrict herself to her own duties. Thus she lives peaceably and joyfully, under the direction of her husband, a very fitting example to those who either communicate all things or nothing with the women. Whoever has a logician for wife cannot even believe in God, unless the wife gives her approval, and he takes oath to all her foolishness as being entirely true. He who has an Athenian, never bears the slightest interruption. What utterly absurd things are done in a republic because the WHY is neither known nor tolerated. The world has faith in the unbelieving, follows the blind, is mortally afraid of the weak, raises the lazy, and admits Heaven knows what absurdities. It ought not, then, take offense when someone laughs at it; it should rather appreciate the talkative ones who keep asking it with importunity why it does and suffers this or that. The world will never regret having been urged from darkness into light, from servitude into freedom.

XXXV.

MEASURE.

As assistant to this second triumvir stands Achitob, the state economist, whose care it is that the state revenues and storehouse supplies are so distributed among the individuals, that not less than his just amount falls to each one. This is not so difficult a task as one might suppose; for since no one lays claim to any prerogative or asks as his right more food than the season of the year and the custom of the city prescribe, but all preserve an equal ratio, the dividing is quickly done in accordance with the number, and the amount of the year's produce; and to see that the food is cleanly and properly cooked, is the special duty and care of the women, who also are to seek out and prepare for the sick those articles of food which are best adapted to them. Achitob has great ability at figuring and he so divides the yearly produce among the citizens that they never hunger, nor yet feast at the expense of their intellectual nature. This is a very desirable arrangement, especially in comparison with those, some of whom suffer hunger and others of whom measure the divine goodness not by plenty, but by superabundance and nausea. They are unworthy of life who seek the chief thing in life on the table or in the stomach, and who pay no attention to the food of heaven; but while the poor-looking servants of God are ascending to heaven, these persons, swelled by the foods of the world, are forced down to hell by the weight of their bellies. Nature is content with but few necessities; neither earth, sea, nor air is sufficient for the gluttony of one man until at length he is tortured in fire without end or measure.

XXXVI.

THE DIRECTOR OF LEARNING.

THE third of the triumvirs, Abida, has the sphere of human learning. I found him, contrary to expectation, without haughtiness or laziness. All about the man was kindly, nothing crabbed. It was thought there was little he did not know; yet in his modesty he professed an ignorance of all things. There was lack of nothing except, among his colleagues, the decorations of titles. He always said that the man who studied as a disciple under the direction of the Holy Spirit, had accomplished something. When I inquired as to the sum of all learning, he mentioned Christ and Him crucified, saying that all things pointed toward Him. He seemed at one time contemning the earth and praising the heavens; and then again he seemed to be estimating the earth highly, and the heavens as of less value. For he insisted that a close examination of the earth would bring about a proper appreciation of the heavens, and when the value of the heavens had been found, there would be a contempt of the earth. At the same time he entirely disapproved of all that literature which did not bring one nearer to Christ; if it tended to separate one from Christ, he cursed it. He centered all importance in the church, which had been tossed about so many thousands of years upon the world-ocean; to the church were due, he said, all tongues, all history, all reasoning, all signs of nature, all arts of the heavens; then finally one might expect the gift of blessed eternity. Only Christians have knowledge, but it is of God. All remaining things are foolishness, because they come out of one's self. These facts surprised me greatly, when I heard all things made light of, which among others are praised highly. But I was convinced when I remembered why we are born into this world, namely, to enjoy Christ, our absolute necessity, our invaluable gain. But when it falls our lot to die, woe to the miserable literature which has fed us for a few days on smoke! Arise, thou sacred science which shall explain to us Christ, that we may here learn things that are not to be unlearned, but to be increased and extended into all ages!

XXXVII.

TRUTH.

I OWE it to the excellent matron, his wife, since she was kind to me, to explain incidentally what kind of a woman she is. Nothing about her is false, everything simple and open. Whatever she sees, against divinity or humanity, she disapproves, but she chooses with kindness and sense. She knows of nothing so objectionable as hypocrisy and sophistry; she looks at all things from top to bottom, and such as she finds them, she makes them known to her husband. She sets no value upon gossip; but rejoices in the silence of the Spirit; if any difference of opinion arises among the women, no one is more fit for conciliation than she is. Her conversation is brief and full of Christ, as is self-evident, and she convinces her adversaries without excitement. She preserves her modesty inviolate, though several times she was wooed by the philosophers on account of the charm of her countenance. Oh, marriage, blessed and much to be preferred by all persons, which unites those who are joined unencumbered with prejudices, cringing flattery, and falsehood! And though they are deceived by them, the deception pleases them and they prefer to hear monstrous fabrication rather than facts that are in accord with their own feelings. Alas for such willing blindness, such voluntary sadness! In the presence of their dead bodies they dream of immortality; in the darkness they dream of clear light; in the midst of crime they dream of a well regulated life; with shackles on their feet, of wings; and what not. How true it is that the number of fools is never greater nor more intolerable than among those who profess wisdom. This most praiseworthy woman has done me this kindness, that she warned me of many mistakes, never before known to me.

XXXVIII.

THE TONGUE.

THE chancellor whom I mentioned above was in the neighborhood. He, too, is anxious to be called a minister of Christians. He is of great importance; hence I would consider him a very bad influence in a wicked state, but an excellent one in a good state. They make sport of us who believe that he hears one thing and speaks another. I have found him frank and even perhaps somewhat heedless. He has good cause for avoiding intemperance; as a matter of fact, he married Moderation, a woman of excellent counsel, and she, as she is very observant of sacred silence, tempers all his conversation very happily. When he has to speak of God, he trembles; when of Christ, he exults; when of the Holy Spirit, he becomes enthusiastic; when his speech concerns man, he grieves; when it concerns nature, he investigates; when Satan, he is disgusted; when the world, he is ashamed; when death, he smiles; when heaven, he looks up. Never does he seem to be doing less than when he discusses daily matters; to such a degree he says we are engaged in details. He values time not to the first minute, but to the sixth or seventh, so that hour-glasses are not at all required. Coins are not cared for elsewhere, as he guards his words, for fear some hateful or poisonous one will escape his lips. And so all around the

Word of God resounds, Jesus speaks, the Holy Spirit breathes, man is ennobled, human nature is controlled, Satan gnashes his teeth, the world laughs, death loses its sting, and the heavens open. It is surely an admirable instrument of God, which guards the oaths and rights of humanity, and is anxious to imitate the Word of God. For what Christ is to the universe, that this interpreter is to this Christian society, in that he brings to light all that is hidden, and makes known the secret corners. If God favors, he praises Him; if He tests misdeeds, he confesses; if He is angry, he intercedes; and if He imposes a cross, he accepts it. If Satan interferes, he disputes the matter; if the flesh oppresses him, he sighs; and if supplies are withheld, he warns; what need of more cases? Whatsoever the Creator commands and is befitting the creature, he attempts according to his own ability and carries out with the readiest obedience, while the carnal-minded carry around burning torches in their mouths with which they set God, men, the world, and themselves afire, so that finally they blaze in inextinguishable flame.

XXXIX.

THE LIBRARY.

WHEN now I had paid my respects to these chief men, I was to be shown the halls of the citadel. There were twelve, destined to preserve the public affairs, all arched, thirty-three feet wide, thirty-three feet long, but not over twelve feet high. In the first room, a library of considerable size, were guarded the creations of great and innumerable natures, divided into groups and distributed according to subject-matter. Whatever we think has been lost, this I found there, to my very great surprise, almost without exception. There is no language on earth which has not contributed something of its own to this place, no mind which is not here represented. Yet the citizens seemed to me not to consider the use of it very highly, and they were satisfied with fewer books—the more thorough ones. The highest authority among them is that of sacred literature, that is, of the Divine Book; and this is the prize which they recognize as conceded by divine gift to men and of inexhaustible mysteries; almost everything else they consider of comparatively little value, yet they are very well read and fortified in advance by this remedy, that they admire nothing that is mere babble. And they write books too, not because of any desire for reputation, but with a view toward spreading the Christian faith, scorning the world, and rebuking Satan. This is the ardent desire of all, to realize how little one really knows, and from this starting-point to aspire to the true knowledge and to disdain the vain boast of the human mind. But there are many things which it is expedient not to know in this life, wherefore a holy simplicity is for many a library in itself. Others say they have enough to study out of the volume of this universe. While very many assert that they find more within themselves and trace the sources of all arts more easily, than out of whole piles of books. And so they are disgusted with all things in the world which do not have in them anything godly, and they collect them for a mockery of the human mind that they may convince their people of the uselessness of such. Farewell then to books, if we follow them only! Hail Christ, the Book of Life, out of which more easily, surely, and safely we may learn all.

XL.

THE ARMORY.

OF the armory, which lies on the other side, they have a still more critical opinion. For while the world especially glories in war-engines, catapults, and other machines and weapons of war, these people look with horror upon all kinds of deadly and death-dealing instruments, collected in such numbers; and they show them to visitors not without disapproval of human cruelty—disapproval, because so much is being contrived for seeking and dealing death, when death itself is so very near, and even hidden in one's bosom; disapproval, that a man will take such a risk to bring upon his nearest brother that at which he himself trembles; that so much danger is being overlooked in the hope, doubtful and for the most part treacherous, of some gain or another; finally that such fierceness and violence is expended upon striving for things of absolutely no value, when a greater and more deadly danger impends from Satan, the world, and even from our own selves. However, they do bear arms, though unwillingly, for keeping off some greater evil, and they distribute them privately among the individual citizens, that they may serve in the homes in the case of sudden emergency. Meantime, they impress all the more seriously upon them that they be mindful of their spiritual armor, never expose their bodies, defenseless and bare of virtues, to Satan, never through drunkenness and gluttony forget their watches, but that they be swift and brave at their stations, elude the enemy in ambush, and when he takes the offensive, repel him, strengthened with the spirit of God.

XLI.

THE ARCHIVES.

THE hall adjoining the library is set apart for preserving the judicial proceedings, laws, and public acts of the state. Here one may see the annals of many periods, from them behold the words and deeds of their predecessors, and compare these with the things accomplished or being accomplished at present. If anything has been honorably and bravely done, it stands out as an example and a stimulus; if otherwise, they have opportunity to change and, as it were, upbraid themselves. No one may be ignorant of the past history of his country; but the latter so strongly re-echoes every age, that they think they have lived in almost any age. Those who have excelled in merit to the advantage of their country, have great reputation; nor do those have less fame who have shone forth in loyalty to God, good sense toward the citizens, bravery against the enemy, or genius in the direction of the arts. When others neglect this, they are not without blame. How few people of to-day know the movements, plans, and transactions of a former age, or hear the lives of predecessors openly and frankly described! Meantime people dream that they all were demigods; and if anyone says they have made a mistake in anything, they resent it. No one really writes about the affairs of the world except flattery, the greatest enemy of posterity. Flattery loves the deceit herself, and so rejoices to pass it along to her children; though her own people accuse each other mutually, though they live basely in fact, yet their lives as pictured by the parasites, are the very images of virtue. Hence it is that many consider the biographies of the elders somewhat doubtfully, when they see that they stand forth from the pens of the authors on a slippery footing. The frankness of just one man, Thanus, received the applause of the public; but though one may praise, he is hardly permitted to imitate. If anyone would attempt the same thing among his own people, he would be flogged. Men are so base that though they do not at all revere the sight of God, yet they themselves can hardly bear to look upon their likenesses represented according to life, nor to expose them to the view of posterity.

XLII.

PRINTING.

NEXT to this is situated the printing shop, the home of an invention that has proved itself for both the advantage and the disadvantage of our age; in this place at least it is harmless. For beyond the Holy Scriptures and those books which instruct the youth and aid the devotion of the citizens, little printing is done. Private copies of the Bible are owned by individuals in their own language, as are also principles of confession, books of hymns and prayers, and such other documents as make for piety. Whatever inquiries benefit the school, are printed in great numbers so that they may serve Christian boyhood. Scattering literature which expresses doubt concerning God, which corrupts the morals or imposes upon man's mind is not permitted. To whatever extent printing presses are defended elsewhere, they nevertheless err to the limit; for though everyone's curiosity is satisfied, one's own ambition and the purse of the printer, yet no concern is felt for God, or the harm to one's neighbor. How many vast volumes of nothingness, what a mass of lies and fallacies are accumulated in the twofold output of the year! One is surprised that there are men who can read through even the titles. For these are the fruits of a learned, boastful age, that the wise and the unwise, side by side and publicly, trifle with such an abundance of productions, and think that unless someone has placed their name in the public market catalogue, it is all up with literature and religion. For nothing can be collected so foolishly, invented so tastelessly, described so crudely, presented so uselessly but the bookshops will keep it.

XLIII.

THE TREASURY.

ADJOINING the armory is the treasury; this has no use at all among the citizens, but is not to be scorned in its relation to foreigners. No one would believe what an amount of coined gold and silver there is here in stock; with it they may pay tribute to Cæsar, support mercenaries when it becomes necessary, trade with foreigners, give to strangers, and support their industries. Whatever has money value, they think has least value; what has been purchased with blood, has the greatest value. The inscriptions on the coins are, on the one side, *If God Be with Us Who Can Be Against Us,* and on the other side, *The Word of the Lord Endures Forever.* The former face bears the representation of an eagle with a cross athwart; the latter, their city resting on a book. And so, money which weakens every other part of the world, lies here unnoticed and of no further value except for its usefulness; and it has no need of an especial guard, since no one in the republic can use it. So here men are served without injury by that which among others is injurious and insuppressible, more than all dragons and monsters. To money is due public corruption; with it the heavens are sold, the soul is fettered, the body bound, hell bought. Whatever sin is committed is attributed to money and not unjustly, when men accuse themselves before having been caught by so very cheap a thing. How easily bought is the human race which has sold its Christian liberty to Antichrist, its natural liberty to tyranny, and its human liberty to sophistry; and has surrendered its wretched efforts for the cheapest return: superstition, servitude, and ignorance!

XLIV.

THE LABORATORY.

BEHIND the treasury is the laboratory, dedicated to chemical science and fitted out with most ingenious ovens and with contrivances for uniting and dissolving substances. No one here need fear because of the mockery, falseness, or falsehoods of impostors; but let one imagine a most careful attendant of nature. Here the properties of metals, minerals, and vegetables, and even the life of animals are examined, purified, increased, and united, for the use of the human race and in the interests of health. Here the sky and the earth are married together; divine mysteries impressed upon the land are discovered; here men learn to regulate fire, make use of the air, value the water, and test earth. Here the ape of nature has wherewith it may play, while it emulates her principles and so by the traces of the large mechanism forms another, minute and most exquisite. Whatever has been dug out and extracted from the bowels of nature by the industry of the ancients, is here subjected to close examination, that we may know whether nature has been truly and faithfully opened to us. Truly that is a humane and generous undertaking, which all who are true human beings deservedly favor. Others, on account of the wickedness of too many or angered by their unhappiness, refuse with foolish haughtiness every investigation of nature and examination of human reason, considering themselves sufficiently wise when they make attempts at the most ingenious art, with one or the other form of mockery, and do not at all remember how infinitely many things they accept and believe only because they have been marked down and mentioned to them; how carelessly they spurn the most evident gifts and remedies of nature, and yet obey the most ridiculous tales of peddlers and quacks. I have transgressed, I suppose, against the haughtiness of many, and against the prejudice of many; but they will grant me their forgiveness when they hear that I did not exercise this art but only watched it; and being of courteous nature, I interpreted it more kindly and advantageously.

XLV.

THE DRUG SUPPLY HOUSE.

OUTSIDE the gate now, stands the pharmacy, and no place in the world has a more carefully selected collection. For inasmuch as the citizens have a strong inclination toward the natural sciences, this pharmacy is for them a veritable miniature of all nature. Whatsoever the elements offer, whatever art improves, whatever all creatures furnish, it is all brought to this place, not only for the cause of health, but also with a view toward the advancement of education in general. For how can the division of human matters be accomplished more easily than where one observes the most skillful classification, together with the greatest variety! This is a very liberal conception, though contrary to the accepted school, and it is entirely inseparable from literature. For what a narrow thing is human knowledge if it walks about as a stranger in the most wholesome creations and does not know what advantage this or that thing bears to man, yet meanwhile wanders about in the unpleasant crackle of abstractions and rules, none the less boasting of this as a science of the highest order! It should rather be the aim, after something has been accomplished with that theory, to prove its practical value to men; after the nomenclature of things, to recognize also the things themselves. Shall theory be so needy that after receiving the precepts of the arts, she should make no attempt at the accomplishment of anything and in the very profession of scholarliness, should consult those who are unlearned? There is enough of our life, if it is spent economically, that we may obtain the best things far more easily than the worst. There is more vexation and irksome labor in the foolishness with which men wear out their powers, than in those things which can raise them aloft and admit them to a contemplation of our earth. So they are whirled around and whirl others about in a perpetual maelstrom—in irrevocable infamy.

XLVI.

ANATOMY.

THEY have also a place given over to anatomy, that is, the dissecting of animals, because nothing is so nearly a miracle as the workshop of the bodies of living things, and especially of man, who may be called a miniature example, an epitome, of the whole world. The value of ascertaining the location of the organs and of assisting the struggles of nature no one would deny, unless he desires to be as ignorant of himself as are the barbarians. And yet there are some persons, even among the educated, who do not know where they live, feel, breathe, digest, or discharge, except that they think these functions are performed somewhere within their skins. For them, right differs very little from left, or lowest from highest. The inhabitants of Christianopolis teach their youth the operations of life and the various organs, from the parts of the physical body. They show them the wonderful structure of the bones, for which purpose they have not a few skeletons and of the required variety. Meantime they also show the anatomy of the human body, but more rarely because the rather sensitive human mind recoils from a contemplation of our own sufferings. Let us, therefore, lament the fact that our little dwelling so carefully formed, snatched from so many dangers, and not a few times clad more delicately than damage to life warranted, should end by passing into such a state of foulness and horror. But even as the origin of our life is a thing to blush at, so the rapidity of our dying has its cause of shame with equal merit. Meantime we do hardly find the number of our diseases, nay even, we rarely compute all the afflictions of one member of the human body. Let us then praise our Christ who, though clad in the same flesh as we, obtained for us the ability of sometime being able to take up again our decaying bodies, purified and refined. In consideration of this we will bear the grievous burden of the flesh, readily and willingly, wherever it pleases Him; we will give over all our members to God; we will dedicate them to His service and will freely return them to Him when He demands them.

XLVII.

THE NATURAL SCIENCE LABORATORY.

UPON this follows the hall of physics, and this cannot be too elegantly described. For natural history is here seen painted on the walls in detail and with the greatest skill. The phenomena in the sky, views of the earth in different regions, the different races of men, representations of animals, forms of growing things, classes of stones and gems are not only on hand and named, but they even teach and make known their natures and qualities. Here you may see the forces of agreement and of opposition; you may see poisons and antidotes; you may see things beneficial and injurious to the several organs of man's body. When I have mentioned these things, it is all of no value unless you shall see everything before your eyes. For if you should wish to examine only those cases even, in which the rare, freakish, and unusual specimens of nature are kept, there would be no end. Truly, is not recognition of things of the earth much easier if a competent demonstrator and illustrative material are at hand and if there is some guide to the memory? For instruction enters altogether more easily through the eyes than through the ears, and much more pleasantly in the presence of refinement than among the base. They are deceived who think that it is impossible to teach except in dark caves and with a gloomy brow. A liberal-minded man is never so keen as when he has his instructors on confidential terms. To what shall we attribute it that we see many professing natural science who hesitate when placed face to face with some little herb, unless we suspect that they have never been admitted to this very pleasant view of nature? If these people should hear citizens of Christianopolis or even boys at their play recognizing, naming, and investigating according to their characteristic marks and signs thousands of herbs, classifying them with respect to diseases, they would blush perhaps, or, what is more to the purpose, they would never leave this auditorium unless they left it instructed with a broader knowledge of nature.

XLVIII.

PAINTING AND PICTURES.

OPPOSITE the pharmacy is a very roomy shop for pictorial art, an art in which this city takes the greatest delight. For the city, besides being decorated all over with pictures representing the various phases of the earth, makes use of them especially in the instruction of the youth and for rendering learning more easy. And so the individual rooms have pictures adapted to them, and they thus advise the youth of the things pertaining thereto. Besides, pictures and statues of famous men, with their manly and ingenious deeds, are to be seen everywhere, an incentive of no mean value to the youth for striving to imitate their virtue. But they are seriously commanded to observe purity, this being taken, I believe, as a result of the audacity and impurity of the world, which poisons the eyes of the innocent with impure pictures. The divisions of this art, or rather the comrades, are architecture, perspective, methods of pitching and fortifying camps, and even sketches of machines and statistics. Whatever of the dramatic spiritual things have, or whatever else there may be like literary elegance, it can all be seen here, purposely prepared for scholars. The very time, which these people spend with a view toward this learned enjoyment, others waste oftentimes in dice, chess, or in other still more foolish games; from these, the latter get the following wonderful use: that for examining into matters and explaining them to other people they have no knowledge at all, but they gaze in useless wonder. How much more happily the others practice with the brush, so that wherever they enter, they bring along their experienced eyes, their hands adapted to imitation, and what is of greater importance, a judgment equal to and already trained for things, not unfruitful or mean. At the same time also the beauty of forms is so pleasing to them that they embrace with a whole heart the inner beauty of virtue itself and the elegance of a Christian life.

XLIX.

MATHEMATICAL INSTRUMENTS.

ADJOINING this workshop is an excavated place for mathematical instruments, a testimony of human acuteness and energy against our mortal chains. For though the sky is so far distant from us and the wings of our original perfection are wanting, yet we are not willing that anything should take place there without our knowledge. Hence we determine the ways of the stars with a number of mechanical devices, and mark them down, to such a degree of accuracy that it is surprising that man could have enough patience and perseverance to enter upon such theories. I will not enumerate the instruments here, inasmuch as nearly all of them are understood from the description of the most eminent Tycho Brahe.[1] A very few have been added, and among these is the very valuable telescope recently invented. The instruments which serve the purpose of geometry are here, and a great number of the common ones which aid the efforts of students. But why do I rehearse these facts, as if I did not know how useless all ingenious implements seem to the masses who make an effort not to be able to use any mathematical instrument! They betray themselves by

[1] Danish astronomer, 1546-1601.

this very fact, in that they throw aside half of learning, and though born for practical human affairs, render themselves useless. Therefore, until those who profess to be broadly educated without mathematics shall return into her favor, I shall not believe nor will I bear witness that they are really educated; I will pronounce them only half educated, and they shall bear testimony to this accusation against themselves whenever they shall suffer themselves to be led forth upon the forum of human sciences. When then they shall recognize the value of the instruments of the liberal arts and the profits of computation, and shall skillfully apply them, they should be honored. If like strangers in a foreign land they shall bring to humanity no assistance or counsel or judgment or device, then I think they deserve to be contemned and classed with the tenders of sheep, cattle, and hogs.

L.

THE MATHEMATICS LABORATORY.

FINALLY, to hasten on, I saw also the neighboring hall of mathematics, remarkable for its diagrams of the heavens, as the hall of physics is for its diagrams of the earth. Here was represented graphically the primary motion as well as those motions derived from it. A chart of the star-studded heavens and a reproduction of the whole shining host above were shown. Whether one cared to see the hemisphere convex, concave, or flattened; the particular and accurate figures of individual stars; the harmony of the heavenly bodies and their mutual, admirable proportions; geographical charts of the earth; different illustrations representing tools and machines, small models, figures of geometry; instruments of mechanical arts, drawn, named, and explained—of all these, nothing was left to be desired. There an opportunity was given to make accurate observations of the positions of heavenly bodies and, a more recent development, observations of the spots on the stars, all made known with incredible care and with an acuteness more than human. Here one's eyes could feed, that is, the eyes of the learned; here were illustrations for short cuts in memorizing. Assuredly when I had observed all these things, I gradually came to be less surprised at the wonderful learning of these people, seeing that it had such mechanical assistance. Generally in the world, though all other things are lavishly spent, no assistance (none at least to speak of) is provided for the youth; on the contrary the students are compelled to struggle with difficulties. If perchance some one of them should break through safely, he has little interest as to how he may draw anyone else out. Nay, if there is advantage to himself in so doing, he blocks the advances of the one struggling to follow, with new dams and new stones. So expenses are made a boast without practical results, arts without instruction, learning without books, charity without a kindly feeling, in short, a drilling-ground for a good mind with no desirable exercises.

LI.

THE DEPARTMENTS OF LEARNING.

WHEN I had been conducted from this place to a higher floor, I saw a school, roomy and beautiful beyond expectation, divided into eight lecture halls where the youths, the most valuable asset of the republic, are molded and trained to God, nature, reason, and public safety. For if injunctions are given to individuals to bring up their children excellently, why should they not do the same for the commonwealth that the best method of education and instruction be entered in upon? For this most important of all duties they have furnished this very elaborate place, that they might thus declare their love and care for these, their children of greatest promise, and that they might, as it were, merit future happiness in advance. All this is not after the infamous example of the world. For when the world seems to love her children most of all, she often shuts them up in some out of the way, unhealthy, and even dirty prison, where they are brought into contact with filth and become accustomed to such jails. Here all is open, sunny, and happy, so that with the sight of pictures, even, they attract the children, fashion the minds of the boys and girls, and advise the youths. They are not baked in summer nor frozen in winter; they are not disturbed by noise nor frightened because of loneliness. Whatever is elsewhere given over to luxury and leisure of palaces, is here devoted to honorable recreation and pursuits, an investment that is nowhere more satisfactory or better paying. For even as the earth when well cultivated returns with interest what has been intrusted to it, so youth when steeped in the life-blood of the republic and impelled to a joyous harvest, pays back everything with usury. This is the summit of happiness, to be able with one and the same effort to preserve the safety of the republic and the adjustment of the future life, so that the children which we bear here, we may find to our satisfaction have been born for the heavens as much as for the earth.

LII.

THE TEACHERS.

THEIR instructors are not men from the dregs of human society nor such as are useless for other occupations, but the choice of all the citizens, persons whose standing in the republic is known and who very often have access to the highest positions in the state. For surely, no one can properly take care of the youth, unless he is also able to discharge the duties of state; and he who succeeds with the youth, has thereby already established his right to serve in governmental affairs. The teachers are well advanced in years, and they are especially remarkable for their pursuit of four virtues: dignity, integrity, activity, and generosity. For if they are not successful with their scholars and disciples and are not highly valued by the public; if they do not excel others in reverence toward God, uprightness toward their neighbor, and in firmness and moderation in their own lives, and are not an example in virtue; if they do not give evidence of skill, wisdom, and the highest power of judgment for instruction and education, as well as a recognition of crises in the natures of their pupils; if they do not prefer to spur their charges on as free agents with kindness, courteous treatment, and a liberal discipline rather than with threats, blows, and like sternness; if these are not their ideals as instructors, then the citizens of Christianopolis do not deem them worthy of organizing this miniature republic, the successor of the greater, nor of being intrusted with the very substance of their future safety. As they succeed so well in keeping up a condition at all times resembling a state government, they can with good grace warn others, not lightly to expose the very valuable, supple, and active youth to the vilest, most vicious, insipid, and coarsest men, merely because such may be had more cheaply. Under such care children are brought up to waste their parents' goods, not by measures but by whole bins; and perhaps later on they in turn leave behind them children even worse than themselves.

LIII.

THE PUPILS.

Now it will be well to mention who the pupils are and of what sort. All the children of citizens in general, children of both sexes, are taken into training. When they have completed their sixth year, the parents give them over to the state, not without prayers and pious vows. The pupils are divided into three classes: the children, the youth, and the mature. Here they eat and sleep, and receive mental and physical training. The more numerous their offspring, the happier the parents are, for they then lack nothing; from this one fact it can be seen how unrestrictedly the citizens live. No parent gives closer or more careful attention to his children than is given here, for the most upright preceptors, men as well as women, are placed over them. Moreover, they can visit their children, even unseen by them, as often as they have leisure. As this is an institution for the public good, it is managed very agreeably as a common charge for all the citizens. They see to it carefully that the food is appetizing and wholesome, that the couches and beds are clean and comfortable, and that the clothes and attire of the whole body are clean. The pupils wash often and use linen towels for drying. The hair is also combed to prevent anything unclean from collecting. If diseases of the skin or body are contracted, the individuals in question are cared for in good time; and to avoid the spreading of the infection, they are quarantined. They do these things as diligently as the world attends to its duties neglectfully. For there is no need of my mentioning here the dirtiness of the schools, the uncleanness of food and beds, and the rudeness of those in charge toward the scholars; inasmuch as those who have suffered these indignities bear witness not so much with cries and complaints, as with bodies feeble throughout all life, for this very reason.

LIV.

THE NATURE OF INSTRUCTION.

THEIR first and highest exertion is to worship God with a pure and faithful soul; the second, to strive toward the best and most chaste morals; the third, to cultivate the mental powers—an order, reversed by the world, if any thought of God still remains among the inhabitants of the latter. Moreover, they feel themselves dedicated to God, by the law of their birth into this world, as well as by the agency of their parents. They begin their study not with some absurd deposition, that is, some prelude of foolishness, but with earnest prayers. From this they proceed through the fixed stages of those beginning, those advancing, and those who have completed the course, with high-sounding titles, it is true; but they unlearn these easily on growing more mature. The titles are a great incentive to the degrees, as a noble mind is raised by praise while it is stimulated by a slight disgrace. There is need of strict uprightness on the part of those who give the titles, lest while they are thus playing, they should haply trifle with the youth. This is where much wrong is done in other places, and all the more so because it is not without gain and loss. For to accept pay and to sell the ignorant to the state, is certainly not just. Punishments are inflicted with fasting and work; if there is need, with whipping; in extreme cases, though rarely, by imprisonment. The young men have their study periods in the morning, the girls in the afternoon; and matrons as well as learned men are their instructors. I do not know why this sex, which is naturally no less teachable, is elsewhere excluded from literature. The rest of their time is devoted to manual training and domestic art and science, as each one's occupation is assigned according to his natural inclination. When they have vacant time, they are permitted to engage in honorable physical exercises either in the open spaces of the town or in the field. Here they may contest in running or wrestling, they may play ball, or even exercise with weapons; or, if they are old enough, they may break horses. You will approve of all these, if you do not forget that moderation and careful supervision are required in everything.

LV.

GRAMMAR, THE FIRST DEPARTMENT.

Now we will examine the schools of the arts, they being also divided into three sections in accordance with the age of the pupils. The first is the school of grammar and languages. There, after the requirements of devotion, prayer, and singing have been satisfied, and sacred as well as other wise sayings that tend toward virtue have been spoken, the work of the boys consists in learning to name all sorts of things and actions in the three languages, Hebrew, Greek, and Latin; in being able to repeat them in classes, inflecting them in the comparisons, cases, tenses, proper persons, and numbers; finally in joining them and defining them with modifiers. Here they see to it that what they read, they actually understand, and what they do not understand, they translate into their native tongue. What audacity it is to teach a boy anything at all comprehensive in Latin, when he does not know what you wish or what he is expected to do; with the same effort and profit you might improve his memory in some other foreign language! And how inconsiderate it is to expect any translations into Latin from the mother tongue before the boy knows what Latin is! They are careful too, that they may not overload delicate, fragile natures with too great a variety or amount of studies, as it is but too certain that immature keenness of mind can be most easily dulled in this way so that the mind will be permanently unsettled. They are foolish who conceive extravagant hopes out of the precocity of childhood, and even further these hopes, when generally such a condition ends in dullness. They want firmly-rooted natures and they obtain these through liberal recreation; in this way the memory is strengthened, power of judgment is drawn forth, individual frankness is fostered, and work is gradually adapted to the talents.

LVI.

ORATORY.

THE more mature students are taught oratory in this same school, where they learn to refute all sorts of arguments in accordance with the rules of the art, and to adorn their speeches with little flowers of elegance. Much stress is laid upon natural force, less upon artificial form; and so he who is able to further the former, is the best instructor for the youth in oratory. Without nature, art is something barren and shows more traces of painstaking than of actual talent. So, oftentimes good theorists in oratory are poor speakers, inasmuch as in life they desire to seem broad because of their natural ability. However, if speech is an indication of the thought, it is easily evident why at times language does not flow fluently from the tongue. Yet there are some people, for the most part foolish men, who hope to rise through mere imitation,—foolish, for as they destroy their own chances and do not reach others, nothing can be quite as split up, rough, and out of place. The thing needed here is native, inborn sense, and a husbanding of whatever peculiar talent God has granted. For there is no master more perfect in eloquence than He who made the language. An admirable instance of this is found in the Holy Scriptures, which do not merely buffet the ears of men, but penetrate the very heart. In this there is no need of exaggeration or of any other extreme foreign form. If one speaks truthfully, modestly, and heartily, he has outdone Cicero in eloquence. To speak briefly, whatever breathes the spirit, will have tremendous effect; whatever smacks of artificiality will be powerless. He has accomplished much who has acquired a taste for God's style; for what fools consider simpleness is nothing other than wisdom. As soon as the orators of the world have ceased talking, the lifeless sound and the elegant form of the words have already escaped; whereas the soul remains unsatisfied. When divine truth calls to us in oratory, the heart glows, the spirit is stirred, one's whole nature becomes active. They should hear these words who are too much satisfied with themselves, as often as they speak without God, nay, even as they confess, with their gods—they who despise Christ to such an extent that they prefer in their speeches any idol, any demon to the holy mysteries of Christianity. Meanwhile they lay claim to all elegance of expression in themselves and are sufficiently talkative if the world demands such; but it is to be feared that the same parties will be speechless before the tribunal of Christ.

LVII.

THE VARIOUS LANGUAGES.

THOSE who are of sufficient age give their attention also to various modern languages; not merely for the sake of knowing more, but that they may be able to communicate with many peoples of the earth—the dead as well as the living; and that they may not be compelled to put faith in every supposed scholar. Learning a language is very easy for them, though other people get so confused. For if they do not acquire fluent use of one language in a year, they think they have accomplished nothing; whereas if other people do not devote ten years to the same task they seem greedy of time. They say that nomenclature is most important, and that a little grammatical study is needed in addition. They begin with easy reading related to a subject already known. One would hardly believe what an advantage the study of cognates is in learning a language. Memorizing and repeated use do the rest. I grieved when I recalled with what disputes I was driven to study so that I did not know what I was doing. Here I learned as if in play, a fact I hardly dare mention lest I awaken envy. Yet I must not omit saying that I learned to consider of comparatively small value the study of languages along with that of literature in general; not that we should throw it all overboard, but that we should not value such study beyond its use. For he is not necessarily wise who speaks in this or the other language, but he who speaks with God. If righteousness and honesty are at hand, it matters little in what tongue they are spoken; if they are absent, it is of no advantage whether one goes astray speaking Greek or Latin. Too easily persuaded are they who attribute to the Latin language the power of making them better educated, rather than to the German. But the Latin language must be preserved because it is in itself valuable in a good many ways, and also because it is biting, and unsympathetic with every trivial contradiction. Then it has what may reproach me, a man woefully untaught in its use, intolerant of its civilization, out of sympathy with its fastidiousness, or, as it itself is wont to insist, barbarous.

LVIII.

LOGIC, THE SECOND DEPARTMENT.

THE second school is called that of logic, being named after one of the noblest of arts. Here the boys, when they have already made some progress, learn to apply the instruments of method to every variety of human affairs, to classify whatever is given them, then to form a syllogism that they may see what is necessarily true, what is possible, and where some fallacy of judgment lurks. Here truth has an especial standard by which it may be tested; but as it is rather unpolished, some people from among the proud have applied it carelessly, not to say faithlessly to divine truth. And this is that Helen, for whose sake the Greeks raised such a tumult, and the Trojans perished. She is beautiful, it is true, but she bears herself all too rudely above her surroundings and tramples her equally deserving sisters under foot. One feels like laughing at those who, while they possess this instrument, think they need nothing else, though they lack everything. But they have horns—let them use them! No skilled workman boasts of his sun-dial pin or his plumb-line alone, unless there is something of his own work on hand to exhibit. These sophists, when they have proved that man is capable of laughing, that the sun has been obscured, or the equality of two angles of a triangle, sing their own praises as if something had been especially well done; and then they rest leisurely for all time to come. Very differently do those, who provide themselves with all sorts of arts, love to arrange them rationally and in orderly manner, and when there is need, draw them forth one at a time from their several places. This they recognize as the chief good of logic; they do not subject all things to it—especially not God. They incite their talented men to recognize what reason has been intrusted to them and to test their own judgment of things lest they find it necessary to seek everything outside of themselves and to bring in the theories from without. For man has within him a great treasure of judging if he prefers to dig it up instead of burying it with mounds and weight of precepts. Yet this is surely the very kernel of all reason, to listen to God obediently who is as far from all falseness and counterfeit as He is always closely joined to the truth. Let us in truth love the true. Let us not seek a reason from Him who is above all reason.

LIX.

METAPHYSICS.

IN this place others hear lectures on metaphysical science, which withdraws from everything concrete, and soars aloft to the first beginnings of creation, a science indeed worthy of a man whose natural bent takes him from earthly things. Here they look at the true, the good, the beautiful, unity, order, and the like, all the more successfully because they have divine light in addition. Where philosophers have groped in darkness, they consult the divine sun and ascend to the known God, who was unknown to the pagans. Moreover it would be surprising if a man who has traveled mentally so far that he can differentiate between elements and things, should return so basely to his own body and should wallow with it in all sorts of filth; or that one who could see the true vision of the good and the beautiful, should be caught and deceived so easily by the false, the evil, and the misshapen. It appears, however, that a slippery place is found wherever man goes out of himself and that he falls staggering. And so, he would stand most firmly grounded in one true and good God, who would deliver to Him a soul stripped of the garments of the flesh. Such a one shall hear things that cannot be related, and he shall behold the universe, as it was created in the original perfection, in a sky, not darkened nor yet overcolored but clear as crystal. So with the greatest delight on his own part, and with no little admiration of others, he will understand the first lines of art and the first points of things. This true beauty, while it is unknown to many, produces in them a nausea for this world and leaves the body itself unattractive because of a number of imperfections and the heaviest burdens of the earth. Thus, persistently and eagerly the citizens of Christianopolis are in this hall that they may acquire the ability to leave themselves and learn to withdraw from earthly matters. By this means they find themselves again, and receive far nobler qualities with interest.

LX.

THEOSOPHY.

THIS same hall serves also for the study of something still higher, and this is theosophy, a science which does not recognize any human invention or research, but which owes its whole existence to God. Where nature ends, this begins; and, taught by the highest divinity, it preserves its sacred mysteries religiously. Few men, even among the most faithful, may embrace theosophy, for it is only God who can work benefits, with His light or with the cross. God reveals Himself in a moment; He keeps Himself long within His shrines; He is always the best, though rarely seen; yet His infinite works have been revealed and in them every true Christian may rejoice. We are without foresight who prefer Aristotle, who value this insignificant little man and not the wonderful works of God, which put him to shame. He never could nor did he wish to believe the FIAT of God, the service of the angels, the spirit of fire, the density of water, the pressure of the atmosphere, the raising up of the earth, the immortality of man, the voice of the dumb animal, the inertia of the sun, the bounds of the earth; yet these are all established facts with us. If we would but give ear to God, far greater wonders than these have been set forth at His throne. Why should we not listen to Him, when His very smallest single act deserves all faith with us, and is invincible? If we believe one miracle, we must accept all which He offers us; for how can we distinguish between the works of Omnipotence? So this school is one of humility and obedience, where young minds learn to submit to the words of God and in His secrets rather to apply a devout silence than unseemly inquisitiveness. Let philosophy worry as it will; theosophy rests easily. Let her contradict, theosophy will give thanks. When the other hesitates, this one sits securely at the feet of Christ. Happy is the man who rises at the first call of God; happier he who follows; and happiest who never once looks back, but continually presses on. This is the chief thing in the prayers and desires of a holy man: if God is pleased, it is well; if He wishes us exercised and crushed because of the weakness of our flesh, God's will be done.

LXI.

ARITHMETIC, THE THIRD DEPARTMENT.

The third hall is named for arithmetic, the very home of all subtleness. He who is One and Three has endowed this with infinite riches. If you consider human need there is no branch of knowledge to which this does not bear some help of first importance. If you consider the undertakings of man's mind, you will discover that man struggles almost with infinity, in this one direction, and worms his way far into the secrets of progression. I am disposed to say that a man who does not know arithmetic is ignorant of a great deal. Hence, this study is pursued by the inhabitants of Christianopolis with the greatest perseverance, and every day they find in it something to admire, something which sharpens their wits and lessens their labors. In algebra they have no equals, because it calls forth all the powers of man, treats physical units in an entirely unique manner, and solves the most intricate problems with incredible keenness. But they do not forget what an effort it requires to untie the snares set by Satan, when even human skill can involve one so far; what power of computing would be needed to unravel the riddles of the world, what need of examination to explain the impossibilities of the flesh, when so much labor is expended in tracing the principles and sources of an art! Even though they strive after nothing at all more lofty, yet they think that such persons should not be tolerated who, out of pure laziness, deprive themselves of a convenience in computing and so variously applicable a short method in problems. And if they should hear that there are among human beings such as these, who nevertheless boast of their learning, I doubt if they could refrain from giving some offense. For among them it is evident that they do not permit their citizens to be ignorant of all these arts and yet strut about as office-holders. If among people of the other type it shall begin to be proper to have real knowledge, and this knowledge be applied to doing things, zealous talent, I imagine, will not be wanting to many, nor will fortune desert them. Meanwhile we will regard those as generous who, though they do not actually favor the arts, at least do not persecute them with extreme hatred.

LXII.

GEOMETRY.

THE next in order are those who study geometry, the own sister of arithmetic, a science which expresses in lines what arithmetic does in numbers. Hence it adapts itself especially to human wants and applies the deepest propositions and theorems to practical matters with admirable diligence. For geometry measures not only the dimensions which are near at hand, as the top or the bottom, nor merely regular shapes, but all figures besides. It passes through them, changes, balances, transfers, raises, and plays a most elegant part in all human labors. If one desires theoretical research, nothing is more subtle; if one desires to apply practical problems, nothing is more convenient or rapid. If you intrust to it any talent, the same is returned nimble and applicable to anything. Hence, the inhabitants of Christianopolis set much store by it, since they see that there is no art which is not rendered easier by it, and that man becomes more expert for taking up such arts. Among the thoughtless this art becomes worthless even as all the rest of mathematics. It is very evident, however, that they pay the penalty for it, in that they have to exert themselves more in their labors, and even watch other people's short cuts with tearful eyes. Why should it be surprising that geometry is neglected when intrigue, avarice, gluttony, vice, and wrath, yea even stupidity and rashness, have no measure and will tolerate none? The citizens of Christianopolis, while they measure various things, first of all make an especial effort to measure and weigh themselves, then also to value the goodness of God. For it is not of so much importance for us to know the acreage of our little fields, as the meagerness of our little bodies, the narrowness of the grave, and the comparative insignificance of the whole earth. In this way the vanity of our brain will most easily contract, and the swelling of our heart will subside. This will help render man forgetful of himself, patient in misfortune, appreciative of God, and mindful of future death that we may prefer to grow in value, rather than that we be brought from our former state of little value, to nothing by an angry God.

LXIII.

MYSTIC NUMBERS.

THOSE who are older rise even higher. God has His numbers and measures, and it is fitting that man should regard them. Surely that supreme Architect did not make this mighty mechanism haphazard, but He completed it most wisely by measures, numbers, and proportions, and He added to it the element of time, distinguished by a wonderful harmony. His mysteries has He placed especially in His workshops and typical buildings, that with the key of David we may reveal the length, breadth, and depth of divinity, find and note down the Messiah present in all things, who unites all in a wonderful harmony and conducts all wisely and powerfully, and that we may take our delight in adoring the name of Jesus. Moreover, these matters are not understood through any human skill, but rest upon revelation and are communicated to the faithful and from one to the other. Therefore they walk into a veritable labyrinth whosoever borrow poles and compasses from human philosophy with which to measure the New Jerusalem, figure out its registers and sacred computation, or fortify it against the enemy. Let it be sufficient for us that Christ has made plain to us all the means which strive to improve and support life; let us all be careful not to approach too hastily everything that glistens, unless the figure of Christ is evident and beckons us into the hidden inner parts. This over-confidence has deceived some of the greatest men, and all the more contrary to expectation, because it seemed to them that they were not speaking without inspiration. In this *cabala* it is advisable to be rather circumspect, since we have considerable difficulty in present matters, grope in events of the past, and since God has reserved the future for Himself, revealing it to a very limited number of individuals and then only at the greatest intervals. Let us then love the secrets of God which are made plain to us and let us not, with the rabble, throw away that which is above us nor consider divine things on an equal basis with human; since God is good in all things, but in His own, even admirable.

LXIV.

MUSIC, THE FOURTH DEPARTMENT.

THE fourth school is spoken of as that of music, and one cannot enter it unless one has had arithmetic and geometry; for it depends to a considerable extent upon measure and number. Here again man has given a specimen of his excellence, inasmuch as he multiplies three tones with limitless variety; so that he excels not only in language but even in the cries of animals and in the songs of birds. He even vies with heaven, where there is always melody. It can never be computed what trivial things man turns to the highest uses. With very few letters he speaks so many tens of thousands of words; with very few tones he produces an infinite symphony. Yet the world has not been able to keep from abusing the legitimate joy of heaven with the evil of Satan, and subjecting it to deceit. So it comes that we have the madness of dancing, the frivolity of vulgar songs, the wickedness of roisterers. All of these things have been long ago driven out of this republic and are now unheard. They like that sort of music which has a prophetic spirit, a whole-souled harmony resounding to the heavens. Whatever the saints have composed, whether it be of a joyful, lamenting, commending, or beseeching nature, this is the material for their music: and daily outbursts of the spirit increase the supply. Here sacred poetry lends its assistance, yet not the sort which sings of Venus and Bacchus. Moreover, they have an exact distribution of voices according to age and sex, so that when they meet in public the tones of all of them can sound forth in harmonious concert. Nothing can be compared with the majesty of this music; for when the favor of the Holy Spirit, the success of the composition, impressiveness of the words, and the force of harmonious volume unite, the greatest charm must result. And they have this advantage too, that the chief points of the Christian religion, examples of an upright life, the most memorable of the deeds of God, are included in their songs and they receive them into their souls by this agreeable medium. More prudent are they than those of the world, who, when among the blandishments of the flesh they have hummed their indecent and foolish songs long enough, are finally compelled amid the stings of death and pricks of conscience to roar something sadder.

LXV.

MUSICAL INSTRUMENTS.

IN the theater of mathematics there is also a place for musical instruments, yet here likewise they are employed in great number and variety. You would have difficulty finding anyone who is not skilled in their use, though each one has the liberty to choose which he is partial to, the lute, the violin, harp, or wind instrument; or the combination of all, as it were, the organ, of which they have very elegant specimens. They are in the habit of recommending to their students very accurate technique, that they may foster promptness toward public affairs, and especially readiness and adaptability of the whole body toward God. For they very frequently admonish them that they should be toward their Creator and their neighbor what the hand which moves, raises, and lowers the fingers according to an inner impulse and outer marks is to music. This might well be mentioned to those who are on all sides subjected to the rules and requirements of an art, but do not care to listen to God who would attune them to His instruments and offer them, what they call a *tabulatura,* of the duty they owe Him. Hence these discords in the various ranks of life, the confusion of human works and ceremonies, and the neglect of divine law—sounds which can never be pleasing to God, but must be ever objectionable. It would be better if they would render the laborious services, which they so readily offer the world, to God who is in no manner so severe or harsh but who is more anxious to preserve and care for His instruments, however fragile they be, than the world is desirous of breaking and casting aside her strongest tools.

LXVI.

THE CHORUS.

THAT they may contribute to public worship as much as possible, they make use of solemn music also. This they do by means of a chorus which passes through the city once every week, in addition to the holidays. All in the school march two by two, men on the one side, girls on the other; and in proper order they traverse the streets of the city, sending up a hymn to God, as much with the voice as with different kinds of instruments. They are arranged according to age in such a way that the voices are well distributed and the less experienced are reinforced by the more mature. When I was there the one hundred and twenty-seventh Psalm was sung, in which the care of the state

was intrusted to God. I have never heard more volume
or better harmony anywhere, than when they walked
with easy step under the arched porticoes. My eyes and
ears were thoroughly delighted, and I wished that I might
always be able to be present during this sacred service
of praise. They do this in imitation of the angelic choir
concerning whose songs God Himself bears witness.
Since they consider the service, protection, warnings, and
instruction of these very highly, and are anxious to have
them as near as possible to themselves, they hope, and not
without reason, that the heavenly chorus may be singing
along in the same measure with them. Who would not believe that these pure souls take more delight in such a public,
spiritual joy than they would in the noise of a city confused
with the power of the world! Or who would doubt that
they offer more to souls raised aloft with a pure joy toward
God, than to those sad and worn out under the torture of
vanity! They say (and I believe it) that they never return
from one of these choral processions except with spirits
strengthened and anointed, as it were, with divine breath;
that they never feel the guardianship of the angels more
closely at hand and remarkably than when their hearts are
bubbling over with a complete joy in God. They say that
in this way God is praised, the soul is enlivened, the flesh
is put aside, the world avoided, and Satan put to flight.
But what about the world? While she is playing the fool,
snoring, and wasting her oil, the Heavenly Bridegroom has
entered and has tightly closed the door behind Him.

LXVII.

ASTRONOMY, THE FIFTH DEPARTMENT.

ASTRONOMY lays claim to the fifth school, and it is as deserving of humankind as any other art. For with incredible diligence it shows us the movements and gentle rotations of the heavens, the orbits and positions of planets, the location of the constellations, their arrangements and differences, then also the number and size of the visible stars and their relations to each other, almost gives entrance into the very sky, and renders the same, as it were, tributary to this our own territory. And surely it is worthy being practiced by the kings of the earth, since it seems to command the sky. The inhabitants of Christianopolis set much store by it, nor do they fear falling away by the motion of the earth or being thrown off by unheard of star-dwellers. The honor is sufficient for them, which Christ bestowed upon the earth when He dwelt upon it as a human being. God shall see to the other things. Yet let us examine those now who look at the sky no more observantly than any beast. As far as they are concerned the sun might rise in the west, and but for their calendar they know no time. If these people make any pretensions to knowledge, it is a great disgrace for them to care nothing about what the holy patriarchs studied with the greatest earnestness; whereas if they have no ambition they are to be reproved for keeping on the ground the countenance which was given man to be raised aloft. Every excuse carries with it its disgrace which deprives man of his humanity, or if you please, his divinity. Surely man has not ascended to those highest abodes on his own legs, nor has he observed those most confusing laws without God's guidance. Hence, only the most noble-minded natures have an inclination toward astronomy; the base and earth-born are satisfied to eat acorns and husks.

LXVIII.

ASTROLOGY.

IN this same hall, astrology, valued highly for many reasons, is offered. For whatever the earth owes the sky, and whatever the sky communicates to the earth, they who have experienced both test out. The all-wise Creator has so made his greatest work interdependent, that it governs and yet obeys itself. Hence the governing influence of the stars is noted, with a greater admiration of human thirst for knowledge than for dependability of the results. Experience fosters confidence, theoretical reason creates doubt; between the two, the earth confesses her inferiority to the sky. The effect of the sun and the moon are the more easily recognized. Of the remaining stars, those who practice the art have as many differences of opinion. I could not understand, when they conversed with me on the subject, what the inclinations of the inhabitants of Christianopolis were. At any rate, they subject their thoughts, however hampered by the hindrances of the body, to God and God alone. They say that it is an uncertain thing to make everything dependent on the first moment of existence and birth, and from this moment to accept judgment of life or death. And so they emphasize rather this, as to how they may rule the stars, and by faith shake off the yoke if any exists. Hence they recognize a new sky, other stars and movements, where Christ is the moving factor.   Through His mercy they break the power of all ill will, of every thing contrary, weak, or foreign.   The most fortunate horoscope is that of adoption into the ranks of sons of God, whose Father, when consulted by prayer, rarely is silent upon anything; when besought rarely refuses anything, so far is it from Him to expose them to wanderings of the stars.   The wanderer on the earth realizes this; and in the shadow of God he fears no storms of the sky.   Those who have wisdom beyond this, are wise to themselves.   Moreover, let us not excuse the stupidity of those who, though they seem to themselves to be in a position to crush everything under their feet and even foolishly scorn the very sky, are men according to the days of the week, now servile, now rebels; to-day admirers, to-morrow scoffers; never fair-minded, always crude.   For he who does not know the value of astrology in human affairs, or who foolishly denies it, I would wish that he would have to dig in the earth, cultivate and work the fields, for as long a time as possible, in unfavorable weather.

LXIX.

THE HEAVEN OF THE CHRISTIANS.

THERE is a great difference between man and man, but a far greater difference between a Christian and a man of the world.   The man of the world does not serve as many things as the Christian has dominion over.   The latter is not only free from all offense of Heaven, but he is even reconciled to the same.   Hence he receives his daily gifts from a friend, as God orders all creatures to be kindly disposed toward the Christian. To what extent the heavens favor the Christian, and how he obeys the impulses of faith, are beyond the conception of the non-believers. How singly he is intent only on the church, no one outside of her knows or comprehends. The sun, the stars, the rainbow, hail, and dew, to mention only a few—with how many blessings have they benefited loyal men! The favor of heaven accompanied the church when it wandered as a stranger from the east into the west, and tamed men whom formerly it had kept as barbarians. The favor of heaven teaches us with prophecies and miracles, rebukes wickedness, raises the heads of the pious, and makes them look up with a hope of restoration. With what wonderful harmony heaven assists the history of the earth and benefits the church in its varying fortunes, it is hardly possible to say. Because only a few care for this, it happens that still fewer grasp the prescribed path of the church in these lands, and though they praise religion, they conclude that flourishing times have come to this age by chance. Meantime they themselves do not consider the words of Antichrist, of Mahomet, and of similar false prophets, nor will they tolerate such investigation on the part of others. Yet they see other clouds arise and they exclaim against them; if they would judge as worthily of the signs of the times, as of the appearances in the sky, they would not have to hear " hypocrites " from Christ. The inhabitants of Christianopolis seek first of all a spiritual heaven and are solicitous for it. They love a physical sky the more because they know it always has been and will continue to be propitious to Christians. As they have founded their city under its blessed auspices and on a favorable anniversary, they know that the ill will of heaven will never come upon the city as long as it honors God.

LXX.

NATURAL SCIENCE, THE SIXTH DEPARTMENT.

The sixth hall has its name from natural philosophy, which I have already suggested in the hall of the same name. How very zealous they are in this field, it is needless to affirm, since the very necessity of the study requires it. For by its help we arrive at a knowledge, general and special, of each world, and examine into the movements, qualities, behaviors, and phenomena of their creatures. By it we discover of what material things are made, what is their form, measure, place, and time; how the heavens move and how they appear, how elements mingle and how they increase, for what purpose living animals and plants exist, of what use metals are, and especially, what the soul, that spark of divinity within us, accomplishes. All these, forsooth, are very beautiful things, and it is below his dignity for man not to know them, after the faithful investigations of so many men. For we have not been sent into this world, even the most splendid theater of God, that as beasts we should merely devour the pastures of the earth; but that we might walk about observing His wonders, distributing His gifts, and valuing His works. For who would believe that the great variety of things, their elegance, advantage, and maturity, and in short, the utility of the earth, had been granted to man for any other reason than for his highest benefit? If anyone believes that all these blessings are due him without gratitude, nay even without consideration on his part, he is basely deceived. It is rather man's duty, now that he has all creatures for his use, to give thanks to God Himself in the place of them all; that is, he should offer to God as much obedience as he observes in His creatures. Then he will never look upon this earth without praise to God or advantage to himself; but with an admonition toward moderate use and exact observation. Blessed are they who use the world and are not used up by it as far as God has generously granted it! He who recognizes Christian liberality will never subject himself to the base servitude of creatures.

LXXI.

HISTORY.

HISTORY, that is, a rehearsal of the events of human tragedy, accompanies natural science. Words cannot do sufficient justice to the importance of this. Yet scarcely anywhere among mortal men does it appear uncorrupted, so deep are the secrets of the human heart, so generous our rating of ourselves, so bold our critical judgment of others, so subtle the apologies for human errors. The inhabitants of Christianopolis grasp truth very firmly, and they prefer to tell the truth though it bring shame to them, than to tell a lie to their glory. And so they want everything written down very plainly, and they confess all their doings, even their faults, frankly in order that posterity may know the events of the past without disguise. It is a very sad thing to look back through so many thousands of years upon the tyranny of Satan, the growth of crime, the monstrous deeds of men, the hideousness of wars, the horrors of massacres, the boasting of conceit, the arrogance of wealth, the confusion of ranks, and the secrets of wickedness. All these conditions suceed each other in the world, recur often, and disturb the entire period. How pleasant it is, on the contrary, to contemplate the champions of God, germs of virtue, dignity of the human soul, abundance of peace, restful quiet, confession of one's shortcomings, the fullness of contentment, varieties of gifts, invincible strength of holiness. There are scholars who are bold enough to be unacquainted with such facts and who rank them with fables; they are very worthy themselves to be told of in fable. Meanwhile, it is clearly evident that as many as are ignorant of past events, are likewise of little value in the present and unprepared for the future, however bold and arrogant they may be as to other things. For as the study of human history makes man gentle, humble, and careful, so the ignorance of it keeps him crude toward himself and others, proud, and hasty toward his own and the state's undoing.

LXXII.

CHURCH HISTORY.

SINCE the inhabitants of Christianopolis make everything in this world second to the church, they are concerned in its history more than with any other. For as this is the only ark which can contain those to be saved, they prefer to be solicitous about it rather than about the waters of the universal flood. So they relate with what immeasurable goodness of God that insignificant little flock was collected, how it was taken up under His covenant, put in order with laws and fortified with the Word; they tell with what weak instruments it was extended, with what very strong

machines it was attacked, with what evident aid it was
defended; with how much blood, with what prayers its
safety was established, with what a roaring on the part of
Satan the banner of the cross triumphed; how readily the
tares grow up, how often its light is drawn back into a
corner, how many eclipses the light suffered, especially
severe and dense under Antichrist; how it emerged oftentimes out of desperate circumstances, and in our own
age under the guidance of the great Luther; with what filth
and spots it is frequently besmirched, how much trouble it
has with the sons of the flesh. Many such points as these,
as well as periodical and harmonious changes in the
church, they have at hand, and impress them carefully
upon the youth that they may learn to trust God, distrust
the flesh, scorn the threats of the world, and bear patiently
the darkness of this age. This is all very well too, however others may boast of their neglect of ecclesiastical history. For how little the latter is required even in the case
of ministers, and how very little, where it is offered, is
done in comparison with one or a second syllogism, need
not be enlarged upon in this place. This is a trick of Satan
who, while he removes from before our eyes the past disputes of the pious, and the scourges of heresy, leaves any
possible clouds of the church, in place of the serene and
unmistakable light, until we under some delay gradually
accustom ourselves to superstition and wickedness. Oh,
if men would but stop to look back at the seriousness of
our reformation, simony and a false impression of security
would not impose upon so many; and oh, that religion would
be guarded more seriously which abhors not only the Roman doctrine, but her morals also! Meantime the inhabitants of Christianopolis think very often not so much of the
church in the larger sense, but also of their own small one

within their hearts, that whatever is done within them for the spirit against the flesh and on behalf of heaven against hell, as often as they are conscious of the divine Presence, they may note it down, that thus they may believe and know that they are the elect and beloved of God.

LXXIII.

ETHICS, THE SEVENTH DEPARTMENT.

THE seventh school has ethics as its chief subject, their guide in all human virtues, in prudence, justice, moderation, bravery, and kindred qualities; not only do they wish her to be careful in precepts and rules, but in very deed, especially shining in daily examples. It is ridiculous to advise others to do what we contradict in our lives. Those who boast of nothing but heaven, should not savor of the earth; those who inculcate justice should do injury to none; those who advocate temperance should not live in extravagance; those who boast of bravery should never be cast down. If there are any who go in advance, those are not lacking who follow, whose examples are very many. Here they give reward for work done; for they drive from the society of good men every item of luck. They say that fortune is purely fictitious and rests upon our own notion; that we seek or shun respectively, what we picture good or bad for ourselves. Since it could be in our power, that conditions be always sufficiently well with us, we accomplish as a result of our own persuasion that we must needs suffer evil and be in want. They say that we will always be in need, as long as we desire what we cannot obtain; that we will always have abundance, as long as we possess only those things of which no one can deprive us. This is altogether true; for no one else is to blame for our unhappiness except ourselves, we who, while we covet individually what is due to all, and while thus keep attacking other people's rights, always have one with whom to quarrel—there is always someone who may conquer or suppress us; or if no one actually disturbs us, surely we never satisfy ourselves. And since the citizens of this ideal city understand these facts, they are not willing that their greatest treasure should dwell anywhere except in their own breasts. And because they do not want a purely imaginative treasure they believe and recognize Christ as the one by whose love they are joined together in perfect mutual friendship, by whose perfect truth they are directed, whose perfect courtesy they obtain, by whose perfect generosity they are covered, or, to mention it all in one, by whose humanity they are ennobled. That it may please us to imitate this, or that it may be permitted through those who usually fill the earth with the basest morals and vainest practices, I do with a whole heart pray God, the author, preserver, and rewarder of a moral and well regulated life.

LXXIV.

THE GOVERNMENT.

MORE subtle than this is government, which very evidently employs a constructive mind for ruling men and for protecting population. I have already said that they have preferred government by aristocracy to other forms, because this approaches more closely to the Christian society. In this they establish three good qualities of man: equality, the desire for peace, and the contempt for riches, as the world is tortured primarily with the opposites of these. They have also put the culture of the soul on a higher plane and have made it known, that anyone may know himself more easily. The chief point with them is that Christians ought to be different from the world round about, in morals as well as in religion, that they ought not be permitted to do everything, though it be right for others; that they ought not tolerate all that others bear. They say that the Gospels require a different government than that of the world, and that the judgment of it lies with the Christian religion. They chide the world for permitting haughtiness among those in high places, immorality among the clergy, dishonesty among office-holders, extravagance among the citizens, deviations from the right by all persons; and only on this one pretext, because they are men. For they say that this merely denotes a lack of serious attempts and a correct constitution of government, since man is really not an untamable animal; afterwards even the very wrestling-grounds of evils are opened so that it is surprising that even now one can resist. They say that very many practices also, which are evil and harmful, are looked upon as good and praiseworthy; and the criticism of these is not permitted. Excellent laws stand out to the view; but if anyone would urge their enforcement, he would be ridiculed. It did not seem to them, they said, that a government was formed after the model of Christ, where God was made of less account than men, the soul less than the body, the body less than riches; where the vices of wealth are not considered a crime; the virtues of poverty not praiseworthy; where the instigator of crime receives a reward; the one corrupted, death; where the soul of a man may be sold for any price.

I could not answer all these arguments, however much I tried. So I referred the matter to the political scientists of our age, who would not portray the world in so many volumes unless they knew what would be profitable to the affairs of mortals. Yet I have thought that many things are said against the morals of our age not unjustly, which could be corrected with no greater difficulty than that with which the world maintains her own. We see that our own affairs can be well enough defended from injury, provided we look upon divine things and the holy name of God with some reverence; since some are said to have observed superstitiously, others fanatically; but only the Christians by their own boasting do not blush to enumerate them among impossibilities.

LXXV.

CHRISTIAN POVERTY.

It is not sufficient for Christians to be good according to the teachings of ethics and government, but they choose as their model Christ Himself, a far higher Master. As He is the most perfect embodiment of the highest virtues, He deserves to have imitators. Moreover these virtues go beyond human excellencies and are included under the symbols of the cross; and those, who have devoted themselves closer to man, have called these Christian proverty, by which we renounce even the things that are permitted the world, that we may possess only Christ. Those who join this group unlearn, leave, and bear everything. They prefer simplicity to intelligence, ignorance to knowledge, silence to eloquence, humility to dignity, credulity to shrewdness, want to abundance, studying to teaching, bearing to doing; and whatsoever things are considered lowly on earth, provided they are harmless, these they desire. Do not believe that these are Roman Minorites,[1] sly and grasping of all that is greatest on this earth; nor yet hypocritical saints of their own understanding and secret pride. It is a happy race of men, and skilled in whatsoever they do on earth. Whatever they have of the gifts of God, they divide in common, reserving almost nothing for themselves. They are not irritated by being offended, nor puffed up by fame; they are not elated by abundance, nor yet depressed by poverty; they do not admire hair-splitting arguments, they do not consider the most insignificant things below their notice; they are not worried by the threats of the age, they are not caught by report of things of the present; they are not disturbed by noise, nor are their wits sharpened by separation from others; they are not afflicted in life nor terrified by death. There are only a very few of these, nor could they easily be other than such as already have penetrated through all things, to whom already human affairs and human knowledge are apparent, to whom after the wanderings on the earth the only thing in their wishes is the certainty of heaven. No one is more voluntarily foolish, none more surely ignorant, none more easily in want, no one more readily serves, than those who, respectively, are experienced in controlling the slipperiness of wisdom, the windings of knowledge, the burdens of possessions, the risks of dangers. Hence those who are accustomed to laugh at and criticise such people, only bear witness by that very fact that they have no taste for human affairs, but wallow about in the very mire out of which they arose by the grace of God.

[1] Franciscans.

LXXVI.

THEOLOGY, THE EIGHTH DEPARTMENT.

Now the eighth school is left, which is devoted to theology, the queen of all that human beings possess, and the mistress of philosophy. This, first of all, teaches the mode of expression of the Holy Ghost in the Holy Scriptures; their strength, elegance, efficacy, and depth, that the students may know what is meant by this or that diction and this or that combination of words; and that they may learn to admire this sort of language more than all the eloquence of this earth. Then they are urged toward a devout imitation of this divine speech that, when they shall have collected for themselves from their boyhood days a mighty treasure of holy thoughts, they may know how to adapt them also to the needs of mortals, and may learn to speak to others with the same spirit, the same words with which the apostles of Christ preached the Gospel to the people. Thirdly, they arm them with the arguments and the firmness of the unconquered Word so that, when they are attacked by heresies or when the father of false argument, Satan himself, battles against them, they may understand how to defend the sincerity of truth borrowed from the source of truth, and that they may learn how to preserve the clear founts of Israel in every time and place from the contamination of earthly mire or human theorizing. This they call scholastic theology, which teaches them to know, imitate, and defend the words of Holy Writ; and in this they train their students so as to remind them that these matters do not of themselves actually accomplish anything in Christianity, but that they do tend toward preparing one for accomplishing something. Moreover, they avoid the names of sects especially, nor do they at all willingly pronounce them; and though they love to hear the name of Lutheran, yet they strive first of all to be Christians. From which I gather that they do not agree with those who, though they admit any translation as safe, and go securely to sleep with the same, are not very much concerned whether the Holy Spirit has said this or something else. Next, that they do not restrict all theology to the experience of addressing an audience, since it may occur that a man, as wicked as he is ignorant, will speak forth to the people borrowed words even though they be holy. On the other hand they do not admire those by whom all theology is converted into daggers, swords, and bows, and who admit no worship of God except it be of a disputatious or contentious nature. Finally I gather, that they do not permit every harmless difference of opinion to generate factions and hate, but teach their pupils in such a way that, as often as there is need, they may be able to form opinions on versions of the Scriptures, address assemblies, defend the truth, avoid schisms, and what is perhaps more fortunate and surely more moderate, that they may prefer to be engaged in the adjusting of a Christian life on the ground that Christ prefers holy men to scholars, obedient ones to logicians; because the very arts of the soul accomplish less in the last oppositions of death than does the strength of conscience, purified by the blood of Christ.

LXXVII.

PRACTICE OF THEOLOGY.

THENCE they gird themselves with a great devotion for practical theology. This teaches them to pray, to meditate, and to stand trial. This is the wisdom which impresses the Holy Scriptures upon us and carries them over into our lives, that we may make known the mysteries of God. Here not merely the approval of the Divine Word is required, but its unanimity and harmony. For as Christ is the sum total of all secrets, so the regeneration in us is the beginning of a new childhood, youth, and even maturity, and urges upon us that which is in agreement not with Adam, but with Christ, our Book of Life. Those who establish their theology according to artificial rules do not comprehend this. For there is need of a biting and bitter acid, taken internally, to tear down the inner structures and break them to pieces. Unless we cease, Christ will not begin; unless we are silent, God will not speak; unless we accept it passively, the Spirit will not be active. This is that sabbath for the sake of which all the pious on earth, throughout all ages, have been ridiculed. Such is the madness of the saints of Christ that they not only believe in Christ crucified, but even are willing to be crucified themselves. Such is the foolishness of the Gospel of Paul to glory in nothing except his own weakness. Here is usually a greater danger from Satan, who, being always evil, is here at his very worst, in that he creeps into man so stealthily that the latter is no longer God's. Hence the evidences of fury, sleeplessness, delirium, and other mockery of a soul not inspired of God but proceeding from itself. So the citizens of Christianopolis are accustomed to advise their own people and others seriously to ask nothing, to attempt nothing for themselves beyond Christian simplicity, without the advice of God.   For we cannot all be snatched into the third heaven as was Paul; yet we can with him become fashioned like Christ.   If we obey the Gospels, if we obey the apostles, this will meet the requirements of true theology, and we will be in no want of revelation or of preaching of angels in any other form.   And even as genuine theology does not consider those coarse and sensuous Christians, so also it does not recognize those who are so extremely precise and those who are drawn out into the realm of the purely mental.   The best moderation of the cross is that which according to the balance of Christ places a fitting weight upon all the children of God, and trains them individually in such a way that they may have a reason for asking aid of God.

LXXVIII.

PROPHECIES.

IF now our very kind Father shall favor one man somewhat beyond others, they do not unceremoniously reject the fact but test the prophesying spirits.   So they have a school of prophecy, not at all that they would give instruction in the virtue of soothsaying which deceives so many, but as a place where they might observe the harmony and truth of the prophetic spirit.   And as this cannot be done without divine suggestion, they confer on the matter in the fear of the Master to see whether any unusual portion of light may have been bestowed upon anyone.   For rarely has anyone who can adjust all types of the Scriptures according to their differences, who can draw forth prophecies out of their most private shrines, who can reconcile the ceremonies of Moses with those of Christ, who can grasp the arguments of the apostles and even Christ, drawn forth from the Old Testament, or accomplish other things like these, under so many interpreters,—rarely has such a one established any faith at all with them. In truth many have caused them doubt as to whether one or another may not have given out judgment too indiscreetly. And so they confess that as far as concerns the forecasting of future events or the interpretation of past, they do not comprehend as yet the oracles of the Holy Spirit, yet none the less they are content in the divine revelation in which eternal salvation rests. Moreover they beseech God that He may be willing in His great indulgence, to make known to His children somewhat of the profound wisdom that lies hidden in the depths of His Word, and to reveal His Son to them in every sacred page. How much they accomplish by this pious prayer, they did not tell me.

Now I have in my uncouth style hastened through the points that were shown me in the Christian schools, and I trust I may not have injured the facts because of my poor writing and perhaps even my forgetfulness. I would hope that some of the facts, though not all and even if only a very few, may please my pious and Christian reader or even give him courage to visit Christianopolis and get surer and more detailed information than I have given. If he will communicate them with the same frankness and freedom as I have done, he will deserve the greatest thanks from those in truth for whom this shall have been so seasonably done; but especially the greatest gratitude from me for assisting and correcting my work.

LXXIX.

MEDICINE.

FOUR rooms are left on this floor which also I was given an opportunity to inspect, two assigned to the study of medicine, two to jurisprudence. I will speak of the former first, however much may be due the other. No one will easily explain the subtlety, method, and reasonableness of the science of medicine. It must be confessed that it is a remarkable gift of God, given over to human dexterity and observation. We say nothing further about it here because it has been very highly praised in the chapters on physics, chemistry, anatomy, and pharmacy, on which it is mainly based. Yet the science has its separate seat here where it examines into diseases and prepares remedies; and where also it gives instruction in case anything outside of the regular schools comes up. Of course each sensible man provides for his own body in such a way that he may live adequately for his daily duties, rather than be slow and dull in spirit. Hence the physicians very often prescribe temperance and exercise for their citizens, as being the safest precautions for health. In the other room surgery is practiced which offers advice and practical assistance for the human body. We human beings are so wretched that we have to be salved, scraped, burned, cut, torn, and emptied, and there is not a single little part of the body which is at all safe from innumerable dangers. So there is need of all sorts of activity and various instruments that these disadvantages may be met and the defects repaired. Moreover it is an excellent thing among all these afflictions of the human body to be mindful of our imperfections or rather the penalties for them, and to lay aside the crests of our vanity the more readily; and then to hasten to that Physician for whom it is very easy not only to heal the sick parts and to restore what has been removed, but to revive the dead and to collect those that have been scattered into the finest dust. Moreover we will respect medicine, not so much because it offers us an unusually long life or sets itself against death, but because our excellent Creator has wished that through His creatures and their use, benefit should be brought to us.

LXXX.

JURISPRUDENCE.

WITH all respect to the lawyers I must say there is no need of them at all among our Christianopolis friends. For as they live by their own laws and are bound to no other law except for a yearly tribute, they do not wish to be bothered by foreign rescripts, codes, pandects, or other legal digests, in canon, indulgence, or extravagance. Here there is nothing that may not be easily explained, nothing more noticeable than justice, and no one enters into legal dispute with another. Hence suits and those who carry them on all amount to nothing. It is an easy matter to settle quarrels and disputes, and there is no need of a *corpus juris*. So they think they have avoided many traps and snares, and especially dangers to the soul with unrest of the body. If they especially minded loss of goods, they would bear this even less. For it is always true that technical law always takes, draws, rubs off, or abjures; presses, beats, hammers, strikes, twists, or shakes out; abducts, purloins, robs, embezzles, sweeps, or carries away something if a person prefers to live by strife rather than tranquillity. However, these methods are to be attributed rather to politicians than to the better scholars of the law. And so the lawyers have a school here also, though it is honorary rather than necessary. Yet that they may not be idle, they serve the political government, and they interpret the Roman laws, which are full of equity and honesty. I noticed about the same situation in the room of the notary; he seemed to be present to fill a place, and did not accomplish anything of great moment in this republic. Yet if anything is to be copied, it is intrusted to these men. And to the art of writing as to a summary of the most valuable invention has been given this honor that it also may have its name in the catalogue of the arts. Some people say also there is some meaning in the forms of the letters as there is in numbers, coming forth out of order and value. The citizens of Christianopolis do not insist upon this; they delight rather in tendering their hearts to God that He may write down with His finger what things will add to the security of the present or the future life. Such is their sacred incantation, such their art of divination, this the sum of their mystic literature, of which they are all the more desirous, as it is more certain.

LXXXI.

THE DWELLINGS OF THE YOUTH.

THE two stories that remain are reserved for bathrooms and dormitory purposes, two sides being given over to the boys and the third to the girls. For since they want this sex also liberally educated, they take particular care that those men who are placed over the youth have such wives as can teach the young women and the girls. The arrangement of the rooms will be plain from the accompanying sketch. This one fact should yet be mentioned, namely, that the boys are so associated with those who are grown up, and the adults so observed by the married men, and the inspection is so carefully carried out all around, that, to the utmost possible extent, moral corruption of the youth is avoided. And as such can happen so rarely under a system of training which has kept up its innocence during a long series of years, it is to be valued above every happiness, especially when we remember what perversion, corruption, and offense of the youth there is elsewhere in schools and public educational institutions. Everyone carries with him domestic, rustic, or even paternal and inborn evil and wickedness, and communicates these to his comrades, with so poisonous a contagion that it spares not even those who ought to be consecrated entirely to God, but winds its way with varying wickedness, deceit, and rudeness, and takes possession of them so entirely that they cannot throw it off throughout their whole lives, and among the most honorable offices; and this is done with lamentable pollution of the innocent, since the plague of one individual spreads to many, and as individuals contribute one is affected. So that now parents have to fear almost nowhere more than where they persuade themselves their children are being most plainly educated toward God. And right here there is especial need of very eager prayers that they may commend their dear ones very carefully to divine custody, whose sole care it is through the angels' guardian power to avert from them those impure and pestiferous lips, to stop their ears, and to strengthen their hearts toward the love of modesty and abhorrence of impurity.

LXXXII.

THE TEMPLE.

AND finally the temple, which is in the middle of the place, was shown me, a work of royal magnificence in which expense and talent vied with each other. This should not be criticised, however, since no one in the republic is in want. The form of the temple is round, its circumference being three hundred and sixteen feet and the height seventy. In the one half where the gatherings take place, seats are cut and excavated from the earth that the structure may ascend less, and that the ears of all may be equally distant on all sides from the voice of the speaker. The other half is reserved for distribution of the sacraments and for music. The senators have a separate place there with the councilmen, not at all far from the speaker's platform, as I have shown in the sketch. But also the sacred comedies, by which they set so much store, and are entertained every three months, are shown here in the temple, in order that the history of divine things may cling the more firmly in the minds of the youth, and that their own talents may be rendered the more skillful and ready in handling such things. I could not sufficiently admire their artistic skill in these matters, as I myself saw the *Jeremia* of Naogeorgus [1] played before the people. The surrounding wall of the temple is full of windows so that it admits light all around. The other parts of the walls are elegantly resplendent with sacred pictures or representations from biblical history. I saw no image except that of the crucified Christ and it was skillfully designed with a view

[1] Thomas Naogeorg, dramatist, 1511-1578.

toward moving even the hardest heart. The rest of the adornments I cannot easily describe unless I wished this done in detail. Suffice to say I could not enough admire the art and beauty, especially when I recalled those who, under the pretext of religion, despoil the churches, and when the desolation of the temples has been effected, do not nevertheless forget to provide for their own domestic luxury. Of a surety they are evangelical Christians with consciences to whom it seems a sin if the gifts of ancient simplicity offend the people anywhere else than in their homes! Oh, the religious reformers who, in order to empty the shrines, have offered their own homes for useless and boastful pomp! Those who forbid the decorating of the temples of God, or who are as tenacious in this matter as they are prodigal in others, might find something here to learn. However, it is not my business here to teach what I think right, but to rehearse what I saw.

LXXXIII.

VOCATION.

As many as have been consecrated to the church regard nothing before or above their calling. This is their confidence, this their shield, and this their crown. The parents wish for and seek in earnest prayer, though they do not buy nor obtain the result through custom, that sometime they may produce in their family interpreters or ministers of God, since they realize that this is the summit of human dignity. So whenever especial gifts of God, and, as it were, intimate acquaintance with the Holy Spirit, become apparent; when a life is permeated, as it were, with heavenly thoughts; when there is even a secret harmony of prayers in favor of one individual, then there arrives at the same time the heavenly and Christian message of a call which corresponds to an inward impulse of the heart and encourages them with a confidence in their spiritual duty. And when public and stated prayers are added to that, and the laying on of hands, they say that divine grace very noticeably appears and that a man, already good before, becomes even better. Hence the calling is valued among the people and is considered effectual; while by the preacher it is a mark of heavenly favor that he has entered into a sacred covenant with God that he might be assisted and taught by Him; that he himself be silent upon nothing which is true or wholesome, nor add anything of human invention, and that he render up life and blood if necessary for the congregation of God; at the same time also that he renounce earthly immunities and express indeed the will of the good spirit. Blessed indeed is that church whose ministers are not dedicated to the ministry for support, condemned to it because of their dull natures, admitted because of some little learning, pushed into it on account of the generosity of their parents, raised to it by the price of blood, promoted because of the agreement of curiosity, merely to find out how much they can accomplish for or against souls! Blessed indeed is that church whose ministers determine their honor by the Word of God, their wealth by the increase of the church, their scholarship by the discomfiture of the Devil, their enjoyment by the putting aside of the flesh, their fame by the testimony of the poor, their purpose by the wreath of faith! Happy indeed is that church in which God calls, man obeys, the angel assists, the government agrees, the people give ear, and the youth grow up! But alas to those who have transformed and debased into a certain frivolity and carelessness of vocation, the solicitude and bravery of their elders, by which they, called of God, fearing for their souls, have freed their necks from the deceits of Antichrist.

LXXXIV.

SERVICES.

OF their sermons which are delivered in the temple, we have already spoken. The presbyter and the diaconus give them; the former explains the Holy Scriptures, the latter the chief principles of religion. There are others subordinate to these who succeed them after death; for it is not permitted here to look longingly at the dead. The service is begun and ended with prayers and sacred psalmody. I saw nothing foreign to our so-called Augsburg Confession; for they disapprove our morals, not our religion. When they pray or hear the Word of God, they fall down on their knees and raise their hands; they even beat their breasts, that they may awaken their souls. To do nonsense in the temple, or to fall asleep, they consider a sin. Though there are daily readings out of the works of holy and devout learned men, none the less they attend in large numbers. For whatever attention is given religion, this they consider the highest occupation. And if half the time of their lives is devoted to this, they still think it is too little. I was surprised at the behavior of these men when I noticed them jumping for joy at times, and often dissolving in tears; for they cannot rehearse either the goodness of Christ or the misdeeds of men without emotion. The events of the life of Christ are so distributed throughout the year that the individual, remarkable acts may have a memorial, and to these times they adapt their festivals, which however are not puffed up by affectation or fancy. In their ceremonies they are not spectacular, for they wish rather to improve than to astonish men. The dress of all is respectable, and that of the ministers is in no respect unusual. The color appropriate for religion is white, that of statesmanship red, of scholarship blue, of the working class green. Yet this fact does not affect Christians so much that they regard distinction of color greater than that of virtues and vices; nor do they regard indifferent ceremonies of such value that all care, examination, and sacred judgments should be annihilated by them. Is it because the vices of men are greater than we can oppose that we whittle straws and strain gnats just to be doing nothing? At Christianopolis, because they sow virtues and uproot vices, they confer regarding trifles at their leisure.

LXXXV.

SACRED PSALMODY.

MUSIC plays not at all the least part in divine worship with them, however much puritanical melancholy may object. They praise God chiefly with the voice, but also with sound of trumpet, harps and zither, drums and chorus, strings and measure, cymbals and various organs. The holy prophets thought this proper, and Christ neither advised against nor prohibited it. Thus Satan is mocked, who never rejoices with his own except when so doing will injure God's cause. They have many sacred songs, and that they may be able to sing them well together, they each bring along their little books and thus supplement their memory. In these songs they admire especially the spirit of the songs of Luther, though they do not spurn others. It is a pleasant thing to hear the whole congregation singing together in four or more parts, and yet not violating the time and rhythm of the composition. The practice of assembling daily for prayers makes this possible. That which has to do with numbers possesses something divine and penetrating into the souls of man. So all the best admire the poetry of David and hold it in high esteem, and favor also the poetry of to-day, if it is pure and Christian. Whosoever lowers the standard of this, is accused of abuse of his talent; whoever traces it down from its source, is considered by them as deserving to be crowned with laurel. Let no one believe that elegance in poetry is out of the question unless mentioning idols; let no one charge the sacred writings of crudeness. It is a trick of Satan, who perverts our hearing so that the music of the zither appeals to us less than the sound of the bagpipe. And what makes sacred song so powerless over us, makes it leap about so wantonly, other than the sluggishness within us toward the good, and the sensational tickle of evil? On the other hand, what quiets or disquiets our thoughts unless it be, respectively, the spirit of sacred song and the shamelessness of worldly music? Whatever genius the worldly songs may possess, they become useless under test of the cross; while however much simplicity the sacred ones have, they refresh the soul beyond belief though previously the words and syllables were neglected. Let us give thanks to God who is ever willing to be near the silent or the prayerful, the grieving and the singing, and willing to hear them compassionately.

LXXXVI.

THE SACRAMENTS.

THE sacraments are administered as instituted by Christ and according to the rites of the early church; frequently, because of their great value; reverently, on account of their high dignity; elaborately, because they are observed by the devout. When children are baptized in the name of the Trinity, they have witnesses of their faith and obligation, first of all the father, but also an honorable married couple and absent friends are bidden; and all these pledge their faith for the sacrament and charge themselves with the care. For they say that godparents should stand in the place of the parents and should render an account to God for their spiritual children. The observation of a guardian should not be more diligent than that of a godfather; while their mutual love will be perchance the greater, as the bonds uniting them through Christ are closer. Those who here seek gold commit a grave fault; those counsel most wisely who require the best observers for their children and monitors of their virtues. As often as the holy supper is offered, as it invites all, so also unless actual necessity prevents, all attend and thus bear witness to their peace with men. The elements consisting of unleavened bread and wine are given at the altar where a haughty countenance can make no change. As many as approach bring along a contrite heart, a faithful soul, and a body ready for correction, and a little later they show by actual deed what they have promised. This is their most welcome tribunal where offenses are adjudged and removed. For he who can be angry at his brother to deny God or not to accept

Him, such a man is a horror to the state and not at all to be tolerated. Then also those stand here who, after having given way to the deceits of the Devil, have again become reconciled to the church; and for their salvation and repentance they are as heartily congratulated as they were lamented at their fall. And especially do they see to it that no crime be charged to church or state; but they free and cleanse themselves and others with the Christian expiation. Those who neglect this, are crushed by their own and others' misdeeds. There was a time when evildoers were interceded for before the church; now, as this turned out evilly, it is different. And yet the world boasts that there is nothing more severe and consistent than her discipline. But this praise surely our predecessors bear; what we shall do, our posterity will speak of sometime, if there be any.

LXXXVII.

ABSOLUTION AND EXCOMMUNICATION.

THE keys which Christ left for binding and loosing, they preserve very religiously, while others use the one to the extreme and hide the other; so that it is said of them that they use the former up and lose the latter. The inhabitants of Christianopolis confess the sum of their sins singly, many of them even into the ears of a friend—for there is no one among them without a rather close friend—or into the ears of a clergyman; and by this frankness they say that their burdens are very much lightened. Through His ministry, Christ promised clemency in return for earnest repentance, eager faith, and careful amendment,

but He threatens strict justice for dissembling. There
is no fear lest anyone grow up ignorant of the Christian
religion, since this is required in the school and carefully
attended to. Moreover, that the consciences may be
strengthened, many ministers are chosen to this very duty,
but only such as are remarkable for innocence of life and
fervor of spirit. If anyone distrusts men, no one is urged
to reveal his secrets, but he is left to God, the reader of
hearts. Against backsliders, especially those who remain
stiff-necked after the vain warnings of brothers, fathers,
and civil authorities, they pronounce the wrath of God, ban
of the church, disgust of the state, and the abhorrence of
every good man, with such success that it seems as if they
have been shut off from the universe, that is, all the creatures of God. They consider this more severe than death
and they all make great effort for the recovery of such a
man. If at last he continues to resist and is stubborn, they
expel him from the republic. Before this is done they tax
him with the most extreme and debased labors or even with
blows, by which means they prefer to punish the sins, than
spill his blood, as far as this is permitted. Surely the world
accomplishes little when it freely punishes the evildoers with
fine, disgrace, or death and does not shake the lethargy out
of their lives by which alone they are so rapidly driven to
destruction, nor breaks their wantonness with hunger and
work that they may either recover or be restrained. Poor
indeed is that physician who is more ready to burn and
to cut, than to cleanse and to revive. Nowhere will a republic be found more fortunate than such a one which preserves
as many of its citizens as possible and destroys the least
possible number. The chief aim of such a state is: that
after divine reverence has been inculcated and the foulness
of sin exposed we learn earlier to be unwilling to sin, than

not to dare to; but if we do dare then that we be not able; and if we break through absolutely, that we be compelled to atone for our acts and cleanse ourselves.

LXXXVIII.

MATRIMONY.

MATRIMONY is undertaken by them with great devotion, approached with great caution, cherished with great gentleness, regarded with great consideration. Yet it is nowhere safer to get married than here. For as the unusualness of the dowry and the uncertainty of daily bread are lacking, it remains only that the value of virtues and sometimes of beauty be made. It is permitted a youth of twenty-four years to marry a girl not under eighteen, but not without the consent of the parents, consultation of the relatives, approbation of the laws, and benediction of God. There is with them the greatest reverence of relationship of blood. The factors considered in joining in marriage are for the most part conformity of natures and propriety; but also, a thing that is elsewhere so rare, recommendation of piety. The greatest fault is considered to be impurity and the laws against such offenders are severe. But by removing opportunities they easily eliminate the sins. The marriages have almost no expense or noise; they do not at all expect worldly foolishness and senselessness. Young men conduct the groom and young women the bride, and they all show their approbation with heart and prayer, when the bond has been joined. Then the parents of both and the nearest relatives come together, shake hands and remind the newly married couple of the value of agreement, work, and moderation, but especially of devotion and patience. And so without any drunkenness, which usually initiates all sacred functions elsewhere, but not without a hymn and Christian congratulations, they are married. There is no dowry at all except the promises of Christ, the example of parents, the knowledge acquired by both, and the joy of peace. Furniture is provided together with the house out of the public store. In this summary fashion they render most safe and speedy, our cross, punishment, torment, purgatory, and however else we are accustomed to call inauspicious marriages. If now there should be any unpleasantness, the difficulties are smoothed and ironed out from the experiences of all the friends; meantime no infidelity comes up, for it is severely punished. The grief which God feels at our desertion, He has not expressed more forcibly than in the case of the forgetting of parental and conjugal love. He has proved His justice with His zeal, in that we may abhor ingratitude and faithlessness, and punish them at the same time. Since the world has turned these two enormities into a joke, there are always worse conditions that follow upon bad ones, always persons who will later outdo former impostors. Hence so many evils of impurity which pour out vices, confuse the dowry-gifts, surround the family with diseases, pour down curses, scatter disgrace, slacken the conscience, cause repletion, scatter filth, squander wealth, call forth the threats of the Master, sow desperation, loose punishment.

LXXXIX.

WOMEN.

THE married women make use of the knowledge which they acquired while in college. For whatsoever human industry accomplishes by working with silk, wool, or flax, this is the material for woman's arts and is at her disposal. So they learn to sew, to spin, to embroider, to weave, and to decorate their work in various ways. Tapestry is their handiwork, clothes their regular work, washing their duty. In addition to this they care for the house and the kitchen and have them clean. Whatever scholarship they have, being mentally gifted, they improve diligently, not only to know something themselves, but that they may sometime also teach. In the church and in the council hall they have no voice, yet none the less do they mold the piety and morals, none the less do they shine with the gifts of heaven. God has denied this sex nothing, if it is pious, of which fact the eternally blessed Mary is a most glorious example. If we read the histories, we shall find that no virtue has been inaccessible to women, and there is none in which they have not excelled. However, rarely do many of them comprehend the value of silence. Yet we have some whom we might compare with or even prefer to men—real Monicas,[1] dedicated to the church, pleasing to their parents, peaceful with their husbands, observing the rites of widowhood, generous toward their children, courteous toward their friends, useful toward those in want, neighborly to all. Among these, filial loyalty requires that I mention my mother. The cases elsewhere, in which very many women are too lordly, are

[1] Referring to the mother of St. Augustine.

rather the fault of those men who are effeminate enough to marry such masculine women. There is nothing more dangerous than situations where the women rule in secret and the men obey openly; on the other hand, nothing is more desirable than that each party takes charge of his or her special duty. It is a rare thing among them, and not at all considered a manly act, for the husband to beat his wife; and the wife who is flogged is rather disgraced among her acquaintances. Their greatest boast is that of peace in the family. It is a monstrous thing to be joined in body and to disagree in spirit. Women have no adornments except that mentioned by Peter;[1] no dominion except over household matters; no permission to do servants' work (a thing that will surprise you), unless disease or some accident demands it. No woman is ashamed of her household duties, nor does she tire of attending to the wants of her husband. Likewise no husband of whatsoever employment thinks himself above honorable labors. For to be wise and to work are not incompatible if there is moderation. Within reasonable bounds, nothing is more sensible than to further the public good with word and deed.

XC.

CHILDBIRTH.

THE crowning accomplishment of women is bearing children, in which they take precedence of all the athletes of the earth; unless mayhap it would seem of greater importance to kill a human being than to give birth to one. It is certainly little short of the miraculous for a woman to

[1] I Peter, III: 3, 4.

bear such pains, and for the child to survive the great dangers. When a child is born the friends offer as congratulation the hope of the heavenly kingdom, they sympathize in the miseries that must be borne in the meantime. But this fact exceeds all others in importance, that we have been reborn by the birth of Christ into life, we who are doomed to die. They have no birthday banquet; for I have already mentioned that they can dispense with wine in their sacred and solemn ceremonies, a thing that others do not wish to do. Midwives are held in the highest regard, but none except the most capable are considered. The more religious a woman is, the more fitted for this office, provided of course the scientific knowledge is not lacking. Unless the case demands it, they do not tolerate nurses, for they desire that the children drink the milk of the mothers. Those who have charge of women in labor and the infants, are for the most part widows, whose special duty this is. There are also young women who take care of children. Baptism is administered in the presence of the congregation unless the child is dangerously ill. If it is deprived of the rite, they know that the seed of the faithful has been washed clean by the blood of Christ, and so they hope for the best. The period of confinement is forty-two days, after the expiration of which they give solemn thanks to God. During these days, lighter food, as is fitting, is brought from the public commissary. For the medical skill even of the women is by no means without results. Meanwhile if the husbands wish to live apart, they can; if not, they are not driven out. They have the greatest desire for conjugal chastity, and they set a premium upon it, that they may not injure or weaken themselves by too frequent intercourse. To beget children is quite proper; but passion of license is a disgrace. Others live together like beasts; yet even the cattle have characteristics which put such persons to shame, who might better with mutual love and mutual aid first care for heaven and later for things of the earth. So the citizens of Christianopolis believe that there may be to a certain extent fornication and pollution even in marriage. Oh, the carnal-minded who are not ashamed to make sin out of lawful as well as unlawful practices! But what can we do, when there are on all sides places for feasting and places of allurements, when even the very names of fasting, temperance, vigilance, and work among us are held in suspicion or are unknown? And so it happens that while we are dreaming that all things are permitted us, we take no pleasure in the things that are really good and healthful, pure and undefiled.

XCI.

WIDOWHOOD.

SINCE no bond survives death, even the closest marriages are dissolved. If a husband dies, his widow leaves the house and withdraws into the home for widows, where she serves the state in some capacity, and marries again if she likes, but not before the expiration of a year, out of respect for her former love. If a woman dies, her widower eats with a neighbor or with others in the public house, till after a year he may marry again. There is no danger at all for the orphans, since all children are brought up with equal care in the college. For there is no one in this republic who has only individual parents. The state itself is a parent to each. The regard of widows is in accordance with their devotion, self-restraint, and industry. So they are honored like mothers, and are employed in bringing up the girls. For it is fitting that those who have experienced the emptiness of this world should advise those who are less protected, should restrain, and correct them. For Satan never operates against us with his secret devices more easily than when he promises pure joys, where in reality there is least of pleasure, very much pain and disgust. Hence as many as take their delight in lusts of the flesh or follow the ways of beasts, we must rightly consider them either entirely without experience or lacking in their senses. It is madness to value the known world, foolishness to long for the unknown. So this is the duty of widowhood, to lessen the reputed value of the flesh among the inexperienced, to curb lustful desires among those who value impurity, since they show by their own example that it is not always necessary to follow after the flesh, nay that it is far better to abstain for reasons of personal advantage, spiritual as well as civil. We may grow warm, but in such a manner that the spirit shall not catch fire; let us restrain the warmth but without extinguishing the spirit; we may grow cool, without allowing the body to freeze; let us keep ourselves warm, yet not so as to kindle the body. Luxury displeases God, marriage pleases Him, widowhood is honored, and virginity is precious to Him. The highest grace and the greatest excellence of a chaste man is Christ's confession of the closest union with him.

XCII.

THE COUNCIL HALL.

THE council hall is situated above the temple, and is intended for the rarest and most august and solemn meetings. In these meetings the highest rulers are created and enter into mutual faith with the people. Here the statutes of the republic are read, here ambassadors from foreign parts are heard. It is of the greatest splendor, either to uphold the majesty of the republic, or that through the eyes it may teach generosity of disposition. For as the history of the earth is expressed here in various ways, so also those shine most brightly who deserve best in the affairs of men. Here I saw among the heroes John Frederick, Elector of Saxony, and of my own sovereigns, Christopher, Duke of Würtemberg, most Christian princes, and others of no less virtues. Here were expressed alternately the advantages and disadvantages of the governing virtue or vice; on the one side the very essence of watchfulness, tares of inactivity, light of humility, whirl of undesirable ambition; on the other side power of love, slipperiness of tyranny, result of good example, chaos of dissoluteness; elsewhere the simplicity of truth, the sound of sophistry, elegance of refinement, the clattering crudeness of barbarism. The form of the divine, of the Christian, of the human, and the Satanic kingdoms, their likenesses and differences, laws and affairs were all here represented, and the result whether fortunate or sad was everywhere attached. Here was shown the likeness of the last judgment in its glad as well as in its horrifying phases, with the rewards of virtues and the punishments for vices all skillfully represented. What shall I say? It seems to me that I saw here, or nowhere ever, the real microcosmos, not with lavish extravagance, but devoted to the real education of man. If now we compare with these the heaven of the gods, the earth of the satyrs, the sea of Neptune, and the Hades of Pluto, how we will grow cool and how we will be laughed at that the human mind stands forth and comes into the open in nothing except foolish fables and dreams, and yet wishes to preserve among men the opinion and reputation of divine culture, love of country, and of scholarly skill.

XCIII.

THE COUNCILMEN.

THE councilors are the most distinguished of all the citizens, conspicuous for their piety, honesty, and industry, and tried out by long experience. In number they are twenty-four, chosen equally from the three orders, honored as well as loved by the citizens because of their high regard for the state. The citizens have elevated these not to remove them from all virtues, but to appoint them as lights of the same, as it were, to all the rest. So they all have a zeal for religion, peace, and learning, out of which comes an abundance of all good things. The councilors take no pleasure in strutting before others, sucking the sap out of others' goods, or fattening lazily. But as the sun shines, so they brighten everyone, consult for all, work for all. If anything rather serious takes place, they themselves pray to God eagerly and require prayers of the people also. They observe the praiseworthy deeds of their predecessors very carefully, and transmit them inviolate to their descendants. I have nowhere seen a more diligent investigation of the past, nowhere a more solicitous care for the future. Hence they examine the present according to models, and if they find that they are deteriorating a single bit, they repair the matter. If on the other hand a thing can be improved in method, they rejoice greatly that opportunity has been given to bear testimony to posterity that they have not lived in vain. Yet they judge this thought to be a praiseworthy one, if they have preserved the flower and safety of the state. No one departs from the path of their former national life lest it might seem that they have become a different people, instead of being the same race, with a more approved skill in their duties. And so a fitting place of honor is preserved for labor and respectable occupation. As they honor the feeble more, so they burden them less, and the younger serve as their prop; so they have twelve additional extraordinary substitutes. If any one of these commits an unusually grave offense, though they say this can hardly occur, he is removed from his position, and the matter seriously looked into. The reward of all is the consciousness of right, in which they exult, namely, that they have been able with divine assistance to propagate the Gospel, to protect their subjects, to ennoble the youth, adorn the land, and to increase the number of dwellers in heaven.

XCIV.

THE GARDENS.

AROUND the college is a double row of gardens, one general and the other divided into plots corresponding to the homes of the citizens; both are fitted out with more than a thousand different sorts of vegetables in such a way that they represent a living herbarium. They are not permitted to confuse the order of the distribution of the plants, which by the skill of the gardener are made to conform to the various zones of the sky, a wonderful and clever combination of colors, representing as it were a painted plate. They have here a number of birds in cages and the bees in their hives are very carefully tended. The plants that are for medicine, cooking, or decorative purposes are all in separate plots. Hence they furnish various uses and pleasures,—fragrance, purifying of the air, honey, drugs, harmonious song of birds, and information. There is plenty of water, which is carried by artistically arranged pipes, nor is the music out of harmony with the water. But they avoid all too great expense. Outside the walls they have their very extensive gardens, in which they raise crops for food purposes, for the others have been planted rather for their elegance. Moreover they learn here to judge the value of human beauty, which is the flower-gathering of a single year. We are born, we grow up, we are in our prime, we droop, and pine away. Out of our death there is again the rise and increase of others. Oh, happy are those who among the wholesome plants learn also to trust in God who feeds the flowers and clothes them without any care on their part; who learn to note down the variety and diverseness of

His gifts, and to connect their pleasant odor with God! But why enumerate what man should learn from the creatures of God, when the smallest leaf contains the whole lesson? Rather let us wonder at those who, though they love the earth most of all, neglect entirely that which is the best of the earth, its use and beautiful decoration. Yet they are not willing to seem to burden the earth, though they tread it with crude feet. Let us lament the lost paradise and long for its restoration. For though we look upon natural objects now with faulty vision, when our sight has been restored through the cross, we will behold all things not on the surface, but in their inmost depths.

XCV.

WATER.

CHRISTIANOPOLIS has water as well as excellent land. I will not now mention navigation in the presence of some who, like fungi, never move from their place. Perhaps sometime I will go into this in detail. Now I must explain what service they have as regards drinking and washing. An abundant supply of very clear water has been introduced into the city which they have distributed first into the streets and then into the houses, so that water abounds everywhere and can be obtained close at hand. Next, by means of underground canals, they have conducted the outlet streams of a lake through the alleys, so that the flowing water frees the houses of their daily accumulations, a scheme that is more conducive to public health than anything else easily thought of. Whence those seem to me to be very wise who want man not only when crested and plumed, that is, dressed according to modesty and fashion, but also when naked and convinced of human necessity, assisted and liberally provided for. For as these conditions accuse us to ourselves and draw us down from the lofty halls of our imagination to the filthiness of our mire, so they also advise us of reasons why we should not live uncleanly. Hence they have baths, that have been in use from early times. But for the most part the baths are private and only those for the children are public, for they fear the temptations of nudity. Then there are sanitary washrooms in quiet places; also washing of clothes, which man soils in various ways; and other arrangements for keeping men clean. Oh, this body of ours! How unclean, how polluted, how moist, how sweaty, how decayed, how filthy! And yet it pleases the soul, dictates to it, wears it out, and at last crushes it! Pity us, Oh Thou source of life, wash and purify that uncleanness, this body of ours, the impure blood, with Thy most holy blood, that we who are so ugly in our impurity may be dressed in the robe of Thine innocence and rendered acceptable in the sight of God; that we may not be ashamed when Thou shalt return to each one according to his deeds!

XCVI.

THE AGED.

THE aged of both sexes stand in the highest esteem, and so they take especial care that they be not afflicted with any trouble, as old age is in itself a disease. So they have appointed people who nurse them, cheer them up, honor and consult them. For since the powers of mind and body fail them together, they have to be kept bolstered up and inspired with young blood; for they grow weak on account of the disgust of human life, and at the memory of so many accidental injuries, and so many errors of their own. Since with great labor and merit toward the republic they have discharged their duties with noticeable faith and care, even up to decrepit old age, no amount of honor and respect is considered enough in gratitude. And since finally they do possess the greatest truths of human life, not merely by way of some subtlety of theory, but through rough practice and experience of material difficulties, nothing can be thought up so ingenious and subtle that when rubbed against the whetstone of old age, it will not give up much of its own opinion, and accommodate itself more nearly to human conditions. If any of the youth but knew with what mistakes, sweat, shame, dangers, and snares the old people have acquired these truths, all of which they have buried within them and which they keep under the one word CAVE, beware!—never would they be so thoughtless as to laugh at the advice of the old, and admire their own plans. But old people also have this advantage, that since they have sent such a throng of acquaintances ahead to their rest; since they have seen the good eventually ascend and very many evil fall; since they have observed the kingdom of God and the little ship of the church stand against the attacks and storms of Satan, and finally triumph; since they have noticed the increasing offspring of virtues and the fruits of piety, they also gladly lay themselves down to the end of life, commend to all the naturalness and ease of death, and precede them all in their familiarity with death. For inasmuch as all our study and all our wisdom are nothing but a consideration of death, it is befitting that those who have spent the most time therein, should be of all mortals the most experienced in matters relating to death.

XCVII.

FOREIGNERS AND PAUPERS.

TOWARD strangers and foreigners they show the greatest kindness and generosity, of which I myself, a man in the deepest straits, am an evident example. Yet they are careful that the citizens do not contract any contagious disease as a result of too great liberty on the part of the guests. Evil practices of taverns, elsewhere so common, are unheard of and unknown to them; and if they did know of them, they would heartily disapprove of them. They keep a guest frugally for a day or two; an exile they support for a long time; and a sick person they care for very kindly. They help the poor sufficiently and do not allow them to leave without material aid. However, they examine them all very closely in their words and behavior, and then do their charity. No beggar is known or tolerated; for they judge that if anyone is really in need, the republic ought not to have to be warned of its duty; neither of which however can happen, and this is right. If a person is physically strong, he is never permitted to deny the republic his efforts, and these are sufficient for the food he gets. Yet elsewhere both these provisions are neglected. For when not rarely those persons starve who accomplish the most hard work, and when breaking down under their load they are deserted and cast aside; on the other hand when those who have basely rejected their heavenly gifts, and who escape all sweat on account of weakness of their flesh, when they are supported for the most part out of the state funds— it cannot but be that the " bread snatched from the children is being cast before the dogs." In this respect we are altogether bound by the rule of the world; for the wealth of the world for the most part, serves the purposes of wickedness and extravagance, rarely, and then very injuriously, giving aid to the works of Christ; and so it is exposed to the thievery of impostors, jugglers, quacks, tramp musicians, and hair dressers, that Christ may appear to be disgusted that such wrongly collected property should have been allowed to pass to so wicked an owner. Meantime, Christ does not lack means to support His own, for whom there is plenty even in their want. Nor are persons wanting who take off their clothes, throw them down, and strew the road for Christ. I myself, though I have always found the world greedy, stingy, and base toward me, have learned among the citizens of Christianopolis that there are still some who, for the sake of Christ and through Christ, desire very much to share their all.

XCVIII.

THE SICK.

As diseases are of various kinds, so also ought our piety be manifold. The citizens of Christianopolis have observed this particularly, who have learned how to care for and comfort the souls, minds, and bodies that are afflicted. All of them strive to be able to come to their own and other people's assistance in case of need. Medicine, surgery, and the kitchen are all equally at the disposal of the sick, and everyone is prompt to assist. He who stands high socially does not exhaust the supply of drugs, while the lowly do not suffer for want of alleviation; crowds of physicians do not linger around the great, nor does loneliness afflict the common people. Yet after all, more rich people on earth are made away with than poor. Married women and widows here have the greatest opportunity and skill, and the state very kindly commends to them the care of the sick; they even have hospitals intended to take care of them. Along with the rest of the medicine they are also accustomed to cheer the spirits of the sick and to remind them of their former strength, lest they lack Christian fortitude. Then they bid them heed their usual moderation that they may not indulge their agitated bodies too far. And last also they urge them toward obedience to the instructions of medical attendance that they may not refuse to accept the unpleasantness of care imposed upon them. With these three the cross of Christ is received, lifted up, and borne. When a plague rages it is wonderful to relate how little effort there is to escape; they await the hand of God. For he who believes that the amount of God's good will is limited, never understands how he may remove himself and withdraw. Persons whose minds are unbalanced or injured they suffer to remain among them, if this is advisable; otherwise, they are kindly cared for elsewhere. This is what is done in case of the violent; for reason commands that human society should be more gently disposed toward those who have been less kindly treated by nature. For even we are not just as God would have us; yet, such as we are, He sustains us with limitless clemency and long-suffering.

XCIX.

DEATH.

WHO will say that those in Christianopolis, though they live correctly, have an unsatisfactory death? Nay, since they die daily, who would doubt that sometime they shall live forever? More than any other this republic does not know death, and yet acts on such confidential terms with it. When they compose themselves to " sleep "—for so they call death—they are very collected. They bear witness to their religion and regard Christ as a pledge of their faith. They also bear testimony to their love of country and seal this with a pious prayer. The rest they leave to God. They have no need of testaments, yet if they have any last wishes, they mention them to their friends. While one is struggling with death, public prayers are sent up for the victory of the Christian warrior. If a soul is in anguish, witnesses of divine truth are at hand and interpreters who demonstrate that God wishes all Christians well. If they suffer physical torment, the assurance of future comfort, health, and everlasting glory counterbalances this. Why do I explain this at such length! Fitting words and deeds are necessary in each individual case, and these are given. Many are present at the deathbed, that they may witness the critical change from human to Christian life. For a single example will accomplish what no warnings can do with us. Yet in their humility and state of equality they have little of which death could deprive them; while our very body is too valuable to us, out of which we are not driven without trembling and which we are horrified to leave behind us. With a whole soul they pray that God, before whom they are about to stand, may be kindly disposed to the departed, and in the place of useless complaint they commend the soul to Him with an appropriate hymn. Finally they pray that when it shall be pleasing to God, they also may find their peaceful sleep with a contrite and faithful heart, one firmly founded on Jesus Christ.

C.

BURIAL.

THE lifeless body they dress in a white robe, and on the day following the death they bear it away with uncovered face; large numbers of people accompany it. Young people sing sacred songs of Prudentius,[1] and other hymns. The nearest relatives follow, for the most part, with calm face, and wearing their usual clothes. For they say that congratulations are more befitting a Christian than grief; and that such sad manifestations have no other result than to weaken the survivors. After the body has been lowered into the grave and covered with the earth from whence it came, they hear the Word of God, intended to give them a cheerful attitude toward death, and to inform them as to life. Rarely is an epitaph of the deceased left, for they say that this can hardly be done with fairness. Such as each one has been, God knows; and posterity will transmit the facts. And this is safer than an inscription that has been bought, forced, or composed. A biographical sketch of those especially deserving is kept in their records, and the

---

[1] Aurelius Clemens Prudentius, 348-410, one of the most noted of early Christian poets.

fact that these are few speaks more loudly than with us where the great number and immense crowd of heroes renders the record suspicious. The cemetery is very spacious and beautiful, but outside the city; for they consider the city to be for the living. I saw a representation of Death leading every order of flesh to the grave, skillfully and ingeniously painted on the walls. No one has any sort of a marker except an iron cross stamped with the name of the deceased. From this the descendants count their ancestors. When this becomes too old it is removed and the name is inscribed in the funeral volume, where it can be more easily found. It is not surprising that they are somewhat careless in these matters, since they count this life of least value and long for the other. So neither these ideas nor other peculiarities of theirs ought to seem absurd to us; since it stands to reason that whoever has a desire for a future blessed life ought indeed believe with us, but must live differently in every respect.

My Christian reader, these are the things which I saw and heard in that blessed republic of God, and which I frankly confess I learned. The thing that grieves me especially is that my memory does not suffice for the great variety of things and that I have not the eloquence to express the things which I do remember; so you will easily see that I am no historian. Moreover I wish now that I had the style of those who can tell more than they saw. As for me, I confess that I can never tell all. So if I have not understood their meaning nor given account of their institution with sufficient skill, there is reason why I should regret my lack of perceptive power and why I should warn my readers not to attribute any fault to the citizens of Christianopolis, but rather to me. It may have happened—

and I really fear it has—that I have overestimated the
value of less important matters, and undervalued greater
ones; that I have told things in reverse order; that I became confused as a result of my admiration of them; that
I was not admitted into the inside of their government.
What would you have of me? I am a young man who has
not as yet grasped the significance of the secrets of statesmanship, but I look at only the external elegance. And
if I should ever be permitted to penetrate into these, my
desire to communicate my observations to others will not be
lacking. It remains now that we hear in what manner I
departed from that place. God forbid that I should ever
suffer myself to be separated from this republic!

Well, when I had inspected everything, I was brought
back to the chancellor that I might report to him
how I felt toward the citizens. "My friend," said
he to me, "you have seen how and where we live.
As all human things are imperfect, we have not
been able to show you anything beyond our mortal lot;
but we have lessened the burdens of our mortality, we
trust, and according to the pattern which we have showed
you. We chose it not because it was more perfect than all
others, but perhaps because it was easier. Whatever disadvantages are connected with it, are gradually removed
by the vigilance of the administration. If it is the object
of life to praise God and love our brothers, then the trifles
of human life will not be of such great moment that they
will render Christians anxious and trouble them. When you
shall have returned to your own people pray be a most gentle
and moderate interpreter in all respects. We aspire to no
praise; we deprecate jealousy; or, if it cannot be helped, we
bear it. Our huts are our own care, let others see to their
palaces. If they rage against us, we will pray that the sea

may not convey them to us. We worship the same God, profess the same religion. If our customs are different, it should not be regarded a crime, as we live in a different quarter of the world. We do not force our manners upon others, nor do we defend them to the limit. Let those who are better than we, judge us, teach us, criticise us; they will find that we are no less teachable than we are patient. If they can find valid excuses for all their conditions we will bring accusation against our own, and will urgently require better. Meantime let them be patient with the contradictory teachings of a single very small island. Do you remain ours, we pray, here and elsewhere."

I did not restrain the tears when I compared the kindness of this man with the stubbornness of others, and I said with trembling voice: "Whatever my people may call me, I will be yours. To you I dedicate this body of mine, since nothing else is left me, that my mind may be freer. Permit that I return to my people and secure an honorable release lest I hear myself called 'fugitive.'" Here the chancellor laughed and said: "Oh you, who are so anxious to comply with the past, yet so timid as to the future! But go, my guest, whithersoever you will, and compare our republic with other better ones, that you may report to us the good and advantageous points which you shall find elsewhere. For we desire not to be preferred to others, merely to be compared with them. No one will be a better friend to us than he who shall make our state conform more nearly to the kingdom of heaven, or (what is the same) remove it farther from the world. Hence we have long wished for an abode situated below the sky, but at the same time above the dregs of this known world." Then I answered: "Unless I am entirely deceived, the place where I shall rest will be with you. If any other land has better conditions, perchance I am not worthy to enjoy them. To this, your republic, I dedicate my labors, my studies, my wishes, my prayers. I give up the guidance of myself to you, who have learned how to control others. I will eat and drink, sleep and watch, speak and be silent at your command. I will worship and adore God with you. Now I ask but one favor, that I may be permitted to invite my friends, excellent men, who are scattered throughout the countries of the world, to come with me also." "By all means," replied the chancellor, "for we do not live too crowded to be able to accommodate a whole boat load of honest men."

While he spoke thus the twelfth hour, noon, sounded forth, and the sweet melody of bells was heard, which is the warning for solemn prayer. So he saluted me in farewell, bade me go in the name of the Master, and return safe under the guidance of God, bringing along as many comrades as possible. And as he extended to me the right hand of Christ's love, he said: "Take heed, my brother, that you do not give yourself over to the world again, and estrange yourself from us." And I answered heartily: "Where thou goest I will go, thy people shall be my people, and thy God, my God. Where thou diest, I will die, and there will I be buried. And so may Jehovah be propitious to me, as death alone shall divide me from thee!" Then I received from him the benediction, with the kiss of peace, and I went away, and am now walking about among you, that, if this republic pleases you, this worship of God, this intercourse of men, this form of education, you may go thither with me at an early day in the name of God. Farewell, and be strong in Christ.

FINIS.

INDEX

INDEX

A

Academe Royal, 53, 118.
Adami, Tobias, 21.
Advancement of Learning, The,
43, 53.
Adversus Cardanum (see *Exercitationes Adversus Cardanum*).
Aesop, 25.
Aiken, Lucy, 49.
Althaus, Friedrich, 107.
Arndt, Johann, 28, 131, 135.
Aristotle, 21, 33, 41, 42, 43, 110, 218.
Athenaeum, The, 45.
Atlantis, 54, 55, 65, 73.
Atlas, 54.
Augsburg Confession, 252.
August von Braunschweig-Lüneberg, 14.

B

Bacon, Francis, 7, 10, 11, 15, 19, 27, 41, 42, 43, 44, 45, 46, 47, 48, 49, 50, 51, 53, 54, 55, 57, 59, 62, 63, 65, 66, 67, 68, 72, 73, 74, 77, 82, 83, 99, 100, 114, 117, 121, 124.
Bacon, Nicholas, 41.
Bacon, Roger, 64.
*Bacon's Life, Letters, and
Works* (Spedding, Heath, and
Ellis), 41, 44, 46, 47, 48, 49.
Bacon's New Atlantis (G. C.
Moore Smith), 42, 46, 55, 57.
Bailey, Margaret L., 101.
Baranza, Father Redemptus, 47.
Baxter, Richard, 78.

Begley, Walter, 15, 77, 78, 79, 80, 84.
Bensalem, 55, 57, 58, 62, 63, 68.
Besold, Christopher, 12.
Boas, Fred Samuel, 7.
Boehme, Jakob, 101.
Boll, F. C., 7.
Bolton, Edmund, 53.
Boyle, Robert, 113, 114, 116, 121, 124.
Boyle's Life and Works (J. and
F. Rivington), 114, 115.
Brahe, Tycho, 203.
Brügel, Julius, 11, 14, 16, 104.
Brüggemann, Fritz, 6, 7, 8.
Bushell, Thomas, 45.
Buwinckhausen, Benjamin von, 52.

C

Campanella, Thomas, 7, 10, 16, 18, 19, 20, 21, 23, 24, 26, 27, 31, 36, 39, 55, 63.
Caphar Salama, 20, 29, 36, 55.
Cary, George, 51.
Casaubon, Isaac, 48, 49, 50, 51, 52.
Charles Stuart II, 49, 52, 113, 117.
Christenburg, Die, 21, 59.
Christianopolis, 19, 29, 31, 34, 35, 37, 58, 63, 70, 93, 94, 95, 98, 99, 110.
Christianopolis, The, 7, 8, 9, 10, 15, 16, 17, 18, 19, 20, 21, 28, 29, 30, 31, 32, 38, 39, 40, 47, 54, 55, 56, 57, 58, 59, 60, 61, 62, 65, 67, 68, 69, 71, 72, 73, 75, 76, 82, 88, 93, 94, 95, 96, 97,

283

98, 99, 104, 105, 108, 110, 111, 119, 120, 121.
Chymische Hochzeit, 26.
Cicero, 212.
Civitas Solis, 7, 16, 17, 18, 19, 20, 21, 23, 24, 25, 32, 36, 38, 39, 40.
Cleveland, John, 77.
College of Six Days' Works, 66, 73.
Comenius, Johann Amos, 10, 15, 67, 80, 99, 100, 101, 102, 103, 104, 105, 106, 107, 108, 109, 111, 112, 113, 117, 119, 123, 124.
Confessio, 26, 39.
Cowley, Abraham, 77, 117, 118.
Crashaw, Richard, 77.

D

Defoe, Daniel, 5.
De Sapientia Veterorum, 53.
Descartes, René, 114.
Descriptio, 11, 14, 16, 18, 20, 21, 25, 27, 28, 40.
Descriptio Globi Intellectualis, 49.
Description of the Famous Kingdom of Macaria, The, 107.
De Thou, Jacques Auguste, 12, 50.
Dextra Amoris Porrecta, 113.
Dialogue of the Holy War, 44.
Didactica Magna, 101, 103, 104, 112.
Duport, James, 77.
Dury (Duraeus), John, 15, 79, 80, 99, 102, 106, 109, 110, 111, 112, 113, 114, 117, 123, 124.
Dutch Annotations on the Bible, The, 116.

E

Eberhardt III, 13.
Elizabeth Tudor, 42.
Ellis, R. L., 49.
Erasmus, Desiderius, 12.

Erection of a College of Husbandry, The, 107.
Enzyklopädie der Pansophie, 107, 108.
Essentials, The Eighty-four, 53.
Evelyn, John, 114, 116.
Exercitationes Adversus Cardanum, 48.

F

Fama Fraternitatis, 11, 14, 26, 39, 40, 54, 59, 72, 73, 74, 119, 120, 121.
Farnaby, Thomas, 77.
Feast of the Family, The, 59, 60.
Fifty-two Discourses, 47.
Figulus, Peter, 112, 124.
Fletcher, Phineas, 77.
Franck, Sebastian, 101.

G

Galilei, Galileo, 49, 113.
Gardiner, S. R., 45.
Gaudentius, John (Bishop), 112.
Gerhardt, John, 135.
Glöckler, J. P., 14, 26.
Goddard, 113.
Goethe, Johann Wolfgang, 5.
Gott, Samuel, 15, 55, 78, 80, 82, 83, 84, 88, 89, 93, 99.
Goulart, Simon, 47.
Great Instauration, The (see Instauratio Magna).
Grüneisen, Carl, 21, 59.
Guhrauer, G. E., 14, 15, 67, 124.
Gussmann, W., 14, 16, 21, 23, 40, 67.
Gustavus Adolphus, 109.

H

Haacke, Theodore, 79, 114, 115, 124.
Happel, Werner, 7.
Harleian Charters, 45, 46.
Hartlib, Samuel, 15, 79, 80, 99,

101, 102, 106, 107, 108, 109, 111, 112, 113, 114, 117, 123.
Heinsius, Daniel, 12, 48, 50.
Henry IV (France), 50.
Herder, Johann Gottfried von, 5, 17, 25, 26.
Hesenthaler, Magnus, 103, 104.
Hierosolyma, 55.
Histoire des Sevarambes, 6, 8, 9.
Hölderlin, Friedrich, 5.
Holy Commonwealth, 78.
Homer, 5.
Höpfner, Ernst, 52.
Hossbach, W., 12, 14, 104.
Hübner, Joachim, 112, 113, 124.
Hudson, Henry Norman, 7.
Hüllemann, Carl, 7, 12, 14, 16, 104.

I

Ideal Commonwealths, 44, 75.
Incomparable Doctor S. Augustine, The, 53.
Insel Felsenburg, 6, 7, 8, 9.
Instauratio Magna, 43, 49.
Insulanischer Mandorell, 7.
Invisible College, The, 114, 115.

J

James Stuart I, 42, 45, 49, 50, 51, 53.
Janua Linguarum Reserata, 101, 107.
Joachim Jungius und Sein Zeitalter, 124.
John Frederick, Elector of Saxony, 265.
Jones, Stephen K., 78.
Judas Maccabaeus, 30.
Jungius, Joachim, 124.

K

Kepler, Johann, 12, 49.
Kemper, O., 30.
Kippenberg, August, 6, 7.
Kleinwächter Fr., 19.

L

Lipsius, Justus, 12, 48.
Lopes, Francisco, 54.
Loyola, Ignatius, 10.
Luther, Martin, 10, 28, 57, 134, 234, 254.

M

Maack, Ferdinand, 11.
Marvell, Andrew, 77.
Massons, 109.
Mästlin, Michael, 12.
Matthew, Toby, 52, 53, 54.
May, Thomas, 77.
Melanchthon, Philipp, 10.
Menippus, 26.
Milton, John, 15, 52, 77, 78, 79, 102, 107, 114.
Milton and Jakob Boehme, 101.
Mohl, Robert von, 14, 15, 16, 17, 18, 26, 37.
Möhrke, Max, 102, 103, 104, 105, 108.
Moller, Mart., 135.
More, Thomas, 7, 8, 16, 19, 20, 21, 22, 23, 24, 26, 27, 31, 55, 62, 63, 64, 75, 141.
Morhof, 101.
Morley, Henry, 44, 75.

N

Naogeorg, Thomas, 249.
Natural History (see *Sylva Sylvarum*).
New Atlantis, The, 7, 15, 19, 26, 42, 43, 44, 45, 46, 47, 54, 55, 56, 57, 58, 59, 60, 61, 62, 63, 64, 65, 66, 67, 68, 69, 70, 71, 72, 73, 74, 82, 99, 124.
Newton, Isaac, 114.
Nicanor, 30.
Niceron, J. P., 47.
Nova Solyma, 81, 82, 87, 90, 91, 93, 94, 95, 96, 98.

Nova Solyma, The, 15, 55, 76, 77, 78, 79, 80, 82, 83, 88, 93, 94, 95, 96, 97, 98, 99, 124.
Novissima Linguarum Methodus, 102.
Novum Organum, 43, 47, 49, 52.

O

Oldenburg, Henry, 114.
Opera Didactica, 102.
Order of the Sun, 91.
Ossian, 5.
Oxenstierna, Axel, 102, 112.

P

Patricius, 48.
Penitent Bandito, The, 53.
Petty, William, 79, 114, 116.
Philosophical College, The, 115, 116.
Philosophia Realis, 21.
Pines, Joris, 6.
Plato, 3, 19, 54.
Praeludia, 107, 112.
Prodromus Pansophiae, 101, 102, 103, 112.
Prudentius, Aurelius Clemens, 276.
Prys, Joseph, 14, 18, 32.

R

Ratke, Wolfgang, 10.
Rawley, William, 41, 42, 43, 44, 45, 46, 65.
Raworth, Francis, 51.
Republic, 3.
Richelieu, A. J. (Cardinal), 113, 118.
Robinsonaden, 6, 8, 9.
Roe, Thomas, 109.
Rosenkreutzerschriften, 11.
Rosicrucians, 19, 28.
Ross, Alexander, 77.
Rousseau, J. J., 5.
Royal Society of London, The, 15, 46, 107, 112, 114, 116, 117, 119, 120, 121, 122, 123, 124.
Rycaut, Paul, 7.

S

Salomon's House, 57, 58, 59, 66.
Scaliger, Joseph Justus, 12, 48, 50.
Schlaraffia Politica, 7, 14, 15, 16.
Schmidt, K. A., 14.
Schnabel, J. G., 6, 9.
Schupp, Johann Balthasar, 19, 101.
Schwenckfeld, Kaspar von, 101.
Serrano, 7.
Sevarambes (see *Histoire des Sevarambes*).
Shakespeare, William, 7, 77.
Sigwart, Christoph, 14, 15, 17, 18, 21.
Smith, G. C. Moore, 42, 45, 46, 54, 55, 57.
Societas Christiana, 102.
Societas Ereunetica, 124.
Society of Gray's Inn, 78.
Socrates, 147.
Sonnenstaat. Der, 21, 23, 36.
Sozialen Utopien, Die, 14, 18, 25.
Spedding, James, 41, 44, 49, 54.
Sprat, Thomas, 116, 117, 118, 119, 120, 121, 122.
Sturm, Johann, 10.
Sudre, 23.
Sylva Sylvarum, 43, 44, 46.

T

Telesio Bernardino, 41, 48, 117.
Teutscher Merkur, 26.
Theophilus, 10, 13, 103, 104, 119.
Thirty Years' War, The, 9, 10, 27, 75.
Thompson, Richard, 50.
Tractate on Education, 79, 102, 107.

U

Underhill, Thomas, 77.
Utopia, 7, 20, 22, 23.

Utopia, The, 8, 16, 19, 20, 21, 22, 23, 24, 26, 39.

V

Vairasse, Denis, 6, 9.
Valerius Terminus, 44.
Vita, ab ipsa Conscripta, 12, 26, 27, 30, 37, 52, III.
Vogt, Carl, 11, 14, 19.
Voigt, Andreas, 8, 14, 18, 25.

W

Wackwitz, Fr., 6.
Wahl, 30.

Wallis, John, 115.
Waterhouse, G., 100, 101.
Weckherlin, Georg Rodolf, 51, 52, 101.
Weigel, Valentin, 101.
Werth, Johann von, 13.
Wessely, Ignaz Emanuel, 21.
Westöstlicher Divan, 5.
Windelband, W., 9.
Wolff, Emil, 43.
Wotton, Henry, 49, 50, 51, 52, 113, 114.
Wotton, Lord of Marley, 50.
Wren, Christopher, 113.
Würtemberg, Christopher, Duke of, 51, 265.

COSIMO is a specialty publisher of books and publications that inspire, inform, and engage readers. Our mission is to offer unique books to niche audiences around the world.

COSIMO BOOKS publishes books and publications for innovative authors, nonprofit organizations, and businesses. COSIMO BOOKS specializes in bringing books back into print, publishing new books quickly and effectively, and making these publications available to readers around the world.

COSIMO CLASSICS offers a collection of distinctive titles by the great authors and thinkers throughout the ages. At COSIMO CLASSICS timeless works find new life as affordable books, covering a variety of subjects including: Business, Economics, History, Personal Development, Philosophy, Religion & Spirituality, and much more!

COSIMO REPORTS publishes public reports that affect your world, from global trends to the economy, and from health to geopolitics.

FOR MORE INFORMATION CONTACT US AT
INFO@COSIMOBOOKS.COM

❋ if you are a book lover interested in our
current catalog of books

❋ if you represent a bookstore, book club, or
anyone else interested in special discounts
for bulk purchases

❋ if you are an author who wants to get published

❋ if you represent an organization or business
seeking to publish books and other publications
for your members, donors, or customers.

**COSIMO BOOKS ARE ALWAYS
AVAILABLE AT ONLINE BOOKSTORES**

VISIT COSIMOBOOKS.COM
BE INSPIRED, BE INFORMED